Religion and Law in the United Kingdom: Great Britain

Religion and Law in the United Kingdom: Great Britain

Third Edition

Mark Hill QC
Russell Sandberg
Norman Doe
Christopher Grout

This book was originally published as a monograph in the International Encyclopaedia of Laws/Religion.

Founding Editor: Roger Blanpain
General Editor: Frank Hendrickx
Volume Editor: Wouter Druwé

Wolters Kluwer

Published by:
Kluwer Law International B.V.
PO Box 316
2400 AH Alphen aan den Rijn
The Netherlands
E-mail: international-sales@wolterskluwer.com
Website: lrus.wolterskluwer.com

Sold and distributed by:
Wolters Kluwer Legal & Regulatory U.S.
7201 McKinney Circle
Frederick, MD 21704
United States of America
Email: customer.service@wolterskluwer.com

ISBN 978-94-035-3495-4

e-Book: ISBN 978-94-035-3500-5
web-PDF: ISBN 978-94-035-3501-2

The Authors

Mark Hill QC lectures at the Open University and is an adjunct Professor at Cardiff University; the University of Pretoria; King's College, London; and Notre Dame University Law School, Sydney; and is a Distinguished Fellow of the Center for the Study of Law and Religion, Emory University. He was Chairman of the Ecclesiastical Law Society (2016–2021), and is Vice-President of the International Consortium for Law and Religion Studies, consultant editor of the *Ecclesiastical Law Journal* and a member of the editorial board of the *Oxford Journal of Law and Religion*. His recent publications include the fourth edition of the practitioner text *Ecclesiastical Law* (2018), as well as the *Routledge Handbook of Freedom of Religion or Belief* (2020), *Christianity and Criminal Law* (2020), *Religion, Law and Security* (2018), *Great Christian Jurists in English History* (2017), *The Confluence of Law and Religion* (2016), and *Magna Carta, Religion and the Rule of Law* (2015). He practises at the Bar in London and has conducted litigation concerning religious liberty in the UK Supreme Court and the European Court of Human Rights.

Russell Sandberg is a Professor of Law at Cardiff University whose research interrogates the interaction between Law and the Humanities. He is author of *Law and Religion* (Cambridge University Press, 2011), the first textbook in the field; *Religion, Law and Society* (Cambridge University Press, 2014), which explored the interplay between the legal and sociological study of religion; and *Subversive Legal History: A Manifesto for the Future of Legal Education* (Routledge, 2021), which argues that history should be at the beating heart of the law curriculum. He is editor or co-editor of seven edited collections and serves as the series editor of three book series published by Routledge: the ICLARS Series on Law and Religion, Transforming Legal Histories and Leading Works in Law.

The Authors

Norman Doe is Professor and Director of the Centre for Law and Religion, Cardiff Law School. He is a Doctor of Civil Law (Lambeth) and a Doctor of Laws (Cambridge). He is an associate professor at the University of Paris, and was President of the European Consortium for Church and State Research (2010). He is author of *Fundamental Authority in Late Medieval English Law* (Cambridge University Press, 1990), *The Legal Framework of the Church of England* (Clarendon Press, 1996), *Canon law in the Anglican Communion* (Clarendon Press, 1998), *The Law of the Church in Wales* (University of Wales Press, 2002) *An Anglican Covenant: Theological and Legal Considerations for a Global Debate* (Canterbury Press, 2008), *Law and Religion in Europe* (Oxford University Press, 2011), *Christian Law* (Cambridge University Press, 2013), *The Legal Architecture of English Cathedrals* (Routledge, 2017) and *Comparative Religious Law: Judaism, Christianity, Islam* (Cambridge University Press, 2018). He is Chancellor of the Diocese of Bangor in the Church in Wales.

Christopher Grout is a barrister who practised in criminal law, before being appointed Registrar of the Qatar International Court and Dispute Resolution Centre where he manages two judicial bodies – the Civil and Commercial Court of the Qatar Financial Centre and the Qatar Financial Centre Regulatory Tribunal. He holds an LLB from Newcastle University and an LLM in Canon Law from Cardiff University. He is a Deputy District Judge of England and Wales (assigned to the South Eastern Circuit) and a Member of the Chartered Institute of Arbitrators.

Table of Contents

List of Abbreviations

ASC	Agreed Syllabus Conference
ASP	Alternatively Secured Pension
BBFC	British Board of Film Classification
BNP	British National Party
CJEU	Court of Justice of the European Union
CTBI	Churches Together in Britain and Ireland
DPP	Director of Public Prosecutions
EAT	Employment Appeal Tribunal
ECHR	European Convention on Human Rights
ET	Employment Tribunal
EWCA	England and Wales Court of Appeal
EWHC	England and Wales High Court
GDPR	General Data Protection Regulations
HE	Higher Education
ICCPR	International Covenant on Civil and Political Rights
IPSO	Independent Press Standards Organisation
NES	NHS Education for Scotland
NHS	National Health Service
NSS	National Secular Society
OFCOM	Office of Communications
PCC	Parochial Church Council
PCP	Provision, Criterion or Practice
PSPO	Public Spaces Protection Order
RE	Religious Education
RI	Religious Instruction
RS	Religious Studies

List of Abbreviations

RVE	Religion, Values and Ethics
SACRE	Standing Advisory Council for Religious Education
SLT	Scots Law Times
UDHR	Universal Declaration of Human Rights
UKHL	United Kingdom House of Lords
UKPC	United Kingdom Privy Council
UKSC	United Kingdom Supreme Court
UN	United Nations

Preface to the Revised 2021 (Third) Edition

The *International Encyclopaedia of Laws* is an ambitious project, building a repository of monographs of national studies addressing a range of legal subjects. The *Religion and Law* series is unusual in the extensive diversity of provision that is made by national legislatures – conceptual, substantive and procedural. Nowhere is that range more evident than in the United Kingdom which sustains within its territorial boundaries a varied selection of models of Church and State. Readers will be continually reminded of distinct differences between the substantive laws of England, Scotland and Wales [1] This has progressively increased with greater devolved powers being exercised in Edinburgh and Cardiff. Indeed the rate of change is such that it is likely that the next edition of this monograph will be limited to England and Wales, and a separate volume will need to be commissioned for Scotland, irrespective of the outcome of a second independence referendum for which there is a growing momentum.

This monograph was first published in 2010, followed by a second edition in 2014. This third edition comprises a complete revision of the text. Few sections are untouched, and many have been substantially rewritten reflecting a rapidly changing society placing greater demands upon its legislators, administrators and judges. The rights-based meta-narrative which has dominated the early twenty-first century has created a more substantial regulatory framework than the much lighter touch which had prevailed hitherto.

The order and division of this work continues to be dictated by a detailed *schema* prescribed by the series editors, designed to achieve uniformity between the national studies so as to promote critical comparison between the provision made for Law and Religion in each of the countries covered. Certain sections comfortably accommodate the position in Great Britain, others less so. Thus there are occasions where the commentary does not sit entirely happily with the given topic or sub-heading: but these occasional incongruities are the small price to be paid in pursuit of the meaningful and rigorous transnational comparison which this Encyclopaedia uniquely provides. The idiosyncrasies of Great Britain's religion law are refracted through the prism of a comprehensive and utilitarian international template.

The preparation of this monograph has involved research within mainstream ecclesiastical jurisprudence and in the wider hinterland of the law relating to employment, property, discrimination, education, charities and human rights. For this third edition, the three original authors have been joined by Christopher Grout,

1. The distinct legal, political and religious situation in Northern Ireland is not covered in this work.

barrister and Registrar of the Qatar International Court and Dispute Resolution Centre. We are indebted to him for bringing fresh insights and for carrying the administrative burden of coordinating the mechanics of revision.

Beyond our own number, we have been considerably assisted by Frank Cranmer, Secretary to the Churches' Legislation Advisory Service, and Parliamentary and Synod Editor of the *Ecclesiastical Law Journal.* We have been acutely aware that while we have been engaged in preparing this third edition, the COVID-19 pandemic has had a life-changing impact throughout the globe. We have each been working remotely and our collaboration has been via Zoom rather than in person. We hope that as the world searches for a vaccine, a degree of normality will return but this is likely to take months or years. Coronavirus is no respecter of national boundaries or juridic concepts. It is all pervasive. We would be failing if we did not acknowledge and discuss its impact upon the religion and law in Great Britain. Mindful that the situation is fast moving – as also is the governmental response – we have not addressed coronavirus within the main body of the text but in a separate, stand-alone section which we have introduced immediately following this editorial Preface.

Irrespective of the unforeseen consequences of COVID-19, religion law remains in a state of growth and of flux. It has changed in many respects, in the ten years since the first edition of this monograph was published, and will doubtlessly continue to do so. It is hoped that this third edition will continue to fulfil the twin ambitions of the original: providing a self-contained and comprehensive snapshot of religion law in Great Britain today; and, through the formulaic arrangement of the topic, to promote detailed comparative analysis of the religion laws of other nations to a high level of specificity.

The law is stated as at 1 March 2021.

Mark Hill QC
Maundy Thursday 2021

The Impact of the COVID-19 Pandemic: A Short Summary

1. COVID-19 is caused by severe acute respiratory syndrome coronavirus 2 (SARS-Co-V-2), and was first identified in Wuhan, China, in December 2019. The World Health Organization declared the outbreak a pandemic on 11 March 2020. Pending the discovery and manufacture of a vaccine, governments have been taking a variety of steps to inhibit the spread of the disease by restricting individual movement and implementing social distancing. This has been achieved through various means including legislation, executive action, public health advice and government guidance. Rather than footnote individual, short-term provisions within the body of the text, this overarching overview is intended as a summary of the impact of COVID-19 on matters of Religion and Law.[2]

§1. Restriction on Movement and Closure of Places of Worship

2. The Prime Minister put the country into lockdown on 23 March 2020. In brief, the population was instructed to stay at home, and only to leave for three specified purposes: to shop for necessities such as food or medicine; to seek medical treatment; and to exercise.[3] The situation fluctuated throughout the remainder of 2020 with different parts of the country being placed into different 'tiers' depending upon the prevalence of the virus within that particular area. The hope of a relaxation over Christmas 2020 did not materialise due to the emergence of a more virulent strain of the virus in Kent. The National Health Service has been effective in providing a large-scale vaccination programme and it is anticipated that restrictions will begin to be eased from April or May 2021. A number of religious buildings were used as emergency vaccination centres, including cathedrals, mosques and gurdwaras.

3. British constitutional law does not make provision for governance by Prime Ministerial decree, whether enunciated in televised press conferences or in the

2. For a comprehensive repository of Covid-related regulations and guidance, together with advice issued by religious organisations see the designated page on the blog-site, *Law and Religion UK* which is regularly updated https://www.lawandreligionuk.com/2020/08/20/covid-19-coronavirus-legislation-and-guidance/.
3. Those in essential employment were exempted from this restriction. Ministers of religion were categorised as keyworkers.

House of Commons. What followed was the hurried passing of primary legislation (Acts of Parliament),[4] secondary legislation (Statutory Instruments) and so-called soft-law (guidelines, advice etc.). The difficulty this presented was that it was less than clear which instructions were mandatory, and reinforced by criminal sanction, and which were merely advisory or aspirational. For the most part, public compliance was high, even in respect of those matters which were not compulsory. The law and guidance was hastily written, unclear, and mutually contradictory in places. The following commentary deals solely with the position in England. Different provisions applied in Scotland, Wales and Northern Ireland.

4. The principal lockdown provisions in England were contained in The Health Protection (Coronavirus, Restrictions) (England) Regulations 2020.[5] This included the closure of business premises. Regulation 5(5) provided that 'A person who is responsible for a place of worship must ensure that, during the emergency period, the place of worship is closed', except for various specific uses, namely funerals, to broadcast an act of worship, whether over the internet or as part of a radio or television broadcast, or to provide essential voluntary services such as food banks, support for the homeless or vulnerable people, blood donation sessions or support in an emergency.[6]

5. In relation to restriction of movement, the Regulations contained more detailed and nuanced provisions than merely the three-fold exemptions outlined by the Prime Minister. Regulation 6(1) provided that 'During the emergency period, no person may leave the place where they are living without reasonable excuse.' A person who breached the regulations without a reasonable excuse commits a criminal offence.[7] A non-exhaustive list of reasonable excuses was set out in Regulation 6(2). These included the three principal exemptions, but also others such as to attend a

---

4. Such as the Coronavirus Act 2020.
5. http://www.legislation.gov.uk/uksi/2020/350/made, made pursuant to powers in s. 45R of the Public Health (Control of Disease) Act 1984. The regulations are dated 26 March 2020, three days after the lockdown was declared by the Prime Minister on national television and are recorded as being made at 1.30 pm, laid before Parliament at 2.30, but coming into force at 1.30 pm. They have been subject to a series of amending regulations, generally intended at clarification or the relaxing of particular provisions.
6. Health Protection (Coronavirus, Restrictions) (England) Regulations 2020, reg. 5(6). Places of worship that served as premises for early years childcare provided by a registered person were permitted to open for this purpose from 1 June 2020: Reg. 5(6)(d) inserted by The Health Protection (Coronavirus, Restrictions) (England) (Amendment) (No. 3) Regulations 2020 (S.I. 2020/558), regs 1(2), 2(5)(b)(ii).
7. *Ibid.*, reg. 10. The offence is punishable by a fine, and police officers are authorised to issue fixed penalty notices. There were some examples of over-zealous policing, and criminal many convictions for breaches of lockdown law were quashed for procedural irregularities. *See*, by way of example only https://www.independent.co.uk/news/uk/crime/coronavirus-fine-police-lockdown-travel-newcastle-marie-dinou-a9444186.html. Section 64 of the Public Health (Control of Diseases) Act 1984 provides that criminal proceedings in respect of offences created by regulations made under this Act (such as these) may not be initiated other than by health protection authorities or other authorised persons. Regulation 11 of Health Protection (Coronavirus, Restrictions) (England) Regulations 2020 states that proceedings for an offence under the regulations may be brought by the Crown Prosecution Service. It would appear that a private prosecution (by a member of the public) is not permissible.

funeral of a member of the person's household or a close family member;[8] and, in the case of a minister of 'religion or worship leader', to go to their place of worship.[9]

6. Although schools were closed, the children of those categorised as 'keyworkers' were permitted to attend school. The Cabinet Office and Department of Education issued *Guidance: Critical workers who can access schools or educational settings*,[10] which was periodically updated, identifying categories of keyworker. Under 'critical workers' was a section entitled 'key public services' which included the category of 'religious staff'. This term was not further defined.[11]

7. The advice from faith leaders invariably followed and adopted government guidance, and occasionally went further than the restrictions imposed by the civic authorities. Controversially, the Church of England instructed its clergy not to enter churches even to livestream liturgy, notwithstanding that this was permitted under the Health Protection (Coronavirus, Restrictions) (England) Regulations 2020 then current. Even at the height of the lockdown, under Regulation 5(6) attendance at places of worship was permissible 'to broadcast an act of worship, whether over the internet or as part of a radio or television'. Anglican priests were instructed not to do so, although subsequently church authorities sought to clarify that this had merely been advice,[12] albeit strongly worded, in order to set an example and encourage churchgoers to remain at home as the lockdown required.

8. The easing of the lockdown, prior to its reimposition, was similarly defined by a lack of clarity, inconsistent messaging and a confusion as to the mandatory or advisory nature of various provisions. In addition, there was an overlay of non-governmental guidance from religious organisations, which in some instances was more restrictive, or at least interpreted as such.[13] The gradual opening up of places of worship was equally unsystematic and somewhat confused. With effect from 13

8. Health Protection (Coronavirus, Restrictions) (England) Regulations 2020, reg. 6(1)(g). A friend was permitted to attend but only if there were no member of the household or family member attending.
9. *Ibid.*, reg. 6(1)(k).
10. https://www.gov.uk/government/publications/coronavirus-covid-19-maintaining-educational-provision/guidance-for-schools-colleges-and-local-authorities-on-maintaining-educational-provision.
11. Also named under key public services are: those essential to the running of the justice system, charities and workers delivering key frontline service, those responsible for the management of the deceased, journalists and broadcasters who are providing public service broadcasting.
12. The Archbishop of Canterbury offered this clarification during a television interview on Easter Day.
13. *See* the Church of England's press release https://mailchi.mp/churchofengland/church-of-england-to-close-all-church-buildings-to-help-prevent-spread-of-coronavirus?e=3746409744 and subsequent Guidance which has been updated periodically https://www.churchofengland.org/more/media-centre/coronavirus-covid-19-guidance-churches.

June 2020, places of worship were permitted to open but only for private prayer by individuals. Private prayer was defined in the Regulations as 'prayer which does not form part of communal worship'.[14]

9. The effect of the lockdown in closing places of worship was the subject of challenge in the courts. The case of *R (on the application of Hussain) v. Secretary of State for Health*[15] concerned the forced closure of places of worship during 'the emergency period'.[16] Swift J refused an application concerning Friday prayers (particularly the Jumu'ah)[17] at a mosque in Bradford.[18] It was argued that the Secretary of State's failure to make provision for the claimant to attend the Mosque for communal Friday prayers was contrary to his right, under Article 9 of the ECHR, to be permitted to manifest his religious belief in worship, teaching, practice and observance.[19] Swift J considered that the undoubted interference with the claimant's Article 9 right was justified: it only inhibited one aspect of the claimant's religious observance, albeit a significant one; the duration of the infringement would be finite, albeit during Ramadan; and the Government had: (a) published a strategy document with a route map to lifting the restrictions as and when it was safe to do so, and (b) consulted with the Places of Worship Task Force, established for this express purpose.[20] The pandemic presented 'truly exceptional circumstances' such that the interference would be justified on grounds of public health:

> The virus is a genuine and present danger to the health and well-being of the general population. I fully accept that the maintenance of public health is a very important objective pursued in the public interest. The restrictions contained in regulations 5 to 7, the regulations in issue in this case, are directed to the threat from the Covid-19 virus. The Secretary of State describes the 'basic principle' underlying the restrictions as being to reduce the degree to which people gather and mix with others not of the same household and, in particular, reducing and preventing such mixing in indoor spaces. I accept that this is the premise of the restrictions in the 2020 Regulations, and I accept that *this*

14. Health Protection (Coronavirus, Restrictions) (England) Regulations 2020, reg. 5(6)(e), inserted with effect from 13 June 2020, by The Health Protection (Coronavirus, Restrictions) (England) (Amendment) (No. 4) Regulations 2020 (S.I. 2020/588), regs 1(2), 2(4)(c)(ii).
15. [2020] EWHC 1392 (Admin).
16. Under reg. 5 of the Health Protection (Coronavirus Restrictions) (England) Regulations 2020.
17. 'Jumu'ah is both an obligation on healthy adult males and a clarion sign of Islam; lifting or suspending that obligation from the community at large is not a step that can or should be taken lightly. Nonetheless, we reiterate that the prime directive for animating this briefing paper is people's health and welfare, particularly protecting the elderly and infirm,' *per* British Board of Scholars and Imams in a Briefing Document published on 16 March 2020.
18. A city in northern England with a large Muslim population.
19. There was no Art. 14 claim because the regulations applied equally in respect of collective worship in a church, synagogue, temple or chapel and, accordingly, no discrimination against Muslims.
20. https://www.gov.uk/government/news/new-taskforce-developing-plan-to-reopen-places-of-worship. The first meeting of the Task Force comprised: the Archbishop of Canterbury; Cardinal Vincent Nichols; Chief Rabbi, Ephraim Mirvis; Shaykh Dr Asim Yusuf, The British Board of Scholars and Imams; Rajnish Kashyap, Hindu Council UK; Jasvir Singh, City Sikhs; Daniel Singleton, Faith Action. It was noted that 'Other faith representatives and government officials may be invited to attend future meetings depending on the Taskforce's priorities'.

> *premise is rationally connected to the objective of protecting public health.* It rests on scientific advice acted on by the Secretary of State to the effect that the Covid-19 virus is highly contagious and particularly easily spread in gatherings of people indoors, including, for present purposes, gatherings in mosques, churches, synagogues, temples and so on for communal prayer.[21]

10. In *Dolan, Monks and AB v. Secretary of State for Health,*[22] a wide-ranging application for a judicial review of the regulations and of school closures was refused. The Claimant also alleged that the prohibition on the use of places of worship for communal acts of worship involved a breach of Article 9 of the ECHR because, as a Roman Catholic, he had not been able to attend communal worship, or receive the sacraments. Lewis J adjourned consideration of this discrete matter because the easing of the regulations with regard to communal worship was already under way,[23] commenting that 'this aspect of the claim may have become academic'. He afforded the parties the opportunity to make submissions on the relevance of the new regulations on this issue. The Court of Appeal granted limited permission to appeal but dismissed the appeal on its merits. An application seeking further permission to appeal was later refused by the Supreme Court.[24]

11. The British Board of Scholars and Imams, in a briefing document published on 16 March 2020, offered guidance which included the following:

> 3. We take seriously our responsibility to minister to the welfare of the Community, both worldly and next-worldly. This involves a recognition of the serious importance that our religion places on life, health, community, and spiritual well-being. To trivialise any aspect of this would be an error. As our scholarly tradition demands, our approach in the Guidance is directed by consideration of what is essential, recommended, and desirable. This includes a keen understanding of when (and which) religious rulings may be suspended due to temporary harms or hardship.

---

21. At para. 19. Conversely, in *Reverend Dr William J U Philip and Others for Judicial Review of the closure of places of worship in Scotland* [2021] CSOH 32, the Outer House of the Court of Session concluded that Scottish regulations relating to the closure of places of worship constituted a disproportionate interference with the Art. 9 rights of the petitioners, Lord Braid observing that the respondents 'have failed to show that no less intrusive means than the Regulations were available to address their aim of reducing risk to a significant extent' (at para.115).
22. [2020] EWHC 1786 (Admin).
23. Following the hearing on 2 July 2020, regulations were made at 10 a.m. on 3 July 2020 which permit places of worship to hold acts of communal worship for up to thirty people with effect from 4 July 2020.
24. In referring the matter for reconsideration by an appellate court, Lord Justice Hickinbottom stated: 'the challenged Regulations impose possibly the most restrictive regime on the public life of persons and businesses ever – certainly outside times of war – but, they potentially raise fundamental issues concerning the proper spheres for democratically elected Ministers of the Government and judges': Reasons for Grant of Permission to Appeal, 4 August 2020. For the substantive judgment of the Court of Appeal, *see* [2020] EWCA Civ 1605. The decision of the Supreme Court, refusing further permission to appeal, is dated 9 December 2020.

5. In the event that government directives are issued overriding any part of the guidance relating to gathering in public or private spaces, then the government directives would take priority.

§2. Opening of Places of Worship for Private Prayer

12. With effect from 13 June 2020, places of worship were permitted to open for private prayer by individuals.[25] Private prayer was defined as meaning 'prayer which does not form part of communal worship'. The Ministry of Housing, Communities and Local Government issued guidance before the changes came into effect:[26] *COVID-19: guidance for the safe use of places of worship during the pandemic*.[27] The Guidance included a roadmap suggesting further easing not before 4 July 2020, subject to scientific advice. It gave examples of activities which were not permitted. These included communal or corporate worship, defined as 'led devotions/worship/service/prayer by a Minister of Religion or lay person, e.g., Evensong, informal prayer meetings, Jummah, Mass or Kirtan'; together with matters such as: services other than funerals; study groups, and out of school settings, including faith supplementary schools such as Sunday schools, madrassas or yeshivas; choir practice or bell ringing; and tourism.[28] The guidance encouraged faith leaders to consider and adopt the general guidance in the document and seek to include changes that could be made to religious rituals that usually involve close contact between individuals. All use of shared objects and food items should be prevented to limit the spread of infection. The guidance set out key principles designed to minimise the spread of infection to vulnerable persons, and to enforce social distancing.[29]

13. The guidance made practical recommendations including staggered entry times, multiple entrances, and a one-way flow of people entering and leaving the building, as well as the provision of hand sanitisers. It was strongly advised that individuals should be prevented from touching or kissing devotional and other objects that are handled communally; that books and communal resources such as prayer mats, service sheets or devotional material should be removed from use; that singing and/or playing instruments should be avoided;[30] that any prerequisite washing/ablution rituals should not be done at the place of worship and shared

25. The Health Protection (Coronavirus, Restrictions) (England) (Amendment) (No. 4) Regulations 2020 (laid before Parliament on 12 June 2020) introduced a new reg. 5(6)(e) into the original regulations adding to restricted categories of purposes for which a place of worship may be used.
26. It was not unusual for government guidance to precede publication the regulations themselves, which they were designed to explain and amplify.
27. https://www.gov.uk/government/publications/covid-19-guidance-for-the-safe-use-of-places-of-worship-during-the-pandemic.
28. *COVID-19: guidance for the safe use of places of worship during the pandemic* (Ministry of Housing, Communities and Local Government, 12 June 2020).
29. *Ibid.*, para. 3.
30. With the exception of organists who are able to use buildings for practice with appropriate social distancing.

washing areas should be closed; and that where possible faith leaders should discourage cash giving and continue to use online giving and resources where possible.[31] The guidance concluded at paragraph 11 with the following exhortation:

> Each place of worship is strongly advised to implement the measures set out in this guidance to ensure that visitors comply with Regulations, and any risk assessments completed for the venue, for the safety of all those who visit and work there. The Government strongly advises each place of worship ensures that visitors comply with the social distancing guidelines.

§3. Opening of Places of Worship for Communal Worship

14. With effect from 4 July 2020, places were allowed to open for collective acts of worship subject to certain conditions.[32] This permitted communal worship subject to social distancing and a risk assessment on the capacity of the building; marriage ceremonies with fewer than thirty people in attendance and adherence to social distancing; funerals subject to like conditions; and 'life cycle ceremonies', again subject to the same conditions. A range of detailed governmental guidance was issued such as: *COVID-19: guidance for the safe use of places of worship during the pandemic*;[33] and *COVID-19: guidance for managing a funeral during the coronavirus pandemic*.[34] Many religious organisations issued their own guidance, either nationally or locally.[35] By way of example only, Church of England Guidance on the reception of the sacrament encouraged each communicant to sanitise their hands before and after removing their face covering to receive the bread, and before and after putting it on again.[36] A revised set of guidance notes was issued by the Church of England on 17 August 2020 and its online coronavirus resources and frequently asked questions continue to be regularly reviewed and updated.[37] Its most recent guidance, as at the time of writing, is dated 20 January 2021 and provides advice for services during the period of Lent, Holy Week, and Easter. The advice covers

---

31. *COVID-19: guidance* (above) para. 4.
32. The remaining parts of the Health Protection (Coronavirus Restrictions) (England) Regulations 2020 were revoked by the Health Protection (Coronavirus, Restrictions) (No. 2) (England) Regulations 2020 (SI 2020 No. 684) with effect from 00.01 hrs on 4 July 2020. This included the restrictions on the use of places of worship under reg. 6 discussed above. The government issued the *COVID-19: Guidance for the safe use of places of worship from 4 July* on 29 June in advance of the revocation of the regulations.
33. https://www.gov.uk/government/publications/covid-19-guidance-for-the-safe-use-of-places-of-worship-during-the-pandemic-from-4-july/covid-19-guidance-for-the-safe-use-of-places-of-worship-during-the-pandemic-from-4-july.
34. https://www.gov.uk/government/publications/covid-19-guidance-for-managing-a-funeral-during-the-coronavirus-pandemic/covid-19-guidance-for-managing-a-funeral-during-the-coronavirus-pandemic.
35. *See*, for example, the Church of England https://www.churchofengland.org/sites/default/files/2020-07/COVID%2019%20advice%20on%20conducting%20public%20worship%20v1.3.pdf.
36. https://mcusercontent.com/14501d5eebc3e98fa3015a290/files/e3431843-273b-403d-9c70-aed1a0678ae7/COVID_19_Advice_on_the_Administration_of_Holy_Communion_v4.1_0.pdf.
37. This included guidance on Baptisms; Weddings; Funerals; Holy Communion; Confirmation; Ordinations and Consecrations; Conducting public worship; Pastoral support in the community including

various issues relating to these important services including the imposition of the sign of the cross on Ash Wednesday, whether palm crosses can be distributed, and whether the Passion Narrative can be said or sung during worship. During what is generally referred to as the third lockdown (commencing in January 2021) the government did not compel the closure of places of worship. However, many religious leaders commended their closure on health and safety grounds.

§4. The Church of England

15. Unlike other religious organisations in the United Kingdom, the Church of England is established by law and therefore has a unique constitutional position. It is regulated by primary legislation and has therefore been reliant on the Westminster parliament to make provision for certain practical difficulties resulting from the COVID-19 pandemic. The General Synod of the Church of England (Postponement of Elections) Order 2020 (SI 2020 No. 526)[38] postponed the date on which the Convocations of Canterbury and York stand dissolved for the purposes of the Church of England Convocations Act 1966 to 31 July 2021. In other words, it prolongs the life of the General Synod (which is the governing body of the Church of England) for a further twelve months beyond the date when the current five-year Synod would have ended. There are ancillary provisions dealing with individual office-holders.

16. When clergy are licensed, the practice of the Church of England has been for oaths to be administered or declarations made 'in the presence of' the bishop or archbishop. In a joint note from senior lawyers in the Church of England,[39] it was declared that:

> We consider that if the oaths and declaration are dealt with via virtual means such as Skype or Zoom, the licence will be valid.

17. The Canon Law of the Church of England prescribes the mandatory holding of certain daily acts of worship. Ordinarily parishes can apply under Canon B 14A to bishops for dispensation from holding the public services in particular circumstances. In the light of the Government's advice on preventing the spread of infection, the Church of England issued advice to the effect that doctrine of necessity can be relied on and that the public services required by the Canons need not – and should not – take place until further notice.[40]

---

care homes; and a Frequently Asked Questions on the vexed question: *Can a choir sing during worship?*. *See* the commentary at https://www.lawandreligionuk.com/2020/08/17/covid-19-further-changes-to-church-of-england-guidance/.

38. Made pursuant to s. 84 of the Coronavirus Act 2020.

39. *Doing Things Virtually*, a Joint Note from the Vicars General and Registrars of the Provinces of Canterbury and York, April 2020.

40. In effect the Government legislation put the canonical requirement into abeyance. The Canon Law requiring specified acts of worship when the statutory provisions were withdrawn on 4 July 2020. *See* Church of England guidance: *COVID-19 Restarting public worship: some legal questions and*

18. The text discusses the anomalous position in England and Wales whereby, subject to certain limited conditions, those resident in parishes[41] have a legal right to be married in the Anglican parish church, irrespective of their religious affiliation.[42] The reading of the Banns[43] is the most common legal preliminary to such weddings.[44] Banns must be called on three Sundays prior to the wedding at the principal service which is defined as that which the greatest number of persons who habitually attend public worship are likely to attend.[45] Given that no public worship took place during lockdown, it has not been possible to call the Banns, which cannot be called via a live-streamed or virtual service with no congregation physically present nor by a notice on the door of a church. Equally, observing remotely an act of worship which is live streamed does not constitute 'attendance' for the purpose of establishing a qualifying connection by means of habitual worship.[46] As an alternative to marriage by banns, marriages may be solemnised in the Church of England on the authority of a common licence or a special marriage licence, the latter being issued under the authority of the Archbishop of Canterbury.[47]

---

answers https://www.churchofengland.org/sites/default/files/2020-06/COVID%2019%20Restarting%20Public%20worship%20some%20legal%20questions%20and%20answers.pdf.

41. And those with a so-called qualifying connection.
42. *See* para. 523 in the main text. There is a corresponding duty on clergy to conduct the marriage service.
43. In effect a public notification of an intended marriage, intended to allow any objection to be made prior to it being solemnised.
44. *See* ss 6–4 of the Marriage Act 1949.
45. If the marriage is not solemnised within three months of the latest of the Sundays on which Banns are read, the process is void and must be repeated.
46. Where couples have shown genuine efforts to establish habitual worship but have been prevented by the lockdown, then Faculty Office is likely to consider the matter favourably and issue an Archbishop's Special Licence.
47. Such special licences may also be issued in cases of emergency, for example, when one of the party's life expectancy is short.

General Introduction

§1. General Background of the Country

I. Geography

19. The expression 'United Kingdom' refers to the United Kingdom of Great Britain and Northern Ireland. The term 'Great Britain' refers exclusively to England, Scotland and Wales as decreed by the Act of Union between English and Scottish Parliaments in 1707. The 'United Kingdom' does not include the Channel Islands or the Isle of Man, although both are represented by the UK Government, as are the colonies and other dependent overseas territories.[48]

20. This monograph focuses entirely upon England, Scotland and Wales. A different legal system operates in Scotland from that in England and Wales. References to England will include Wales unless otherwise stated.[49] The distinct legal, political and religious situation in Northern Ireland is outside the scope of this work.

21. The United Kingdom has a population of almost 67 million people and is situated in Western Europe. It lies between the North Atlantic Ocean and the North Sea, northwest of France. It covers an area of 244,820 square kilometres and has a coastline of 12,429 kilometres, making it slightly smaller than the US State of Oregon.

22. It is one of five permanent members of the UN Security Council and a founding member of the North Atlantic Treaty Organization (NATO). The United Kingdom withdrew from the European Union on 31 January 2020.[50] It remains, however, a member of the Council of Europe. The United Kingdom is a member of the Commonwealth of Nations, often known simply as the Commonwealth. This is an intergovernmental organisation of fifty-four nation States, most of whom were

48. The Interpretation Act 1978 makes it clear that the phrase 'British Islands' includes the United Kingdom, the Channel Island and the Isle of Man but not the Republic of Ireland.
49. Act of Union 1536.
50. The decision to withdraw followed a UK-wide referendum in June 2016 in which 52% of voters voted to leave the EU, with 48% having voted to remain. The 31 January 2020 withdrawal date began a transition period which is due to end on 31 December 2020. During this time, the UK remains subject to EU law and remains part of the EU customs union and single market. The position post 31 December 2020 will be dependent upon the outcomes of the negotiations between the UK and the EU during the transition period.

formerly part of the British Empire. The Queen is Head of the Commonwealth and is also the Monarch of sixteen members of the Commonwealth (these countries are known informally as the Commonwealth Realms).

II. Constitution

23. The United Kingdom does not have a single document comprising a formal written constitution.[51] Instead, the institutions of government, their powers, limitations and relations with each other and with the citizen are regulated by a wide range of constitutional rules found in a number of sources. In addition to legal sources, such as Acts of Parliament, secondary legislation created under the authority of parliamentary statute and the decisions of the common law courts, constitutional rules are to be found in quasi-legal principles, customs and conventions.

24. The principal characteristics of the constitutional tradition of the United Kingdom include a long-established constitutional monarchy, representative elected government, deference to the rule of law, the supremacy of the House of Commons over the House of Lords in Parliament, the independence of the judiciary and the making of decisions at local government level.

25. The Constitution of the United Kingdom entrusts unlimited power to make law to Parliament by means of the doctrine of the supremacy of Parliament.[52] This is often also referred to as the sovereignty of Parliament. Parliament can create any law it pleases on any subject.[53] The courts cannot challenge the validity of a statute on the basis of its morality[54] or on the grounds that Parliament has broken its internal procedure.[55] However, Parliament cannot bind its successors.[56]

26. There is no constitutional court in the United Kingdom. From 13 October 2009, a Supreme Court has existed, but the Court is markedly different from its United States namesake. Apart from its location and name, the new Supreme Court does not differ substantially from the Appellate Committee of the House of Lords,

51. For a fuller account, *see*, e.g., J. Alder & K. Syrett, *Constitutional and Administrative Law* (11th ed., Palgrave Macmillan 2017). For a classic account, *see* A.V. Dicey, *An Introduction to the Study of the Law of the Constitution* (10th ed., Palgrave Macmillan 1959).
52. *See* J. Alder & K. Syrett, *Constitutional and Administrative Law* Ch. 9 (11th ed., Palgrave Macmillan 2017).
53. *Mortensen v. Peters* [1906] 14 SLT 227; *Manuel v. AG* [1985] 3 All ER 786; *R v. Kelly* [1982] AC 665.
54. *Cheney v. Conn* [1968] 1 All ER 779 at 782. Compare: *Dr Bonham's Case* (1610) 8 Co Rep 107a at 118.
55. *British Railways Board v. Pickin* [1974] 1 All ER 609.
56. *Vauxhall Estates v. Liverpool Corporation* [1932] 1 KB 733; *Ellen Street Estates v. Minister of Health* [1934] 1 KB 590. Note, however, the case of *Thoburn v. Sunderland City Council* [2003] QB 151 concerning references to 'constitutional statutes'.

the body which it replaced. It remains the highest appellate court[57] but the Supreme Court, like the Committee before it, is subordinate to the legislative will of Parliament.

27. The domestic courts of the United Kingdom decline to give effect to the provisions of treaties or other pan-national conventions save to the extent that they have been expressly incorporated into domestic legislation[58] or are mirrored in United Kingdom common law.[59] Domestic effect was given to directly applicable community law by dint of the European Communities Act 1972, while the Human Rights Act 1998 gave further effect to the rights and freedoms guaranteed under the European Convention on Human Rights (ECHR).

28. The European Communities Act 1972 required English courts to give effect to certain laws made by European institutions and to follow the decisions of the European Court of Justice.[60] By virtue of the United Kingdom's decision to withdraw from the European Union, the European Communities Act 1972 was repealed by the European Union (Withdrawal) Act 2018, albeit that its provisions were 'saved' by the European Union (Withdrawal Agreement) Act 2020 and remain in force until the end of the 'transition period'.

29. The Human Rights Act 1998 requires courts to interpret United Kingdom legislation so far as is possible in a manner compatible with the rights outlined in the ECHR,[61] and in so doing they must take into account[62] .– though not necessarily follow[63]– the decisions of the European Court of Human Rights at Strasbourg. In the event of the courts issuing a declaration of incompatibility, the domestic legislation prevails subject to a 'fast-track' system of executive action to bring English law into line with the Convention.[64] The Act also makes it unlawful for public authorities to act in a way which is incompatible with a Convention right.[65]

30. In addition to the enactment of the Human Rights Act 1998, the other most significant change to the constitution in recent years has been the devolution of powers to Scotland and Wales following public referenda.[66] The nature and mechanics of devolution in Wales and Scotland differ considerably.

57. Except in criminal cases in Scotland where there is no onward appeal from the Court of Criminal Appeal.
58. *A-G for Canada v. A-G for Ontario* [1937] AC 326; *Rayner (Mincing Lance) Ltd v. Department for Trade* [1990] 2 AC 418.
59. Note also Constitutional Reform and Governance Act 2010 s. 20 concerning the laying of Treaties before Parliament prior to ratification.
60. Section 2(1).
61. Section 3(1).
62. Section 2(1).
63. *R (Alconbury Developments Ltd) v. Secretary of State for the Environment, Transport and the Regions* [2001] UKHL 23, para. 26.
64. *See* s. 4 (declaration of incompatibility) and s. 10 (remedial action).
65. Section 6.
66. *See* further Part IV, Ch. 3 below.

31. In respect of Scotland, the Treaty of Union 1707, though merging the Parliaments of England and Scotland, preserved Scotland's separate judicial, education and local government systems. The Scotland Act 1998 provided for the creation of a new Scottish Parliament which has legislative competence over all matters except those stated in section 29 of the Act. A referendum took place on 18 September 2014 in Scotland asking, 'Should Scotland be an independent country?' 55.3% voted against Scottish independence; 44.7% voted in favour.

32. In respect of Wales, the Acts of Union 1536–1542 resulted in a common legal, education and local government system for England and Wales. The Government of Wales Act 1998 created a National Assembly for Wales, now the Senedd Cymru, or 'Welsh Parliament',[67] and a system of executive devolution. This gave the Assembly powers which were generally the same as given to central government Ministers in relation to England. This has been buttressed by the Government of Wales Act 2006 which, following a successful referendum in 2011, provided a system of legislative devolution.

§2. Social Facts about Religion

33. According to the 2011 Census, 59.3% of the population of England and Wales regarded themselves as Christian, 4.8% Muslim, 0.50% Jewish, 0.4% Buddhist, 1.5% Hindu, 0.8% Sikh, 0.4% other and 25.1% none with 7.2% of respondents giving no answer. The 2011 Census figures for Scotland showed similar figures: Christians (54%), Muslims (1.4%), Jews (0.1%), Buddhists (0.2%), Hindus (0.3%) and Sikhs (0.2%), 37% ticked the box saying none while 7% declined to answer. Both sets of census results saw a significant decline in the number of Christians as compared to the 2001 census.[68]

34. Generally, sociological evidence has pointed to a steady decline in the membership of most Christian churches, and a decline in religious beliefs albeit not so fast a decline as seen in relation to religious practice. This trend of a widespread 'unchurched and residually Christian religion'[69] has been captured by a number of sociological phrases such as 'believing without belonging'[70] and the concept of 'vicarious religion'.[71]

35. Moreover, at the start of the twenty-first century, Al-Qaeda terrorist attacks in New York on 11 September 2001 and in London on 7 July 2007 have meant that the place of religion in the public sphere has attracted great prominence and debate. Indeed, social historians have commented that from the last decade of the twentieth

67. *See* the Senedd and Elections (Wales) Act 2020.
68. For further discussion of the census statistics and their reliability *see* R. Sandberg, *Religion, Law and Society* Ch. 2 (Cambridge University Press 2014).
69. G. Davie, *Europe the Exceptional Case* ix (Longman and Todd 2002).
70. G. Davie, *Religion in Britain since 1945* (Blackwell 1994).
71. G. Davie, *Europe the Exceptional Case* 19 (Longman and Todd 2002).

century onwards in, 'the midst of overall decline in popular religiosity, British religion showed signs of increasing seriousness and militancy', facilitated in part by the growth of modern technology such as the Internet which helped to foster the 'growing opportunities for vigorous minorities' both liberal and conservative to 'argue their cases, achieve success and push forward agendas'.[72]

36. Three developments may be discerned from the sociological literature a changing moral framework,[73] the rise of consumerism which has led to religion becoming seen as a consumer choice,[74] and the arrival of new forms of religion from outside Europe which have challenged the widely held assumption that 'faith is a private matter'.[75]

§3. Historical Background

I. Overview

37. Different historical relations between religion and the State exist within each of the nations of the United Kingdom. The following brief summary of a complex historical process is confined to England where four broad overlapping but conceptually distinct phases can be discerned.[76]

II. Temporal/Spiritual Division (1066–1530s)

38. The first phase applied in the pre-Reformation period where the jurisdictional boundaries of the English (royal) common law and the Roman (papal) Canon Law were stable and broadly settled. English canonists applied law which came from one of three sources: the papal Canon Law of Rome, the native and provincial laws of the Church in England and the *ius commune* of Western Christendom.[77] Broadly speaking, the common law and the royal courts dealt with 'temporal' matters, while Canon Law and the ecclesiastical courts dealt with 'spiritual' matters; but

---

72. C.G. Brown, *Religion and Society in Twentieth-Century Britain* 297, 309 (Pearson 2006). *See also* R. Griffitih Jones, *Islam and English Law* (Cambridge University Press 2013).
73. R.W. Fevre, *The Demoralization of Western Culture* (Continuum 2000).
74. *See*, e.g., Z. Bauman, *Society under Siege* (Polity Press 2002).
75. G. Davie, *Is Europe an Exceptional Case?* Hedgehog Review 23, 32 (2006). *See*, further, R. Sandberg, *Religion, Law and Society* (Cambridge University Press 2014).
76. *See* N. Doe, *National Identity, the Constitutional Tradition and the Structures of Law on Religion in the United Kingdom*, in *Religions in European Union Law*, Proceedings of the European Consortium of Church and State Research 93–118, 109–110 (Guiffrè 1997); J. Gunn, *Religious Liberty (Modern Period)*, in *Encyclopaedia of Christianity* Vol. 4, 605–617 (E. Fahlbusch et al. eds, Wm. B Eerdmans 2005); J. Rivers, *The Law of Organized Religions* Ch. 1 (Oxford University Press 2010) and R. Sandberg, *Law and Religion* Ch. 2 (Cambridge University Press 2011).
77. *See* W. Stubbs, *Historical Appendix*, in *Report of the Commissioners into the Constitution and Working of the Ecclesiastical Courts* Vol. I (The Society for Promoting Christian Knowledge 1883) and R.H. Helmholz, *The Oxford History of the Laws of England; Volume 1, The Canon Law and Ecclesiastical Jurisdiction from 597 to the 1640s* (Oxford University Press 2004).

this distinction is notoriously artificial, given the partnership of and intersections between secular and church life and government.[78]

III. Discrimination and Intolerance (1530s–c.1689)

39. The Reformation statutes of the 1530s led to the ousting of papal jurisdiction, the liberation of the Church of England from foreign jurisdiction and religious intolerance towards all other religious groups.[79] Since 'subject' was synonymous with 'member of the Church', other religions, most notably Roman Catholics and extreme Protestant dissenters, suffered legal disabilities: oaths were to be taken acknowledging the royal supremacy, and those who failed to attend church were penalised. There were two exceptions: Mary's reign (1553–1558), when papal authority was restored, and the period of the Commonwealth (1648–1660) when there was a 'toleration' of dissenting Protestant groups.

40. Following the Restoration of the monarchy in 1660, the Church of England regained its position and restrictions were placed, once again, on Roman Catholics and Protestant dissenters. All civic office and military holders had to be communicants of the Church of England under the Corporation Act 1661 and the Test Act 1673 and attendance at a religious assembly other than the Church of England was forbidden by the Act of Uniformity 1662 and Conventicle Act 1664.

IV. Religious Toleration (1689–2000)

41. The accession of the Protestant William and Mary led to limited and piecemeal toleration. Most notably the Toleration Act 1689 allowed dissenters their own places of worship, provided they met with unlocked doors and with notice to the local Church of England bishop. However, the Test and Corporation Acts were not repealed. In 1714, the Schism Act forbade nonconformists from having their own schools, but this was repealed in 1718.

42. This lifting of disabilities continued in the nineteenth and twentieth centuries leading to the development of the concept of religious freedom. The Act for the Relief of Catholics 1828 allowed Roman Catholic schools and places of worship and also allowed them entry to the legal profession and relief from taking the oath of royal supremacy. In the same year, the Corporation and Test Acts were repealed. Jews were admitted to Parliament in 1858 and atheists in 1888.

78. R.H. Helmholz, *Roman Canon Law in Reformation England* 4–20 (Cambridge University Press 1990).

79. *See* E. Duffy, *The Stripping of the Altars* (Yale University Press 1992).

43. In the twentieth century, this protection of religious freedom was furthered by limited overlapping protection afforded by the Race Relations Act 1976,[80] the granting of exemptions from generally applicable rules,[81] the recognition of conscientious objection[82] and the conferral of some positive rights.[83]

44. However, this did not amount to a general right to religious liberty.[84] At common law, religious liberty existed as a broad and largely negative freedom rather than a positive right.[85] Legal mechanisms generally favoured individual freedom of action: in the absence of a legal prohibition people were permitted to do as they wished. Although the common law was able to define long-stop boundaries when the circumstances so demanded, the stance adopted by the legislature and judiciary was generally that of passive accommodation as opposed to prescriptive regulation.[86]

V. Positive Religious Freedom (2000–Onwards)

45. As already noted, the Human Rights Act 1998, in force from October 2000,[87] has marked a further substantial shift by protecting religious freedom as a positive legal right rather than a negative accommodation. The Act provided domestic courts with the 'jurisdiction directly to enforce the rights and freedoms' under the ECHR, including freedom of religion under Article 9. The codified rights enforced by the Human Rights Act 1998 and the different rules of interpretation clashed with aspects of the English constitutional heritage, bringing judges more clearly into the political arena and leading to an increase in litigation.[88]

46. Moreover, the Act has been followed by a plethora of laws affecting religion enacted, interpreted and administered in the early years of the twenty-first century – most notably a law on religious discrimination[89]– which cumulatively may be said

---

80. *Mandla v. Dowell Lee* [1983] 2 AC 548; *Seide v. Gillette Industries Limited* [1980] IRLR 427; *J H Walker Limited v. Hussain and Others* [1996] ICR 291.
81. *See*, e.g., Employment Act 1989, s. 11, Motorcycle Crash Helmets Religious Exemption Act 1976 (now *see* Road Traffic Act 1988 s. 16); Welfare of Animals (Slaughter or Killing) Regulations 1995 (SI 1995/731) reg. 2.
82. For example, conscientious objections to military service (Military Service Act 1916, s. 2), oath taking (Promissory Oaths Act 1868; Oaths Act 1978), and abortion (Abortion Act 1967, s. 4).
83. *See*, e.g., the law on education and adoption (e.g., Education Act 1996; Children Act 1989).
84. M. Hill & R. Sandberg, *Is Nothing Sacred? Clashing Symbols in a Secular World*, Public Law 488–506, 489 (2007).
85. *See* generally, M. Hill, *The Permissible Scope of Legal Limitations on the Freedom of Religion or Belief in the United Kingdom*, 19(2) Emory International Law Review 1129 at 1131–1132 (2005).
86. *See* S. Poulter, *Asian Traditions and English Law* 1 (Trentham Books 1990).
87. The Act was in force from 1999 in Scotland and Wales (in relation to the National Assembly). The first case before the domestic courts in which the Human Rights Act 1998 was pleaded was *Starrs v. Ruxton* [1999] Scot HC HCJ 259 (11 November 1999).
88. M. Hill & R. Sandberg, *Is Nothing Sacred? Clashing Symbols in a Secular World*, Public Law 488–506, 490 (2007).
89. Employment Equality (Religion or Belief) Regulations 2003; Equality Act 2006; Equality Act 2010. *See* Part VII, Ch. 7 below.

to be indicative of an abrupt shift from passive religious tolerance to the active promotion of religious liberty as a basic right. These trends are subject to detailed analysis in the text that follows.[90]

90. *See also* the essays contained in *Law and Religion: New Horizons* (N. Doe & R. Sandberg eds, Peeters 2010) and R. Sandberg, *Law and Religion* (especially) Ch. 10 (Cambridge University Press 2011).

Part I. Legal Framework and Sources

Chapter 1. Constitutional Position of Religion

§1. Overview

47. The constitutional position of religion differs in the separate component nations of the United Kingdom. Formerly in all four nations there were established churches. However, legislation disestablishing the national church has been enacted in respect of Ireland and Wales. There are different established churches in England and Scotland respectively. The Church of England is an Episcopal Anglican Church; the Church of Scotland is Presbyterian. The Monarch is the head of the former and a member of the latter.

48. This section will examine the constitutional position of religion in relation to each of England, Scotland and Wales, focusing upon the established churches in the cases of England and Scotland and the mechanism and result of disestablishment in respect of Wales. The legal status of other religious communities is explored in Part III while Part II explores the right to religious freedom in United Kingdom law.

§2. England

49. In England, the established Church of England enjoys a unique relationship with the State. The following explores this relationship beginning with an account of the legal features of establishment (often referred to as the 'incidents of establishment'). Particular attention is then paid to three legal characteristics of establishment: the role Parliament plays in the law-making of the Church, the legal status of the Church courts and rights afforded to parishioners in relation to baptism, marriage and burial.

50. The Church of England consists of the provinces of Canterbury and York. Anomalously, the Diocese of Gibraltar in Europe is 'deemed to be' within the Province of Canterbury.[91] In addition, a number of national and provincial churches have been declared in communion with the See of Canterbury, forming the Anglican

91. Constitution of the Diocese in Europe (1995) para. 2. The Constitution was made pursuant to the Diocese in Europe Measure 1980.

Communion.[92] While offices and institutions exist at the global level of the Anglican Communion, namely the Instruments of Communion (i.e., the office of Archbishop of Canterbury, the Lambeth Conference, the Primates' Meeting and the Anglican Consultative Council), there is no body at this level competent to make decisions binding on individual churches. Two developments in the worldwide Anglican Communion are worthy of note, however, namely the unwritten common law of the Anglican Communion[93] and the Anglican Covenant,[94] as recommended in October 2004 by the Lambeth Commission on Communion, which produced the *Windsor Report* (2004).

I. The Church of England

51. The Reformation legislation of the 1530s resulted in the detachment from Rome, through a series of Acts of Parliament, of the Church of England, as a Church established by law.[95] The concept of establishment, its meaning, effect and future, is 'a complex matter of history, ecclesiology, sociology and politics' which informs 'its legal relationship with the State and the manner of its self-regulation'.[96] There are many divergent meanings of establishment:[97] it has been judicially noted that establishment does not make the Church of England a department of State, rather establishment is a process whereby 'the State has accepted the Church as a religious body in its opinion truly teaching the Christian faith, and given to it a certain legal position, and its decrees, if rendered under certain legal conditions, certain legal sanctions';[98] the Church of England has 'special links with central government' but 'remains essentially a religious organisation' with the relationship with the State 'being one of recognition, not of devolution'.[99]

52. Although 'the juridical nature of the Church [of England] is, notoriously, somewhat amorphous',[100] several incidents of establishment may be identified. The Monarch is the Supreme Governor of the Church of England.[101] The Act of Settlement 1700/1701 requires that the heir apparent must be a 'protestant' (although a person is no longer disqualified from succeeding to the Crown as a result of marrying a Roman Catholic)[102] and that the Monarch 'shall join in communion with the

92. *See* N. Doe, *Canon Law in the Anglican Communion: A Worldwide Perspective* (Oxford University Press 1998).
93. *See The Principles of Canon Law* (Anglican Consultative Council 2008).
94. *See* N. Doe, *An Anglican Covenant: Theological and Legal Considerations for a Global Debate* (SCM Canterbury Press 2008).
95. The Church of England is 'established according to the laws of this realm under the Queen's Majesty, belongs to the true and apostolic Church of Christ': Canons of the Church of England, Canon A1.
96. M. Hill, *Ecclesiastical Law* para. 1.19 (4th ed., Oxford University Press 2018).
97. *See* the discussion in *AG (Victoria) ex relator Black v. Commonwealth* (1981) 146 CLR 559.
98. *Marshall v. Graham* [1907] 2 KB 112.
99. *Aston Cantlow v. Wallbank* [2003] UKHL 37 [2004] 1 AC 546.
100. *Ibid.*, Lord Rodger of Earlsferry, para. 154.
101. Canons of the Church of England, Canon A7.
102. Succession to the Crown Act 2013, s. 2(1).

Church of England as by law established'. In determining the succession to the Crown, the gender of a person born after 28 October 2011 does not give that person, or that person's descendants, precedence over any other person (whenever born).[103] At succession, the Monarch must make a declaration to uphold and maintain the established church.[104] The Monarch, while not a minister of the word of God or the sacraments,[105] enjoys significant rights of patronage, appointing all bishops and archbishops, twenty-six of whom sit in the House of Lords.[106] There are several other connections between the Church of England and Parliament. The Church Commissioners, for instance, are accountable to the House of Commons in the form of Parliamentary questions and prayers are held at the beginning of every sitting in both Houses of Parliament.[107]

II. The Law of the Church of England

53. The law of the Church of England is part of the general law of England.[108] The term 'ecclesiastical law', though problematic,[109] is often used to describe both the internal law of the Church and State legislation and common law relating to the Church.[110]

54. Today, there are various other sources of law pertaining to the Church of England, 'some imposed by the State, others made by the Church with the concurrence of the State and others created internally by the Church itself at national, provincial or diocesan level'.[111] It has been judicially recognised that although 'its enforcement is divided between the ecclesiastical courts and the temporal courts' nevertheless the 'unity and coherence of the law is not affected by the division of jurisdiction as to its enforcement'.[112]

55. The historical position of the Church of England means that two forms of its internal regulation have a special constitutional and legal status. Measures have the status of primary legislation and Canons have the status of secondary legislation.

103. *Ibid.*
104. Accession Declaration Act 1910; Coronation Oath Act 1688.
105. Thirty-Nine Articles of Religion, Art. 37.
106. Appointment of Bishops Act 1533; Manchester Bishopric Act 1847.
107. *See* Part V, Ch. 2.
108. *Mackonochie v. Lord Penzance* (1881) 6 App Cas 424.
109. N. Doe, *The Legal Framework of the Church of England* 12–13 (Clarendon 1996).
110. *Wallbank v. PCC Aston Cantlow* [2001] 2 All ER 363, Sedley LJ.
111. M. Hill, *Ecclesiastical Law* 1.02 (4th ed., Oxford University Press 2018).
112. *AG v. Dean and Chapter of Ripon Cathedral* [1945] Ch. 239, Uthwatt J.

A. Measures

56. The enactment of Measures[113] is regulated by the Church of England Assembly (Powers) Act 1919.[114] Measures are legislation 'passed by the General Synod' which form 'part of the law of the land.'[115] The General Synod of the Church of England has 'power ... in regard to legislation touching matters concerning the Church of England'.[116]

57. Measures are dealt with in Synod in a manner analogous to a Bill in Parliament, and are considered by the Ecclesiastical Committee of Parliament, comprising members of the major parties in both Houses. The Ecclesiastical Committee drafts a report on the nature and effect of the proposed Measure which is communicated to the Legislative Committee of Synod.[117] If the report is unfavourable, the Synod may withdraw the proposed Measure; there is no provision for amending it. If approved, Measures are sent for the Royal Assent.

58. A Measure is defined as 'a legislative measure intended to receive Royal Assent and to have effect as an Act of Parliament'.[118] A Measure has 'the force and effect of an Act of Parliament on Royal Assent being signified thereto in the same manner as to Acts of Parliament'[119] and 'may extend to the amendment or repeal in whole or in part of any Act of Parliament'.[120]

59. A Measure is classified as primary legislation for the purposes of the Human Rights Act 1998.[121] This means that regardless of when enacted, Measures must be read and given effect in a way which is compatible with the ECHR.[122] If a court is satisfied that it is not compatible, it may make a declaration of incompatibility.[123] Remedial action under section 10 does not apply to Measures.

---

113. *See* M. Hill, *Ecclesiastical Law* 1.24–1.26. (4th ed., Oxford University Press 2018).
114. The statute is commonly known as the Enabling Act. This power has been transferred under the Synodical Government Measure 1969 to General Synod.
115. N. Doe, *Canon Law in the Anglican Communion* 17 (Oxford University Press 1998).
116. Church of England Assembly (Powers) Act 1919, preamble. For interpretation *see R v. Ecclesiastical Committee of Both Houses of Parliament, ex parte Church Society* (1994) 6 Admin 670.
117. The procedure governing the enactment of measures is found in the Church of England Assembly (Powers) Act 1919, the Synodical Government Measure 1969, and the Standing Orders of General Synod.
118. Church of England Assembly (Powers) Act 1919, s. 1(5). *See R v. Archbishops of Canterbury and York Ex parte Williamson* (1994) The Times 9 March.
119. Church of England Assembly (Powers) Act 1919, s. 4.
120. *Ibid.*, s. 3(6).
121. Human Rights Act 1998, s. 21.
122. Section 3.
123. Section 4.

B. Canons

60. The General Synod also has the power to legislate by canon[124] under the Synodical Government Measure 1969.[125] Canons, before promulgation by the archbishops, must receive the assent and licence of the Monarch.[126] No parliamentary approval is required. Canons must not be contrary to the royal prerogative, customs, statutes or laws of the realm,[127] and those dealing with liturgy and doctrine cannot be contrary to the doctrine of the Church of England as determined by General Synod.[128]

61. Unlike Measures, a canon may be challenged in the State courts on the basis that it is *ultra vires*.[129] Canons are binding on the clergy but not upon the laity.[130] For the purposes of the Human Rights Act 1998, canons are understood to be 'subordinate legislation',[131] i.e., 'other instrument made under primary legislation'.[132] This means that they must be read and given effect in a way which is compatible with the ECHR.[133] In the case of incompatibility, the status of canons as subordinate legislation means that remedial action could conceivably be taken under section 10. If a court is satisfied that there is incompatibility it may amend or revoke the subordinate legislation unless the primary legislation concerned prevents removal of the incompatibility in which case a declaration of incompatibility may be made as for primary legislation.[134]

62. Parliament, of course, retains its law-making capacity over the Church of England. However, it is sometimes claimed that there is a constitutional convention that Parliament will exercise this power only with the consent of the Church of England.[135] That said, provisions found in the Civil Partnership Act 2004 provide that Ministers may amend or repeal 'church legislation'.[136] It has been contended

124. *See* M. Hill, *Ecclesiastical Law* 1.27–1.29 (4th ed., Oxford University Press 2018).
125. The power 'shall be exercisable' in accordance with the constitution of General Synod (s. 1(2)). Prior to 1970, the power to create canons had been exercised on a provincial basis by the respective convocations of Canterbury and York.
126. Synodical Government Measure 1969, s. 1(3)(a).
127. *Ibid.*, s. 1(3)(b).
128. Church of England (Worship and Doctrine) Measure 1974, s. 4.
129. *Brown v. Runcie* (1990) The Times, 20 February; but *see* M. Hill, *Ecclesiastical Law* para. 1.28 (4th ed., Oxford University Press 2018).
130. *Middleton v. Crofts* (1736) 2 ATK 650.
131. Burton J, *Calvert v. Gardiner and Others* [2002] EWHC 1394 at para. 38, approving M. Hill, *Ecclesiastical Law* para. 1.27 (2d ed., Oxford University Press 2001).
132. Human Rights Act 1998, s. 21.
133. Section 3.
134. Section 4. However, the provisions of the Human Rights Act 1998 may not apply to some canons promulged prior to the Synodical Government Measure 1969 since it may be argued that they were not made under primary legislation. *See* M. Hill, *Ecclesiastical Law* 1.29 (4th ed., Oxford University Press 2018).
135. *See*, e.g., Lord Sainsbury, in debate on the Civil Partnership Act 2004 (Overseas Relationships and Consequential etc. Amendments) Order, 19 July 2005 Columns GC192-3.
136. *See* ss 255 and 259.

that 'while its exercise is currently benign, the words of the statute are broad, giving power to the executive to legislate for the Church of England' but that 'reliance must be placed on the continuance of the constitutional convention that the government does not legislate for the Church of England without its consent.'[137]

III. The Courts of the Church of England

63. The courts of the Church of England and their jurisprudence form part of the law of the land.[138] The following is a very broad outline.

64. Several courts and tribunals currently function within the Church of England. Traditionally they have been seen as exercising two separate jurisdictions: civil and criminal. In modern parlance and practice the distinction is better made between the subject matter exercised, namely the faculty jurisdiction in the case of courts established under the Ecclesiastical Jurisdiction Measure 1963 (as amended by the Ecclesiastical Jurisdiction and Care of Churches Measure 2018), and the discipline of clergy, now under the auspices of statutory tribunals pursuant to the Clergy Discipline Measure 2003.

A. *Faculty Jurisdiction*

65. Each Diocese has a Consistory Court (in the Diocese of Canterbury it is known as the Commissary Court). This is the court of the bishop presided over by the diocesan chancellor. The chancellor is appointed by the bishop (after consultation with the Dean of Arches and Lord Chancellor); candidates must have seven years general qualification[139] or hold high judicial office. The chancellor is independent of the bishop.[140] The Consistory Court is administered by the diocesan registrar to whom the chancellor may delegate certain functions. Its primary jurisdiction concerns the grant or refusal of faculties permitting alterations to the fabric or structure of church buildings and other matters concerning consecrated land, particularly reservation of grave spaces and exhumation.[141] In faculty cases, an appeal from the Consistory Court is to the Court of Arches (in the Province of Canterbury), presided over by the Dean of Arches, or to the Chancery Court (in the Province of York), presided over by the Auditor. The Dean and Auditor (now a single office) is appointed by the archbishops jointly, with approval of the Monarch. If a faculty case

137. M. Hill, *Ecclesiastical Law* 2.07 (4th ed., Oxford University Press 2018). *See also* S. Slack, *Church Autonomy and the Civil Partnership Act 2004*, 9 Ecclesiastical Law Journal 206 (2007).
138. *See* M. Hill, *Ecclesiastical Law* 2.49–2.64 (4th ed., Oxford University Press 2018).
139. Courts and Legal Services Act 1990.
140. *Re St Mary's, Barnes* [1982] 1 WLR 531.
141. *See* M. Hill, *The Faculty Jurisdiction Rules 2013: Simpler Process, Equal Portection*, 16 Ecclesiastical Law Journal 47 (2014).

involves a matter of doctrine, ritual or ceremonial, the appeal lies to the Court of Ecclesiastical Causes Reserved (comprising five persons appointed by the Crown).[142]

B. Clergy Discipline

66. Formerly, under the Ecclesiastical Jurisdiction Measure 1963, cases involving clergy discipline fell into two categories: conduct cases, involving the commission of ecclesiastical offences, such as neglect of duty or conduct unbecoming a cleric, and so-called reserved cases (involving doctrine, ritual or ceremonial). Different procedures applied to archbishops and bishops, and to priests and deacons. For priests and deacons, conduct cases were determined by interview with the bishop, reference to Examiners, and trial in the Consistory Court and an appeal thereafter. For archbishops and bishops, process was by Committee of Enquiry, trial by a Commission of Convocation and appeal to a Commission of Review. Penalties (or censures) included deposition, deprivation, inhibition, suspension, monition and rebuke.

67. The Ecclesiastical Jurisdiction Measure 1963 continues to apply to reserved cases but no longer applies to conduct cases. Since 1 January 2006, the provisions of the Clergy Discipline Measure 2003 have stripped the Consistory Court of its criminal jurisdiction and established a Clergy Discipline Commission for the Church of England instead. Where, following preliminary scrutiny, and formal investigation, the President of the Clergy Discipline Commission decides there is a case to answer; the complaint is referred to a Bishop's Disciplinary Tribunal constituted from a panel of chairmen, clergy and laity for the purpose. A tribunal has jurisdiction to determine disciplinary proceedings against a priest or deacon in the diocese for misconduct and for officiating without authority. The Vicar-General's Court of each province determines these cases with respect to bishops and archbishops.[143]

68. It is generally thought that the decisions of Church courts are subject to judicial review by the High Court.[144] Section 81 of the Ecclesiastical Jurisdiction Measure 1963 states that the High Court has power to enquire into contempt of the Consistory Court upon certification by the chancellor[145] and recognises the supervisory jurisdiction of the High Court over ecclesiastical courts.[146] It has been held

142. *See* M. Hill, *Ecclesiastical Law* para. 7.78 (4th ed., Oxford University Press 2018).

143. For a discussion of the practice and procedure of Clergy Discipline Tribunals, *see* M. Hill, *Ecclesiastical Law* Ch. 6 (4th ed., Oxford University Press 2018); A. Iles, *The Clergy Discipline Measure 2003: A Canter Through Its Provisions and Procedures*, 9 Ecclesiastical Law Journal 250 (2007) and A. Iles, *The Clergy Discipline Measure 2003: A Progress Report*, 16 Ecclesiastical Law Journal 3 (2014).

144. *See* M. Hill, *Judicial Review of Ecclesiastical Courts*, in *English Canon Law* 104–114 (N. Doe, M. Hill & R. Ombres eds, University of Wales Press 1998).

145. Section 81(3).

146. Section 81(2).

that mandatory and prohibiting orders (as they are now styled) lie to prevent or compel the exercise of jurisdiction by the ecclesiastical courts of the Church of England.[147] While it has been a long-settled principle that a quashing order (formerly certiorari) does not lie to overturn the decision of an ecclesiastical court,[148] this rule has been the subject of criticism[149] and may be no longer sustainable, particularly in the light of general developments in judicial review.[150] For the purposes of the Human Rights Act 1998, all courts and tribunals of the Church of England are public authorities and as such must act in a way which is compatible with Convention rights.

IV. Public Ministry

69. Historically, at least, membership of the Church of England was synonymous with citizenship.[151] Accordingly, English law recognises various rights for all who are resident in parishes of the Church of England regardless of their religious belief or practice: parishioners cannot be excluded from public worship[152] nor can those who are confirmed be refused Holy Communion without lawful excuse.[153] Parishioners also have the right to be married[154] and to be buried[155] in the parish church. Every prison must have a chaplain and, if large enough, may also have an assistant chaplain.[156] Both must be clergy of the Church of England. The Secretary of State may also appoint prison ministers representing denominations other than the Church of England.[157]

§3. Wales

70. There is no established church in Wales. The Welsh Church Act 1914 disestablished the Church of England in Wales and created the Church in Wales. However, certain vestiges of establishment continue to apply to the Church in Wales, meaning that the Church in Wales enjoys some constitutional links with the State.

147. *See*, e.g., *R v. North, ex parte Oakey* [1927] 1 KB 491.
148. *R v. Chancellor of St Edmundsbury and Ipswich Diocese, ex parte White* [1948] 1 KB 195.
149. *R v. Chancellor of Chichester Consistory Court, ex parte News Group Newspapers Ltd* [1992] COD 48.
150. *See R v. Exeter Consistory Court, ex parte Cornish* (1998) 5 Ecclesiastical L. J. 212.
151. *Town of Pawlet v. Clark* (1815) 13 US 292.
152. *Cole v. PC* [1937] 1KB 316.
153. Sacrament Act 1547, s. 8, save in cases of necessity.
154. *Argar v. Holdsworth* (1758) 2 Lee 515. This does not include the marriage of same sex couples under the Marriage (Same Sex Couples) Act 2013. *See* Part X, Ch. 1.
155. *Kemp v. Wickes* (1809) 3 Phil Ecc 26; Burial Law Amendments Act 1880. *See also Re St Mary Woodkirk* [2020] ECC Lee 3.
156. Prison Act 1952, s. 7.
157. Section 10.

I. The Church in Wales

71. From 31 March 1920, the Church of England, so far as it extended to and existed in Wales, ceased 'to be established by law'.[158,159] The Crown lost all powers of appointment and no bishops of the Church in Wales were to sit in the House of Lords.[160] However, the Welsh Church Act 1914 did not simply disestablish the Church in Wales;[161] its objective was also 'to re-establish the Church in Wales on a contractual basis'[162] as a 'voluntary organisation'.[163]

II. The Law of the Church in Wales

72. The Welsh Church Act 1914 provided that the 'ecclesiastical law of the Church in Wales' would cease to exist in Wales as the law of the land.[164] However, the Act also provided that the existing law of the Church of England would continue to bind members of the Church in Wales 'in the same manner as if they had mutually agreed to be so bound', subject to modification or alteration, according to the constitution and regulations of the new institutional Church in Wales.[165]

III. The Courts of the Church in Wales

73. The Welsh Church Act 1914 stipulated that the existing ecclesiastical courts ceased 'to exercise any jurisdiction'.[166] Although the Act permitted the Church in Wales to establish courts, such courts cannot exercise coercive jurisdiction and their decisions cannot be appealed against.[167]

IV. Public Ministry

74. Despite disestablishment, many legal rights and responsibilities have remained[168] such as the right to marry,[169] burial rights[170] and the requirement that Welsh prison chaplains must be clerics of the Church in Wales.[171]

---

158. *See* generally N. Doe, *The Law of the Church in Wales* Ch. 1 (University of Wales Press 2002) and N. Doe, *The Welsh Church Act 1914: A Century of Constitutional Freedom for the Church in Wales?*, 22 Ecclesiastical Law Journal 2–14 (2020).
159. Welsh Church Act 1914, s. 1.
160. *Ibid.*, s. 2(2).
161. *Representative Body of the Church in Wales v. Tithe Redemption Commission* [1944] 1 All ER 710.
162. *Powell v. Representative Body of the Church in Wales* [1957] 1 All ER 400 at 403.
163. Welsh Church Act 1914, s. 3; *Re Clergy Orphan Corporation Trusts* [1933] 1 Ch. 267.
164. Welsh Church Act 1914, s. 3(1).
165. *Ibid.*, s. 3(2).
166. *Ibid.*, s. 3(1).
167. *Ibid.*, s. 3(3). *See R v. Provincial Court of the Church in Wales ex parte Clifford Williams* (1999) 5 Ecclesiastical L. J. 217.
168. *See* T.G. Watkin, *The Vestiges of Establishment: The Ecclesiastical and Canon Law of the Church in Wales*, 2 Ecclesiastical Law Journal 110 (1990).

§4. SCOTLAND

75. There are two major Protestant Churches in Scotland: the (Presbyterian) Church of Scotland and the (Anglican) Scottish Episcopal Church of Scotland.[172] Although only the Church of Scotland is established, a brief mention should be made of the Scottish Episcopal Church.

76. Although it is a member of the Anglican Communion, the Scottish Episcopal Church is historically distinct from the Church of England.[173] And, although the Church generally has the legal status of any other non-established religious group, State legislation has granted a few benefits and disabilities that are exclusive to the Church. For example, provided that meetings and worship are not held in the (Church of Scotland) Parish Church, then Sheriffs, Magistrates and Justices of the Peace are 'strictly required' to give protection, aid and assistance to worshippers.[174] All Episcopalian Ministers are 'obliged and required to present [their] Letters of Orders' to the Justices of the Peace to be recorded for a small fee. And Episcopalian Ministers have the right to 'administer the Sacraments and marry'.[175]

I. The Church of Scotland

77. Like the Church of England, the Church of Scotland has been 'a creature of legislation' from the sixteenth century onwards.[176] The organisation of the Church is Presbyterian.[177] The Church of Scotland has famously been described as being 'both established and free'[178] and as enjoying a 'lighter form of establishment' than the Church of England.[179] Although the Monarch swears an oath on Accession to protect the Church and the Presbyterian form of Government, he or she is not Supreme Governor of the Church. The Monarch is a Member of the Church and (unless she chooses to attend in person) is formally represented at the Annual General Assembly by the Lord High Commissioner.[180]

169. Welsh Church (Temporalities) Act 1919, s. 6; Marriage Act 1949, s. 78(2) This does not include the marriage of same sex couples under the Marriage (Same Sex Couples) Act 2013 but note s. 8 of the Act. *See* Part X, Ch. 1.
170. Welsh Church (Burial Grounds) Act 1945.
171. Prison Act 1952, s. 53(4).
172. *See*, generally. A. Rodger, *The Courts, the Church and the Constitution* (Edinburgh University Press 2008).
173. Scottish Episcopalians Act 1711, s. 1; Episcopal Church (Scotland) Act 1864, s. 5; Episcopal Church (Scotland) Act 1964, s. 1.
174. Scottish Episcopalians Act 1711, s. 1.
175. Section 5.
176. Confession of Faith Ratification Act 1560 (Scotland).
177. There are no Bishops or leaders as such: Church of Scotland Act 1921, Articles Declaratory, Art. II.
178. T.M. Taylor, *Church and State in Scotland*, Juridical Review 121 (1957).
179. C.R. Munro, *Does Scotland Have an Established Church?,* 4 Ecclesiastical Law Journal 639 at 645 (1997).
180. C.G. Brown, *The Myth of the Established Church of Scotland*, in *The Scottish Churches and the Union Parliament 1707–1999* at 48 (J. Kirk ed., Scottish Church History Society 2001).

78. The Church of Scotland Act 1921 recognised the Church of Scotland's independence in 'matters spiritual' by recognising the Articles Declaratory passed by the Church General Assembly, which are appended to the Act.[181] It stated that no civil authority has 'any right of interference with the proceedings or judgments of the Church within the sphere of its spiritual government and jurisdiction'.[182] The Articles Declaratory also acknowledge the 'mutual duties' of Church and State to one another.[183] Ministers of the Church of Scotland are 'holders of a public office having a right to ecclesiastical titles'.[184]

79. In *Percy v. Church of Scotland Board of Mission*,[185] a sex discrimination claim brought against the Church of Scotland by a former minister of the Church, it was held by the House of Lords that the claim was not encompassed by the category 'matters spiritual' under section 3 of the Church of Scotland Act 1921 and therefore was not within the exclusive cognisance of the Church of Scotland and its own courts. Lord Nicholls of Birkenhead opined that although the term 'matters spiritual' is not defined, the ordinary understanding of the expression did not extend to the exercise of statutory rights attached to a contract of employment.[186]

II. The Law of the Church of Scotland

80. Section 1 of the Church of Scotland Act 1921 states that the Articles Declaratory are lawful and that all existing laws be 'construed in conformity' with the Articles and be subordinate to them. All 'statutes and laws insofar as they are inconsistent with the Articles Declaratory' were repealed.

III. The Courts of the Church of Scotland

81. Section 3 of the Church of Scotland Act 1921 provides that nothing in that Act 'shall affect or prejudice the jurisdiction of the civil courts in relation to any matter of a civil nature'. Although the courts of the Church of Scotland are courts of the realm,[187] they are treated as a parallel jurisdiction and the secular courts have traditionally refused to review their decisions.[188]

181. All existing laws were said to be 'construed in conformity' with the articles and be subordinate to them: Church of Scotland Act 1921, s. 1.
182. Articles Declaratory, Art. IV.
183. Article VI.
184. R. King Murray, *The Constitutional Position of the Church of Scotland*, Public Law 155 at 159 (1958).
185. [2005] UKHL 73.
186. At para. 40. *See also* Lord Hope of Craighead at paras 133–134.
187. *Presbytery of Lewis v. Fraser* (1874) IR 888; *Logan v. Presbytery of Dumbarton* 1995 SLT 1228.
188. *Lockhart v. Presbytery of Deer* (1851) 13 D 1296; *Wight v. Presbytery of Dunkeld* (1870) 8 M 921; F. Cranmer, *Judicial Review and Church Courts in the Law of Scotland*, Denning Law Journal 49 (1998).

IV. Public Ministry

82. The Articles Declaratory state that as 'a national Church', 'the Church of Scotland' 'acknowledges its distinctive call and duty … to the people in every Parish of Scotland'.[189] Only Church of Scotland ministers are automatically entitled to solemnise a marriage;[190] and the Marriage (Scotland) Act 1977 recognises as valid any form of ceremony recognised by the Church of Scotland 'as sufficient for the solemnisation of marriages'.

189. Church of Scotland Act 1921, Articles Declaratory, Art. III.
190. Marriage (Scotland) Act 1924, s. 18.

Chapter 2. Other Legislation with Regard to Religion

83. Laws affecting religious communities generally are covered in Part III. Other important legislation such as discrimination law[191] and criminal laws[192] affecting religion are addressed at the relevant place in the monograph. Part II explores the right to religious freedom in UK law, focusing upon the impact of the Human Rights Act 1998.

191. *See* Part VI, Ch. 7.
192. *See* Part VI, Ch. 8.

Chapter 3. Typology of the System

84. The modern general framework of State law on religion in Great Britain is characterised by a number of complexities, ambiguities and, sometimes, contradictions.[193] The product of history means that a mild preference exists in respect of the established and disestablished churches described above but it has been argued that these are outweighed by their burdens. Indeed, instances of all three of the models of Church-State relations (State Church Systems, Separation Systems and Hybrid or Cooperationist Systems)[194] can be found in the United Kingdom, leading commentators to suggest that the United Kingdom as a whole may be best understood as a microcosm, including elements of all three models of Church– State relations characteristic of European countries.[195]

193. For a fuller account *see*: R. Sandberg & N. Doe, *Church-State Relations in Europe*, 5(1) Religion Compass 561 (2007); R. Sandberg, *Church-State Relations in Europe: From Legal Models to an Interdisciplinary Approach*, 3(1) Journal Religion Europe 329 (2008); F. Cranmer & J. Oliva, *Church-State Relationships: An Overview*, 4 Law and Justice 162 (2009) and N. Doe, *Law and Religion in Europe* (Oxford University Press 2011).

194. *See*, e.g., G. Robbers, *State and Church in the European Union*, in *State and Church in the European Union* 578–580 (G. Robbers ed., Nomos 2005).

195. M. Hill, *Church and State in the United Kingdom: Anachronism or Microcosm?* in *Law and Religion in the 21st Century* 199–210 (S. Ferrari & R. Cristofori eds, Ashgate 2010).

Part II. Religious Freedom in General

Chapter 1. Individual Religious Freedom

§1. Overview

85. Individual and collective religious freedom is reflected in both international human rights norms and the common law. Often no meaningful distinction can be drawn between individual and collective religious freedom.[196] In international law, freedom of religion provisions are often framed as individual rights which can be exercised in association with others. Religious groups enjoy such rights, although claims are generally made by individual adherents. In domestic law, protection is sometimes afforded to adherents of certain religions: for instance Sikhs are exempt from the requirement to wear a safety hat on a construction site and from the law relating to the wearing of protective headgear for motor cyclists;[197] while Jews and Muslims enjoy exemptions from rules on animal slaughter.[198] More commonly, special provision is afforded on grounds of religion. For instance: it is a defence to charge of having a blade in a public place if the blade is carried 'for religious reasons';[199] and section 1 of the Adoption and Children Act 2002 (and various other statutes regarding the care of children) recognises the right of children to have 'due consideration' given to their 'religious persuasion'. There is provision in the Marriage (Same Sex Couples) Act 2013 relieving religious organisations from any compulsion to solemnise same sex weddings.[200]

196. For a general discussion of how English law protects religion as both an individual and a collective right, *see* R. Sandberg, *Religion and the Individual: A Socio-Legal Perspective*, in *Religion and the Individual* 157–169 (A. Day ed., Ashgate 2008).
197. Employment Act 1989, s. 11; Road Traffic Act 1988, s. 16. For a full account, *see* S. Poulter, *Ethnicity, Law and Human Rights* Ch. 8 (Oxford University Press 1998). *See also* J. Dingemans et al., *The Protections for Religious Rights: Law and Practice* (Oxford University Press 2013).
198. Welfare of Animals (Slaughter or Killing) Regulations 1995, SI 1995/731, reg. 2.
199. Criminal Justice Act 1988, s. 139.
200. Marriage (Same Sex Couples) Act 2013, s. 2. The protection of religious organisations is generally referred to as the 'quadruple lock'. Those religious organisations that wish to solemnise gay marriage may elect to opt in.

86. Traditionally these privileges were rare and hard fought.[201] For instance, the law provides no special protection for Rastafarians for their use of cannabis on religious grounds[202] nor would a defence to a criminal charge grounded on divine law be sustainable.[203] However, two developments in religion law have led to greater prominence being given to freedom of religion.

87. First, the Human Rights Act 1998 gave further effect to the rights and freedoms guaranteed under the ECHR. Whereas previously the ECHR merely had the status of a treaty obligation under international law,[204] Convention rights (including freedom of religion under Article 9) became part of domestic law, justiciable in domestic courts, with effect from 1 October 2000.[205]

88. Second, the Employment Equality (Religion or Belief) Regulations 2003[206] and the Equality Act 2006 prohibited for the first time discrimination on grounds of religion or belief in employment and the provision of goods and services. These provisions are now to be found in the Equality Act 2010.[207]

89. Although there are many ways in which the law of the United Kingdom facilitates religious freedom, this part will focus upon the protection afforded under the Human Rights Act 1998. Other provisions will be examined at the relevant place elsewhere in the text. The law on religious discrimination is examined in Part VII, Chapter 7.

§2. Article 9 ECHR

90. By dint of the Human Rights Act 1998, Article 9 of the ECHR is directly justiciable in domestic courts. It provides:

(1) Everyone has the right to freedom of thought, conscience and religion; this right includes freedom to change his religion or belief, and freedom, either alone or in community with others and in public or private, to manifest his religion or belief, in worship, teaching, practice and observance.

---

201. *See* M. Hill, *Historical Hinterlands for Religious Freedom in the United Kingdom*, 33(2) *Studies in Christian Ethics* 147–155 (2020).
202. *R v. Taylor* [2001] EWCA Crim 2263, *R v. Andrews* [2004] EWCA Crim 947.
203. *Blake v. DPP* [1993] Crim LR 556.
204. Although individual petition to the European Court in Strasbourg had been permitted since 1966. *See* further Part IV.
205. The withdrawal of the United Kingdom from the European Union has no effect on continuing obligations under the ECHR, and the jurisdiction of the European Court of Human Rights in Strasbourg, which are creatures of the Council of Europe. Whether at the future date, the United Kingdom Parliament passes legislation to revoke or amend the Human Rights Act 1998 or resolves to withdraw from the Council of Europe is a matter of political speculation.
206. SI 2003/1660.
207. Notwithstanding the United Kingdom's withdrawal from the European Union, this domestic legislation will remain in force in the United Kingdom, as will EU law generally, unless and until expressly abrogated by later legislation passed by Parliament.

(2) Freedom to manifest one's religion or beliefs shall be subject only to such limitations as are prescribed by law and are necessary in a democratic society in the interests of public safety, for the protection of public order, health or morals, or the protection of the rights and freedoms of others.

91. Article 9 provides a positive right to both the freedom of thought, conscience and religion and the manifestation of religion or belief. The right to freedom of thought, conscience and religion is absolute. It includes the right to hold a religion or belief and to change it free of State interference.[208] In contrast, the right to manifest one's religion or belief is limited by Article 9(1) in that the manifestation must be 'in worship, teaching, practice and observance' and, more importantly, by the possible qualifications in Article 9(2) which permits the State to interfere with the right if the three tests in Article 9(2) are met. The interference must be 'prescribed by law', have one or more of the legitimate aims listed in Article 9(2) and be 'necessary in a democratic society'. Thus, in relation to the right to manifest, litigants need to show that there has been an interference with their manifestation of religion or belief under Article 9(1), the onus then falls on the State to show that this interference is justified under Article 9(2).[209]

92. Most disputes concern manifestation. The case law on individual religious freedom under the Human Rights Act 1998 may thus be conceptualised as involving two broad questions: first, whether there is an interference with the right to manifest under Article 9(1) and second, whether that interference with the right to manifest is justified under Article 9(2). The reminder of this chapter focuses on these two questions. It should be noted, however, that in the language of the Human Rights Act 1998 such claims can only be made against public authorities.[210] The next chapter on collective religious freedom will explore the case law on whether religious groups may bring cases under the Human Rights Act and have cases brought against them.

§3. INTERFERENCE UNDER ARTICLE 9(1)

93. The European Court of Human Rights in Strasbourg generally takes a formulaic approach to Article 9 cases. The Court invariably begins by stressing the importance of the right, citing the leading case, *Kokkinakis v. Greece*,[211] which

208. *Manoussakis v. Greece* (1997) 23 EHRR 387; *Metropolitan Church of Bessarabia v. Moldova* (2002) 35 EHRR 306. *Moscow Branch of the Salvation Army v. Russia* [2006] ECtHR (No. 72881/01) (5 October 2006).

209. *See* M. Hill & K. Barnes, *Limitations on Freedom of Religion and Belief in the Jurisprudence of the European Court of Human Rights*, in *The European Court of Human Rights and the Freedom of Religion or Belief: The First 25 Years Since Kokkinakis* 82–102 (J. Temperman, T.J. Gunn & M. Evans eds, Brill Nijhoff, 2019).

210. As to whether the component parts of the Church of England constitute public authorities, *see Parochial Church Council of Aston Cantlow v. Wallbank* [2004] 1 AC 546.

211. (1994) 17 EHRR 397.

described how 'Freedom of thought, conscience and religion is one of the foundations of a "democratic society" within the meaning of the Convention'. The *Kokkinakis* justification is twofold, stressing both the social and personal functions of religion.[212] The European Court of Human Rights permits a 'margin of appreciation' allowing States to differ from each other in relation to their laws and policies to some extent to allow for their different cultures. While previously Strasbourg has spoken of the existence of a wide margin of appreciation in the sphere of morals and religion (especially in relation to attacks on religious convictions),[213] recent decisions suggest a degree of inconsistency in the deference which the Strasbourg Court will afford to national legislatures on matters of religion.[214]

94. The Court then asks whether there has been an interference with Article 9(1) and if there is whether that interference is justified under Article 9(2). The question of whether there has been an interference is often a formality. The question is sometimes expressed as asking whether Article 9 has been engaged. Some cases suggest that these are two separate tests; others suggest that they are the same question expressed differently.[215]

95. Strasbourg has employed three 'filtering devices' to determine whether Article 9 is engaged: the definition of belief, the manifestation/motivation requirement and the specific situation rule.[216]

I. The Definition of Belief

96. The European Court of Human Rights has taken a liberal approach to the definition of religion. Strasbourg institutions have considered claims concerning scientology,[217] druidism,[218] pacifism,[219] communism,[220] atheism,[221] prolife,[222] Divine Light Zentrum,[223] the Moon Sect,[224] as well as 'splinter' groups within larger traditions,[225] and have invariably done so without questioning whether the objects of

212. P.W. Edge, *Current Problems in Article 9 of the European Convention on Human Rights*, Juridical Review 42 at 47 (1996).
213. *See*, e.g., *Otto Preminger-Institut v. Austria* (1995) 19 EHRR 34 at para. 56.
214. *See* e.g., *Sahin v. Turkey* (2005) 41 EHRR 8 and *Lautsi v. Italy* (2011) 30 BHRC 429.
215. For a full discussion, *see* T. Alves Pinto, *An Empirical Investigation of the Use of Limitations to Freedom of Religion or Belief at the European Court of Human Rights*, 15 Religion and Human Rights 96–133 (2020).
216. R. Sandberg, *Law and Religion* Ch. 5 (Cambridge University Press 2011).
217. *X and Church of Scientology v. Sweden* (1978) 16 DR 68.
218. *Chappell v. United Kingdom* (1987) 53 DR 241.
219. *Arrowsmith v. United Kingdom* (1978) 19 DR 5.
220. *Hazar, Hazar and Acik v. Turkey* (1991) 72 DR 200.
221. *Angeleni v. Sweden* (1986) 51 DR 41.
222. *Plattform 'Ärtze für das Leben' v. Austria* (1985) 44 DR 65.
223. *Omkarananda and the Divine Light Zentrum v. Switzerland* (1981) 25 DR 105.
224. *X v. Austria* (1981) 26 DR 89.
225. For example, *Serif v. Greece* (1999) 31 EHRR 561 (Mufti elected by Mosque congregations in opposition to the Mufti appointed by the Government).

such claims are protected.[226] The general practice of the Court may be illustrated by *X v. Austria*[227] where the question of whether Nazism was outside the scope of Article 9(1) was not addressed; the Commission simply relied on Article 9(2) to hold that the interference was justified. Alternatively, the question of definition may be posed but left unanswered: in *Chappel v. UK*,[228] for instance, although the existence of Druidism as a religion was questioned, the case was decided on the grounds that State restrictions on the celebration of the summer solstice at Stonehenge were justified under Article 9(2).

97. On occasions, however, Strasbourg will require claimants to prove the existence of the religion in question: in *X v. UK*,[229] for example, an application from a prisoner who sought to be registered as a follower of Wicca failed on the grounds that the applicant had 'not mentioned any facts making it possible to establish the existence of the Wicca religion', what Wicca was and why there was a breach. However, 'more recent decisions suggest more generous acknowledgment of non-mainstream religions'.[230]

98. Strasbourg case law tends to revolve around the definition of 'belief', rather than the definition of 'religion'. The term 'belief' is considered in Strasbourg jurisprudence to require a worldview rather than a mere opinion: it was defined in *Campbell and Cosans v. United Kingdom*,[231] in reference to Article 2 of the first protocol to the ECHR,[232] as denoting 'views that attain a certain level of cogency, seriousness, cohesion and importance'.[233] However, provided this threshold is satisfied, the Court has held that 'the state's duty of neutrality and impartiality is incompatible with any power on the state's part to assess the legitimacy of religious beliefs or the ways in which those beliefs are expressed'.[234] Strasbourg has only been prepared to use the belief filter in exceptional cases, such as in relation to a strong 'personal motivation' to have your ashes scattered at home,[235] support of the notion of assisted suicide,[236] and preferences on the part of prisoners as to prison uniform.[237]

226. R. Ahdar & I. Leigh, *Religious Freedom in the Liberal State* 153 (2d ed., Oxford University Press 2013); P.M. Taylor, *Freedom of Religion: UN and European Human Rights Law and Practice* 207 (Cambridge University Press 2005). *See also* J. Martinez-Torron, *Manifestations of Religion or Belief in the Case Law of the European Copurt of Human Rights*, in *The European Court of Human Rights and the Freedom of Religion or Belief: The First 25 Years Since Kokkinakis* 57–81 (J. Temperman, T.J. Gunn & M. Evans eds, Brill Nijhoff 2019).
227. (1963) 13 CD 42.
228. (1987) 53 DR 241.
229. (1977) 11 DR 55.
230. M. Taylor, *Freedom of Religion: UN and European Human Rights Law and Practice* 208 (Cambridge University Press 2005), citing *Omkarananda and the Divine Light Zentrum v. Switzerland* (1981) 25 DR 105, *X v. Austria* (1981) 26 DR 89 and *Chappel v. UK* (1987) 53 DR 241.
231. EHRR 4 (1982): 293.
232. *See* Part IX.
233. Paragraph 36. This definition has also been applied to Art. 9: *Eweida and Others v. United Kingdom* (2013) 57 EHRR 8 at para. 81: 'The right to freedom of thought, conscience and religion denotes views that attain a certain level of cogency, seriousness, cohesion and importance'.
234. *Eweida and Others v. United Kingdom* (2013) 57 EHRR 8 at para. 81.
235. *X v. Germany* (1981) 24 DR 137.
236. *Pretty v. United Kingdom* (2002) 35 EHRR 1.

99. The Strasbourg approach has been replicated at the domestic level. In the House of Lords decision of *R v. Secretary of State for Education and Employment and others ex parte Williamson,*[238] discussed below, Lord Nicholls noted that the protection of 'religion or belief' meant that the question of 'deciding whether a belief is to be characterised as religious ... will seldom, if ever, arise under the European Convention' because it does not matter whether the belief is religious or non-religious.[239] Moreover, Lord Nicholls noted that 'Freedom of religion protects the subjective belief of an individual'.[240] Lord Walker of Gestingthorpe, in particular, doubted whether it was right for courts, except in extreme cases, 'to impose an evaluative filter' at the stage of identifying whether there was a belief, 'especially when religious beliefs are involved'.[241]

100. Lord Nicholls held that 'a belief must satisfy some modest, objective minimum requirements'.[242] His Lordship explained that to be protected under Article 9 beliefs 'must be consistent with basic standards of human dignity or integrity' and 'must relate to matters more than merely trivial. It must possess an adequate degree of seriousness and importance'. For Lord Nicholls, 'The belief must also be coherent in the sense of being intelligible and capable of being understood'. These requirements applied to 'a non-religious belief, as much as a religious belief'; moreover, a non-religious belief 'must relate to an aspect of human life or behaviour of comparable importance to that normally found with religious beliefs.'[243] This test was applied in *Whaley v. Lord Advocate,*[244] concerning the hunting ban. For Lord Hope, the current jurisprudence did 'not support the proposition that a person's belief in his right to engage in an activity which he carries on for pleasure or recreation, however fervent or passionate, can be equated with beliefs of the kind that are protected by Article 9' since that would make it difficult to 'set any limits on the range of beliefs that would be opened up for protection'.[245]

237. *McFeely et al v. UK* (1980) 20 DR 44.
238. [2005] UKHL 15, [2005] 2 AC 246.
239. Paragraph 24.
240. Paragraph 22.
241. Paragraph 57.
242. Paragraph 23.
243. Paragraph 24. In respect of philosophical beliefs under the provisions of the Equality Act 2010, *see Grainger plc v. Nicholson* [2010] ICR 360, which concerned belief in climate change.
244. *Whaley v. Lord Advocate* [2007] UKHL 53.
245. *Whaley v. Lord Advocate* [2007] UKHL 53 at para. 18. In a different legislative context, the Supreme Court attempted a definition of religion in *R (on the Application of Hodkin) v. Registrar General of Births, Deaths and Marriages* [2013] UKSC 77. Lord Toulson stated at [57] that for the purposes of the Places of Religious Worship Registration Act 1855, a religion could be described as 'a spiritual or non-secular belief system, held by a group of adherents, which claims to explain mankind's place in the universe and relationship with the infinite, and to teach its adherents how they are to live their lives in conformity with the spiritual understanding associated with the belief system'.

101. Generally, however, domestic courts have not relied upon the definition of belief as a filter in their interpretation of Article 9.[246] This is shown by two cases concerning religious drug use:[247] in *R v. Taylor*[248] and *R v. Andrews*,[249] cases concerning respectively the possession and importing of cannabis by Rastafarians, the Court of Appeal held that anti-drug laws could be justified under Article 9(2). It was assumed without comment that Rastafarianism was a religion and that drug-taking was capable of being a manifestation of that religion under Article 9(1).

102. The High Court decision in *R (on the Application of Ghai) v. Newcastle City Council*[250] suggested however that Article 9 only affords protection to activities that are at the core of religious life. The case was brought by Hindus and Sikhs who sought to have cremations on open air funeral pyres. Cranston J held that Hindu beliefs about an open air funeral pyre satisfied what he styled 'the *Williamson* thresholds': they had 'the requisite degree of seriousness and importance' and were 'concerned with central rather than peripheral matters'.[251] He held that there had been interference with Article 9(1) but that this interference was justified under Article 9(2). In contrast, Cranston J held that 'Article 9 accords no protection to the Sikh tradition of using open air funeral pyres' because it was conceded that their use was 'simply a matter of tradition' and 'not a matter of dogma and belief'.[252] This somewhat arbitrary distinction is unlikely to be applied in future cases in consequence of the subsequent ruling of the European Court of Human Rights in *Eweida* which rejected the doctrinal mandate test (*see* below).

II. The Motivation/Manifestation Requirement

103. The second filter used in relation to Article 9(1) is the manifestation/motivation requirement, whereby the claimant's actions manifest their religion or belief as opposed to being merely motivated by it.[253] This has been criticised on the basis that the presence or absence of religious motivation may actually serve as a good indicator of whether a belief should be protected and that a rigid adherence to

---

246. Compare this with the case law on religious discrimination. For a discussion of recent case law, *see* A. Hambler, *Beliefs Unworthy of Respect in a Democratic Society: A view from the Employment Tribunal*, 22 Ecclesiastical Law Journal 234–250 (2020).
247. *See* P.W. Edge, *Religious Drug Use in England, South Africa and the United States of America*, 2(1) Religion & Human Rights 165–177 (2006); M. Gibson, *Rastafari and Cannabis: Framing a Criminal Law Exception*, 12 Ecclesiastical Law Journal 324 (2010). R. Sandberg, *Judging Religious Drug Use: The Misuse of the Definition of 'Religion'*, in *The Internationalization of Ayahuasca* 389 (H. Jungaberle & B.C. Labate ed., Lit Verlag 2011).
248. [2001] EWCA Crim 2263.
249. [2004] EWCA Crim 947.
250. [2009] EWHC (Admin) 978.
251. Paragraph 101.
252. Paragraph 102. Although the High Court's decision was later reversed on appeal ([2010] EWCA Civ 59), the Court of Appeal held that the accommodation of the claimant's wishes would not in fact necessarily infringe the legislation relating to cremation. The appellate judgment, therefore, did not focus upon the Art. 9 claim.
253. *Arrowsmith v. United Kingdom* (1981) 3 EHRR 218.

the manifestation requirement 'would seem to discriminate against religions without an established cultural base in European States' whose devotions 'take different forms, such as sexual intercourse, ritual violence, or refusal to pay taxes to a centralised state hostile to their beliefs'.[254]

104. It is not surprising, therefore, that this filter has been applied inconsistently by the Strasbourg Court.[255] In recent Strasbourg decisions the test has often been rephrased as requiring, for example, that the action is 'intimately linked' to the claimant's religion or belief,[256] or whether the actions 'give expression' to their religion or belief.[257] These requirements are seemingly less strict. In *Eweida and Others v. United Kingdom*,[258] the Strasbourg Court held that 'acts or omissions which do not directly express the belief concerned or which are only remotely connected to a precept of faith fall outside the protection of' Article 9.[259] The Court stressed that, although 'an act of worship or devotion which forms part of the practice of a religion or belief in a generally recognised form' would provide an example of an act which was intimately linked to the claimant's belief, 'the manifestation of religion or belief is not limited to such acts'. Whether the act is intimately linked will be fact -specific but the Strasbourg Court noted that 'there is no requirement on the applicant to establish that he or she acted in fulfilment of a duty mandated by the religion in question'.[260]

105. The decision of the Strasbourg Court in *Eweida and Others v. United Kingdom* corrects a confusion found in some domestic judgments concerning whether an act had to be compelled by the religion in question in order to be a manifestation. In *R v. Secretary of State for Education and Employment and others ex parte Williamson*,[261] head-teachers, teachers and parents of children at four independent schools where discipline was enforced by the use of mild corporal punishment alleged, *inter alia*, that the new ban on corporal punishment in schools[262] breached Article 9 as being incompatible with their belief that physical punishment was part of the duty of education in a Christian context.[263]

254. P.W. Edge, *Current Problems in Article 9 of the European Convention on Human Rights*, Juridical Review 42 at 45–47 (1996).
255. S. Knights, *Freedom of Religion, Minorities and the Law* (Oxford University Press 2007), 44; R. Sandberg, *The Changing Position of Religious Minorities in English Law: The Legacy of* Begum, in *Legal Practice and Cultural Diversity* (R. Grillo et al. eds, Ashgate 2009).
256. *C v. UK* (1983) 37 DR 142, 144; *Hasan and Chaush v. Bulgaria* (2002) 34 EHRR 55; *Eweida and Others v. United Kingdom* (2013) 57 EHRR 8.
257. *Knudsen v. Norway* (1985) 42 DR 247.
258. (2013) 57 EHRR 8. For a discussion of the court's decision, *see* M Hill, *Religious Symbolism and Conscientious Objection in the Workplace,* 15 Ecclesiastical Law Journal 191 (2013).
259. At para. 82.
260. *See also* the para. 2 of the partly dissenting opinion of judges Bratza and Björgvinsson.
261. [2005] UKHL 15, [2005] 2 AC 246.
262. Education Act 1998 s. 548 (as amended in 1998).
263. *See*, for instance, Proverbs 13:24.

106. While the Court of Appeal dismissed the claim, holding that the infliction of corporal punishment was not a manifestation for the purposes of Article 9,[264] the House of Lords dealt with Article 9 'overtly and comprehensively, paying careful attention to freedom of religion and belief'.[265] The House of Lords held that although there had been an interference with the applicant's Article 9 rights, this was justified under Article 9(2) as being prescribed by law,[266] necessary in a democratic society for the protection of the rights and freedoms of others,[267] and as having a legitimate aim to protect children as a vulnerable group and promote their well-being.[268]

107. Although Lord Nicholls did note the motivation requirement, stating that "Article 9 does not 'in all cases' guarantee the right to behave in public in a way 'dictated by a belief'",[269] he held that this should not exclude the claim. He further noted that if 'the belief takes the form of a perceived obligation to act in a specific way, then, in principle, doing that act pursuant to that belief is itself a manifestation of that belief in practice' and that 'in such cases the act is "intimately linked" to the belief'.[270] However, he added this did not mean 'that a perceived obligation is a pre-requisite to manifestation of a belief in practice'.[271] That a belief was obligatory was simply good evidence that the exercise of that belief was manifestation protected by Article 9; it was not the case that a belief had to be obligatory to be protected by Article 9.

108. Later cases have not always adhered to Lord Nicholls's analysis.[272] In *R (on the Application of Playfoot (A Child)) v. Millais School Governing Body*,[273] the judge held (questionably) that the absence of a doctrinal obligation to wear a purity ring meant that the practice did not constitute a manifestation of that belief.[274] In *R on the Application of Bashir v. The Independent Adjudicator and HMP Ryehill and the Secretary of State for Justice,*[275] concerned a prisoner who was charged with failing to obey a lawful order contrary to the Prison Rules 1999 when he failed to provide an adequate urine sample as a result of a voluntary religious fast.[276] The judge considered that the fact that the fast was voluntary rather than obligatory was

264. [2002] EWCA Civ 1926.
265. S. Langlaude, *Flogging Children with Religion: A Comment on the House of Lords Decision, in Williamson,* 8 Ecclesiastical Law Journal 335, 345 (2006).
266. Since the ban was 'prescribed by primary legislation in clear terms', Lord Nicholls at para. 48.
267. Lord Nicholls at para. 49.
268. *Ibid.* The means chosen to achieve that aim were appropriate and proportionate: Lord Nicholls at para. 50.
269. Paragraph 30.
270. At paras 32–33.
271. *Ibid.*
272. R. Sandberg, *Controversial Recent Claims to Religious Liberty*, 124 Law Quarterly Review 213 (2008).
273. [2007] EWHC Admin 1698.
274. Paragraph 23.
275. [2011] EWHC 1108 (Admin).
276. A similar matter of principle arose in *Korostelev v. Russia* 29290/10 [2020] ECHR 314, where a Muslim prisoner was reprimanded for praying during the prison's obligatory night-time sleeping period. The reprimand decreased the applicant's chances of early release, and the proportionality of

not a relevant consideration. The correct interpretation of *Williamson* was that 'there is nothing within Article 9 that requires there to be a perceived, much less an objectively demonstrable, obligation for the manifestation of religious belief to be protectable'.[277] This interpretation was reaffirmed by the Strasbourg Court in *Eweida and Others v. United Kingdom,*[278] following which the domestic courts have held that determining whether or not an act is a core component of a religion is not a relevant consideration under Article 9.[279]

III. The Specific Situation Rule

109. The third filtering device may be styled the 'specific situation rule': it recognises that a person's Article 9 rights may be influenced by the particular situation of the individual claiming that freedom. This principle is not of universal application: it only applies where someone voluntarily submits to a voluntary system of rules. Strasbourg has recognised the application of this rule in relation to a detained person,[280] a person who voluntarily submits to military service,[281] a person who voluntarily enter into a contract of employment[282] and those who voluntarily enrol at a university.[283] However, in *Jewish Liturgical Association Cha'are Shalom Ve Tsedek v. France*[284] Strasbourg institutions seemed to go further by imposing an 'impossibility test': the Court commented that an 'alternative means of accommodating religious beliefs had ... to be "impossible" before a claim of interference under Article 9 could succeed'. This broader approach has not been followed in subsequent Strasbourg cases.[285] For instance,[286] in *Thlimmenos v. Greece*[287] the Court simply accepted that the 'set of facts' complained of fell 'within the ambit' of Article 9 since it was 'prompted' by the claimant's religion or belief.[288] The Court noted

---

that sanction was not properly assessed by the domestic courts. The Court concluded that the interference did not strike a fair balance between the competing interests and was disproportionate to the aims identified by the Government, and accordingly could not be regarded as having been necessary in a democratic society. It was held to constitute a violation of Art. 9: paras 64 and 65.

277. Paragraph 21.
278. (2013) 57 EHRR 8.
279. *Mba v. Mayor and Burgresses of the London Borough of Merton* [2013] EWCA Civ 1562. Note, however, the different reasoning of the Court of Appeal judges.
280. *X v. United Kingdom* (1974) 1 D&R at 41–42.
281. *Kalaç v. Turkey* (1997) 27 EHRR 552.
282. *Stedman v. United Kingdom* (1997) 5 EHRLR 544; *Ahmad v. United Kingdom* (1981) 4 EHRR 126.
283. *Karaduman v. Turkey* (1993) 74 DR 93.
284. (2000) 9 BHRC 27.
285. S. Knights, *Freedom of Religion, Minorities and the Law* 44 (Oxford University Press 2007); R. Sandberg, *The Changing Position of Religious Minorities in English Law: The Legacy of* Begum, in *Legal Practice and Cultural Diversity* 267 (R. Grillo et al. eds, Ashgate 2009).
286. The Court has not applied the specific situation rule in the case of a non-religious claimant who has voluntarily submitted to a religious situation. *See Lautsi v. Italy* [2009] ECtHR (Application No. 30814/06).
287. (2001) 31 EHRR 15.
288. Paragraph 42.

that it did 'not find it necessary' to examine whether the facts 'amounted to interference with his rights under Article 9(1)'.[289]

110. In *Eweida and Others v. United Kingdom*[290] the Strasbourg Court held that the specific situation rule should be considered only in relation to the Article 9(2) question of justification and not the Article 9(1) question of interference. It consequence, it is factor to take into account rather than a determinative filtering device. Although a number of previous decisions suggested 'that the possibility of resigning from the job and changing employment meant that there was no interference with the employee's religious freedom', the Court had 'not applied a similar approach in respect of employment sanctions imposed on individuals as a result of the exercise by them of other rights protected by the Convention'.[291] The Court therefore concluded that 'given the importance in a democratic society of freedom of religion, the Court considers that, where an individual complains of a restriction on freedom of religion in the workplace, rather than holding that the possibility of changing job would negate any interference with the right, the better approach would be to weigh that possibility in the overall balance when considering whether or not the restriction was proportionate'.[292]

111. The decision of the Strasbourg Court in *Eweida and Others v. United Kingdom* corrected a confusion found in some domestic judgments concerning the application and scope of the specific situation rule, such as *Copsey v. WBB Devon Clays Ltd.*[293] Elias LJ in *Mba v. Merton London Borough Council*,[294] observed that the question under Article 9 is whether the interference of that right by the employer is proportionate given the legitimate aims of the employer. In substance the justification is likely to relate to the difficulty or otherwise of accommodating the religious practices of the particular individual claimant.

112. The House of Lords decision in *Williamson* recognised the existence of the specific situation rule, but found that it did not apply it to the facts of the case. As Lord Nicholls noted, 'What constitutes interference depends on all the circumstances of the case, including the extent to which in the circumstances an individual can reasonably expect to be at liberty to manifest his beliefs in practice', meaning

289. Paragraph 43.
290. (2013) 57 EHRR 8.
291. At para. 81.
292. *See also* the para. 2 of the partly dissenting opinion of Judges Bratza and Björgvinsson. For a discussion of the implications of *Eweida v. United Kingdom*, *see* M. Hill, *Religious Symbolism and Conscientious Objection in the Workplace*, 15 Ecclesiastical Law Journal 191 (2013).
293. [2005] EWCA Civ 932. *See also Kuteh v. Dartford and Gravesham NHS Trust* [2019] EWCA Civ 818, in which the Court of Appeal upheld the dismissal of a nurse who had inappropriate discussions with patients about her religious faith. Singh LJ noted that the hospital had not imposed a blanket ban on religious speech in the workplace and that, citing *Kokkinakis*, *improper* proselytism is not protected by Art. 9. The nurse's dismissal was a disciplinary matter based on her disobedience of a management instruction and a failure to comply with the provisions of *Good Medical Practice*.
294. [2013] EWCA Civ 1562 at para. 34.

that an individual 'may need to take his specific situation into account'.[295] Lord Nicholls rejected as unrealistic the submission of the Secretary of State that there has been no interference since the ban on corporal punishment 'left open to the parents several adequate, alternative courses of action' such as home education.[296]

113. The opposite approach, however, was employed in some subsequent domestic decisions on Article 9: in response to cases on religious dress, judges relied upon the specific situation rule and applied the rule outside its original contractual setting meaning that English law effectively adopted the 'impossibility' test elucidated in the Jewish Liturgical case.[297] In *R (on the application of Begum) v. Headteacher and Governors of Denbigh High School*,[298] the claimant contended that her school's ban on wearing a *jilbab* was a breach of her Article 9 rights. The House of Lords held unanimously that there was no such breach, with the majority (Lords Bingham of Cornhill, Hoffmann and Scott of Foscote) holding that there had been no interference with the applicant's rights under Article 9(1) because of the specific situation rule. Lord Bingham stated that:

> The Strasbourg institutions have not been at all ready to find an interference with the right to manifest religious belief in practice or observance where a person has voluntarily accepted an employment or role which does not accommodate that practice or observance and there are other means open to the person to practise or observe his or her religion without undue hardship or inconvenience.[299]

He concluded that the Strasbourg case law indicated that 'interference is not easily established'.[300]

114. The approach in *Begum* was applied by the High Court in *R (on the application of X) v. Y School*,[301] and *Playfoot* (above), where no interference with Article 9 was found since the respective claimants had each voluntarily accepted the school's uniform policy. Subsequent cases show a growing reluctance to rely upon the specific situation rule as a filtering device to dismiss claims. In *R on the Application of Bashir v. The Independent Adjudicator and HMP Ryehill and the Secretary of State for Justice*[302] the argument that the claimant should be treated as having voluntarily accepted the restrictions implicit in a prison environment by committing

295. At para. 38.
296. At para. 41.
297. *See* M. Hill & R. Sandberg, *Is Nothing Sacred? Clashing Symbols in a Secular World, Public Law* 488–506 (2007).
298. [2006] UKHL 15.
299. At para. 23.
300. At para. 24.
301. [2006] EWHC (Admin) 298.
302. [2011] EWHC 1108 (Admin).

the offences for which he had been convicted was rejected.[303] The case of *Lyons v. R*[304] concerned a medical assistant in the navy who appealed his conviction for intentionally disobeying a lawful command on the basis that the order contravened his Article 9 rights as a conscientious objector. The Court of Appeal applied the specific situation rule, but as part of the Article 9(2) question of justification rather than the Article 9(1) issue of interference.[305] This interpretation was adopted by the Strasbourg Court in *Eweida and Others v. United Kingdom*,[306] and accordingly, the reasoning in *Begum* should no longer be followed.[307] The fact that a child could go to another school to manifest his or her religion is a factor that falls for consideration under Article 9(2), and accorded such weight as the court or tribunal deems fit.

§4. Justification under Article 9(2)

115. In Strasbourg jurisprudence the focus invariably shifts from the question of interference under Article 9(1) to the Article 9(2) qualifications, which are used to determine whether the interference by the State was justified.[308] The same is also true of domestic decisions, though for the reasons discussed above, in many cases the consideration of Article 9(2) by a domestic court has often been *obiter*, the Court having rejected the claim on the question of interference under Article 9(1). Nevertheless the vast majority of decisions address the three tests laid out in Article 9(2) applying them one by one: to be justified the interference must be 'prescribed by law', have a 'legitimate aim' and be 'necessary in a democratic society'. The remainder of this section explains the ambit of these tests by reference to the Strasbourg jurisprudence and considers how these tests have been applied in the domestic courts.[309]

---

303. At para. 22. *See also National Secular Society v. Bideford Town Council* [2012] EWHC 175 (Admin) at para. 75 and *The Mayor, Commonality and Citizens of London v. Tammy Samede* [2012] EWHC 34 (QB) at 162, and approved at [2012] EWCA Civ 160 at para. 34.
304. [2011] EWCA Civ 2808.
305. Paragraph 28.
306. (2013) 57 EHRR 8. This has been recognised by the Supreme Court: *Bull v. Hall* [2013] UKSC 73 at para. 47.
307. M. Hill, *Religious Symbolism and Conscientious Objection in the Workplace*, 15 Ecclesiastical Law Journal 191, 198 (2013); M. Hill & R. Sandberg, *Is Nothing Sacred? Clashing Symbols in a Secular World,* Public Law 488 (2007) and R. Sandberg, *Law and Religion* 91 (Cambridge University Press 2011).
308. Where the interference with Art. 9 was not directly attributable to the State, since it was the actions of a private company, for instance, then 'the Court must examine whether in all the circumstances the State authorities complied with their positive obligation under Article 9; in other words, whether [the applicant's] right freely to manifest her religion was sufficiently secured within the domestic legal order and whether a fair balance was struck between her rights and those of others': *Eweida and Others v. United Kingdom* (2013) 57 EHRR 8 at para. 91.
309. *See* M. Hill, *The Qualified Right to Freedom of Religion: An Examination of the Limitations Contained in Article 9 of the European Convention on Human Rights*, in (2020) Studia z Prawa Wyznaniowego (forthcoming) and T.A. Pinto, *An Empirical Investigation of the Use of Limitations to Freedom of Religion or Belief at the European Court of Human Rights,* 15 Religion and Human Rights 96–133 (2020).

I. Prescribed by Law

116. This first test requires that the interference must have some basis in domestic law. Strasbourg has defined 'law' broadly to include statutory law and 'written law' encompassing enactments of lower rank than statutes,[310] regulatory measures taken by professional regulatory bodies under independent rule-making powers delegated to them by Parliament,[311] as well as judge-made law and 'unwritten law'.[312] Implicit within this test is the requirement that the interference complies with European rule of law standards.[313] The operation of the law must not be arbitrary.[314] This test has not proved problematic for the domestic judiciary: for instance, the House of Lords has held that both a rule 'prescribed by primary legislation in clear terms'[315] and a school uniform policy[316] was prescribed by law. In relation to the latter, emphasis was given to the fact that schools and their governors were permitted under statutory authority to make rules on uniform and those rules had been very clearly communicated to those affected by them.[317]

II. Legitimate Aim

117. The second test is that the interference fulfils one of the aims listed in Article 9(2). These permitted aims overlap substantially. At Strasbourg, this requirement is often a formality: Taylor has noted that the margin of appreciation adopted by European institutions means that they 'tend to accept rather than challenge the aim claimed by the State, and accordingly pass over this pre-condition with little detailed analysis'.[318] For example, the Strasbourg Court has suggested that a 'wide margin of appreciation' is to be given to domestic authorities where the legitimate aim is health and safety given that local decision-makers are 'better placed to make decisions about clinical safety than a court, particularly an international court which

---

310. *De Wilde, Ooms and Versyp v. Belgium* (1979–1980) 1 EHRR 373.
311. *Barthold v. Germany* (1985) 7 EHRR 383.
312. *The Sunday Times v. United Kingdom* (No. 1) (1979–1980) 2 EHRR 245. In a recent case, the Strasbourg Court considered the confiscation of religious materials on the grounds that they had not been authorised for import. The confiscation was held not to have been prescribed by law where there was clear evidence that the religious material had in fact been so authorised: *Nasirov and Others v. Azerbaijan,* 20 February 2020, European Court of Human Rights, Application No. 58717/10, paras 63 and 66.
313. C. Evans, *Freedom of Religion under the European Convention on Human Rights* 138 (Oxford University Press 2001).
314. *Religious Community of Jehovah's Witnesses of Kryvyi Rih's Ternivksy District v. Ukraine* 3 September 2019, European Court of Human Rights, Application No. 21477/10.
315. *R v. Secretary of State for Education and Employment and others ex parte Williamson* [2005] UKHL 15, [2005] 2 AC 246.
316. This was accepted by all of the Appellate Committee in *Begum*.
317. Lord Bingham at para. 26.
318. P.M. Taylor, *Freedom of Religion: UN and European Human Rights Law and Practice* 301–302 (Cambridge University Press 2005).

has heard no direct evidence'.[319] A similar approach appears to be taken at a domestic level. Although in most cases the legitimate aim is protecting the rights and freedoms of others,[320] referring to the Convention rights of others,[321] a wide range of legitimate aims have been cited by courts. The question of how narrow a legitimate aim may be was addressed by the Court of Appeal in *R (on the Application of Swami Suryananda) v. Welsh Ministers*[322] concerning the decision by the Welsh Assembly Government to order the slaughter of a sacred bullock at the claimant's Hindu temple, who had tested positive for bovine tuberculosis.[323] The claimant contended that there had been a violation of Article 9 because the sacredness of life was a cornerstone of Hindu beliefs. The High Court[324] granted the application for judicial review and quashed the decision by the Welsh Ministers. The Court of Appeal allowed the appeal and on the question of the legitimate aim held that, although there is a risk that an objective may be framed so narrowly that it becomes coincident with the results sought, in the instant case the Welsh Ministers had a public health objective – the eradication or control of bovine tuberculosis.

III. Necessary in a Democratic Society

118. The third test has been the subject of clarification by Strasbourg. For the interference to be necessary in a democratic society, two tests must be met: the interference must correspond to a 'pressing social need' and it must be 'proportionate to the legitimate aim pursued'.[325] This requires a 'balancing exercise' whereby the court asks 'whether the interference with the right is more extensive than is justified by the legitimate aim'.[326] Most cases concerning Article 9(2) focus upon the issue of proportionality. The court in weighing the proportionality of the measures taken operates 'within a margin of appreciation' but is concerned with whether a 'fair balance' has been 'struck'.[327] There needs to be a 'reasonable relationship of proportionality between the means employed and the aim sought to be achieved'.[328] The Court 'generally allows the national authorities a wide margin of appreciation when it comes to striking a balance between competing Convention rights'.[329] Since 'the

319. *Eweida and Others v. United Kingdom* (2013) 57 EHRR 8 at para. 99.
320. *See Begum*, Lord Bingham at para. 26, Lord Hoffmann at 58 and Baroness Hale at 94.
321. The Supreme Court has questioned, however, whether 'the "rights of others" for the purpose of Art. 9(2) (and indeed the other qualified rights in the Convention) are not limited to their Convention rights but include their rights under the ordinary law': *Bull v. Hall* [2013] UKSC 73 at para. 44.
322. [2007] EWCA Civ 893.
323. *See* R. Sandberg, *Controversial Recent Claims to Religious Liberty*, 124 Law Quarterly Review 213 (2008).
324. [2007] EWHC (Admin) 1736.
325. *Serif v. Greece* (2001) 31 EHRR 20.
326. D. Feldman, *Civil Liberties and Human Rights in England and Wales* 57 (2d ed., Oxford University Press 2002).
327. *Eweida and Others v. United Kingdom* (2013) 57 EHRR 8 at para. 91.
328. *Francesco Sessa v. Italy*, App No. 28790/08, Judgment of 3 April 2012, para. 38.
329. *Eweida and Others v. United Kingdom* (2013) 57 EHRR 8 at para. 106. Note the Resolution of the Parliamentary Assembly of the Council of Europe (30 September 2018) in which 'the Assembly reminds States of their obligation to ensure that all the religious communities which accept shared fundamental values are able to benefit from an appropriate legal status guaranteeing the exercise of

notion of proportionality will always contain some subjective element and depend significantly on the context',[330] it is not surprising that different judges have taken differing approaches to this test. In *Begum*, for instance, the House of Lords conceptualised the question largely in terms of proportionality, giving scant attention to identifying a pressing social need.[331] Lady Hale concluded that the school's uniform policy was a thoughtful and proportionate response to reconciling the complexities of the situation.[332]

119. In *R on the Application of Bashir v. The Independent Adjudicator and HMP Ryehill and the Secretary of State for Justice*,[333] the High Court held that 'some care needs to be taken before a Court accepts at face value assertions of an un-particularised sort that making reasonable adjustments would be too administratively inconvenient or too expensive to be contemplated'.[334] The judge concluded that the interference had been disproportionate because there 'was no evidence before the Adjudicator which enabled him to conclude (as apparently he did) that it was proportionate to require all Muslim prisoners engaged in personal fasting to break that fast as and when required to do so for the purposes of providing a [sample] regardless of the circumstances'.[335]

120. In *Bull v. Hall,*[336] Lady Hale accepted that 'the scope for reasonable accommodation is part of the proportionality assessment, at least in some cases'.[337] Her Ladyship also confirmed that following *Eweida and Others v. United Kingdom*[338] the specific situation rule was 'to be taken into account in the overall proportionality assessment, which must therefore consider the extent to which it is reasonable to expect the employer to accommodate the employee's right'.

---

freedom of religion. In the Assembly's view, Member States and religious communities should work together to promote coming together, dialogue and mutual respect: there is no better way of effectively combating all fanaticism and extremism, religious or anti-religious' http://assembly.coe.int/nw/xml/XRef/Xref-XML2HTML-en.asp?fileid=22199&lang=en.

330. C. Evans, *Freedom of Religion under the European Convention on Human Rights* 145 (Oxford University Press 2001).
331. Lord Bingham para. 26, Lady Hale at para. 94.
332. Paragraph 98. Drawing upon *Sahin*, Lord Bingham concluded that that the interference with the Art. 9(1) right was proportionate since the school 'had taken immense pains to devise a uniform policy which respected Muslim beliefs but did so in an inclusive, unthreatening and uncompetitive way': para. 34.
333. [2011] EWHC 1108 (Admin).
334. At para. 29.
335. Similar reasoning appears in the Strasbourg decision of: *Korostelev v. Russia* 29290/10 [2020] ECHR 314.
336. [2013] UKSC 73.
337. At para. 47.
338. (2013) 57 EHRR 8. This has been recognised by the Supreme Court: *Bull v. Hall* [2013] UKSC 73 at para. 47.

§5. OTHER CONVENTION RIGHTS

121. Several other Articles of the ECHR have an impact on religion. They are relevant for two main reasons: first, because the ECHR is a living document, Articles must be interpreted in the spirit of the entire Convention. Second, religious claims may be advanced under Articles other than, or in addition to, Article 9.

122. For instance, registration cases are sometimes argued primarily under Article 11 (peaceful assembly and association). For example, in *Moscow Branch of the Salvation Army v. Russia,*[339] the refusal to grant re-registration to the Moscow Salvation Army on the grounds, *inter alia*, that it was and 'in essence … a quasi-military religious organisation that has a rigid hierarchy of management' was argued to be a breach of Article 11 read in the light of Article 9. It has been suggested that the Strasbourg Court 'has tended to accord a greater degree of scrutiny to the application of restrictions under Article 11(2) than under Article 9(2)'.[340] In *Church of Scientology Moscow v. Russia,*[341] the Court stressed that States 'have only a limited margin of appreciation' under Article 11(2).[342] In *Kimlya v. Russia*[343] it was held that the ability to establish a legal entity in order to act collectively in a field of mutual interest was one of the most important aspects of freedom of association under Article 11 and that a refusal to recognise a legal entity would also constitute interference with the right to freedom of religion under Article 9.

123. Further, the enjoyment of all Convention rights is subject to Article 14. Article 14 forbids discrimination on, *inter alia*, grounds of religion but only does so in regard to 'the rights and freedoms set forth in this Convention'. Article 1 of Protocol 12 extends this to 'any right set forth by law' but this has not been ratified in the UK.

124. This does not mean that a 'violation of a substantive Article need to be established at all in cases involving discrimination' under Article 14.[344] Strasbourg has confirmed that 'a measure which in itself is in conformity with the requirements of the Article enshrining the right or freedom in question may however infringe this Article when read in conjunction with Article 14 for the reason that it is of a discriminatory nature',[345] that is, if the distinction has no objective and reasonable justification.[346] In *O'Donoghue and Others v. United Kingdom,*[347] it was held that a

339. (2007) 44 EHRR 46.
340. M.D. Evans, *Freedom of Religion and the European Convention on Human Rights: Approaches, Trends and Tensions*, in *Law and Religion in Theoretical and Historical Context* 291, 310 (P. Cane et al. eds, Cambridge University Press 2008).
341. (2008) 46 EHRR 16.
342. At para. 86.
343. (2013) 57 EHRR 27.
344. P.M. Taylor, *Freedom of Religion* 182–183 (Cambridge University Press 2005).
345. *Case Relating to Certain Aspects of the Laws on the Use of Languages in Education in Belgium* EHRR 1 (1979–80): 252 (at 282).
346. Infringement with Art. 14 may be justified if it pursues a 'legitimate aim' and if there is a 'reasonable relationship of proportionality between the means employed and the aim sought to be realised' (*Darby v. Sweden* (1991) 13 EHRR 774). The factors to be weighed in the balance when

scheme which exempted those who married in the Church of England from being required to have a certificate of approval was not a breach of the Article 9 rights of two Catholics wishing to marry but did constitute a breach of Article 14 when read together with Article 9.

125. Other Articles will often interact with Article 9, for instance, where freedom of expression clashes with freedom of religion. Strasbourg has held that the freedom to manifest religion does not include a right to be protected from all criticism[348] and freedom of expression contains 'a duty to avoid expressions that are gratuitously offensive to others and profane'.[349] The importance of Article 12 which protects the right to marry and Article 2 of the First Protocol (which protects the right of parents to ensure such education and teaching in conformity with their own religions and philosophical convictions) are explored later.[350]

---

assessing the proportionality of the measure under Art. 14 taken in conjunction with Art. 9 are similar to those considered when assessing proportionality under Art. 9: *Eweida and Others v. United Kingdom* (2013) 57 EHRR 8 at para. 101.

347. ECHR Application No. 34848107.

348. *ÌA v. Turkey* (2007) 45 EHRR 30 at para. 43: 'Those who choose to exercise the freedom to manifest their religion, irrespective of whether they do so as members of a religious majority or a minority, cannot reasonably expect to be exempt from all criticism. They must tolerate and accept the denial by others of their religious beliefs and even the propagation by others of doctrines hostile to their faith.'

349. *ÌA v. Turkey* (2007) 45 EHRR 30 at para. 39.

350. *See* Parts IX and X below.

Chapter 2. Collective Religious Freedom

§1. Overview

126. As noted above, English law recognises and regulates collective religious freedom in a number of other ways. Religious groups enjoy a number of exceptions from general rules, including those in discrimination law. These will be addressed at the relevant points elsewhere in the text.

127. This chapter will focus upon the protection provided under the Human Rights Act 1998. At first sight, section 13 of the Human Rights Act 1998 seems to accord a special protection for the religious freedom of religious organisations. It reads:

> (1) If a court's determination of any question arising under this Act might affect the exercise by a religious organisation (itself or its members collectively) of the Convention right to freedom of thought, conscience and religion, it must have particular regard to the importance of that right.

In this section 'court' includes a tribunal.

128. Section 13 was the result of lobbying by religious groups during the passage of the Human Rights Bill through Parliament.[351] Evangelical Christians, were joined by the Roman Catholic Church, the Chief Rabbi, the Church of Scotland and the Plymouth Brethren, to express concern at the ramifications of the Act.[352] Section 13 was therefore added as 'an attempt to reassure the Churches' about the impact of the Act:[353] the Government contending that religious groups would not generally be 'public authorities' (and thus susceptible to claims under the Act) with the exception of where they stood in the place of the State providing a public service.[354]

129. While, by analogy, certain cases on a parallel provision on freedom of expression and the press have hinted that section 13 might give presumptive priority to religious freedom,[355] it has also been held that section 13 does not allow religious freedom to trump other rights such as Article 6.[356] In practice, it seems the enhanced protection which was envisaged has been ineffective: section 13 hardly

351. *See* S. Lee, *The Cardinal Rule of Religion*, in *Magna Carta, Religion and the Rule Law* Ch. 18 (R. Griffith-Jones & M. Hill eds, Cambridge University Press 2015).
352. P. Cumper, *Religious Organisations and the Human Rights Act 1998*, in *Law and Religion in Contemporary Society* 72 (P.W. Edge & G. Harvey eds, Ashgate 2000).
353. Jack Straw, then Home Secretary, Commons Hansard 20 May 1998: Column 1021.
354. *Ibid.*, Column 1017.
355. *Douglas v. Hello! Ltd* [2001] QB 967, *per* Sedley LJ; *Lakeside Homes Limited v. BBC* [2000] WL 1841602, *per* Cresswell J.
356. *The Queen on the Application of Ullah v. Special Adjudicator* [2002] EWHC 1584 (Admin) *per* Harision J.

features in higher court judgments concerning freedom of religion.[357] Commentators seem agreed that the section is 'rather mild',[358] largely symbolic[359] and 'at best an articulation and codification' of the pre-Human Rights Act position.[360]

130. Notwithstanding the limited effect of section 13, as Article 9 makes clear, the right to manifest religion or belief may be exercised 'either alone or in community with others and in public or private'. This means that religious groups enjoy the protections afforded by the Human Rights Act and may bring claims under the Act. The following sections explore the extent to which religious groups may use human rights and the extent to which the Human Rights Act 1998 applies to religious groups. Before doing so, however, it is necessary to explore briefly the approach taken at Strasbourg to collective religious liberty.

§2. THE STRASBOURG APPROACH

131. Strasbourg has held that Article 9 permits religious autonomy and diversity in terms of the regulation of religious groups. Convention organs have accepted a variety of Church-State relations as being part of the contracting State's margin of appreciation. Mild forms of State preference for one religion over another do not violate the ECHR. It was noted in *Darby v. Sweden*:[361]

> A State Church system cannot in itself be considered to violate Article 9 of the Convention … . However, a State Church system must, in order to satisfy Article 9, include specific safeguards for the individual's freedom of religion.

132. The Grand Chamber in *Refah Partisi v. Turkey*[362] made it clear that States are required to facilitate religious freedom, noting that 'the State's role as the neutral and impartial organiser of the exercise of various religions, faiths and beliefs, … is conducive to public order, religious harmony and tolerance in a democratic society'.[363]

357. M. Hill, *Ecclesiastical Law* para. 1.26, n 81 (4th ed., Oxford University Press 2018): 'this provision has been largely ignored or not applied … '. Note however, *Hamat (Article 9: Freedom of Religion)* [2016] UKUT 286 (IAT) in which Upper Tribunal Judge Jordan stated that [19] 'A distinctive feature of the Human Rights Act's treatment of the right to freedom of thought, conscience and religion is to place it in a distinct category of protection and to create a statutory right which is independent of the Article 9 Convention right'.
358. R. Ahdar & I. Leigh, *Religious Freedom in the Liberal State* 359 (Oxford University Press 2005).
359. P. Cumper, *The Protection of Religious Rights under Section 13 of the Human Rights Act 1998*, Public Law 265 (2000) and J. Wadham & H. Mountfield, *Blackstone's Guide to the Human Rights Act 1998* 55 (Blackstone 1998).
360. M. Hill, *Judicial Approaches to Religious Disputes*, in *Law and Religion* 419 (R. O'Dair & A. Lewis eds, Oxford University Press 2001).
361. (1991) 13 EHRR 774.
362. (2003) 37 EHRR 1.
363. Paragraph 91.

133. Strasbourg has admitted claims by religious groups. Under Article 34, to have standing an applicant must be a person, a non-governmental organisation or group of individuals and that the applicant must be a victim. While originally Strasbourg maintained a line that religious groups only enjoyed Convention rights as individual rights bestowed on members but not grounded in their own right,[364] it has since been accepted that this is an artificial distinction and that a religious group 'is capable of possessing and exercising the rights ... in its own capacity as a representative of its members'.[365] It remains the case, however, that the religious group must be a non-governmental body. The fact that there may be a close affinity between the religious group and the State does not preclude the group from seeking redress in Strasbourg.[366]

§3. Human Rights Claims by Religious Groups

134. Domestic courts have followed Strasbourg in admitting claims by religious groups.[367] In *Gallagher (Valuation Officer) v. Church Of Jesus Christ Of Latter-Day Saints,*[368] the Church of Jesus Christ of Latter-Day Saints (LDS) appealed from the ruling of the Court of Appeal[369] which had held, *inter alia*, that the Temple and several associated buildings were not entitled to the exemption from non-domestic rates as a 'place of public worship' under paragraph 11 of Schedule 5 to the Local Government Finance Act 1988 since it was open only to those 'Patrons' in possession of a 'recommend' as proof of good standing. The House of Lords had previously decided in *Church of Jesus Christ of Latter-Day Saints v. Henning (Valuation Officer)*[370] that the words 'place of public religious worship' could not apply to a place where entry was denied to members of the public. A human rights argument based on Article 9 read in conjunction with Article 14 (discrimination) was raised for the first time at the House of Lords in *Gallagher*, but it was not pursued with any great vigour.[371] Only Lord Scott held there to have been an interference with Article 14 in conjunction with Article 9, notwithstanding there being no breach of the substantive Article. However, he held the discrimination to be justifiable: States were entitled to conclude that religion was capable of being divisive and since 'secrecy in religious practices provides the soil in which suspicions and unfounded prejudices can take root and grow' there was 'every reason why a state should adopt

364. *Church of X v. United Kingdom* (1968) 29 CD 70.
365. *X and the Church of Scientology v. Sweden* (1979) 16 DR 68.
366. *Holy Monasteries v. Greece* (1995) 20 EHRR 1.
367. *See also New Testament Church of God v. Stewart* [2007] EWCA Civ 1004, discussed in Part VI.
368. [2008] UKHL 56.
369. [2006] EWCA Civ 1598.
370. [1964] AC 420.
371. The lack of detailed treatment in the judgment was criticised, for example, in R. Sandberg, *Underrating Human Rights: Gallagher v. Church of Jesus Christ of the Latter-Days Saints*, 11 Ecclesiastical Law Journal 75–80 (2009).

a general policy under which fiscal relief for premises used for religious worship is available where the premises are open to the general public and is withheld where they are not'.[372]

135. The matter was pursued in the European Court of Human Rights: *Church of Jesus Christ of Latter-day Saints v. United Kingdom.*[373] The majority judgment declared the substantive claim admissible, indicating that the taxation status of religious buildings was capable of having an impact on the manifestation of religious belief (as in *Association les Témoins de Jéhovah v. France*[374]), and thus coming within the ambit of Article 9.[375] However, it concluded that the tax exemption was a neutral law which did not have a discriminatory effect on the Church concerned; that any minor prejudice to the LDS was objectively justified; and that the provision fell within the State's margin of appreciation being a matter of economic or social strategy.[376]

§4. Human Rights Claims Against Religious Groups

136. The Human Rights Act 1998 had the potential to be used against religious groups, particularly the established Church of England. If a religious group is regarded as a 'public authority' in the language of the Act then human rights claims may be levelled at it.

137. The case of *Aston Cantlow v. Wallbank*[377] concerned a Parochial Church Council (PCC) of the Church of England which sought to enforce the appellant's liability under the Chancel Repairs Act 1932 to pay for chancel repairs.[378] They contended that the PCC was a 'public authority' and therefore compelled to act in a manner compatible with Convention rights. The House of Lords held that the PCC was not acting as a public authority. It was not a 'core' public authority exercising functions which were governmental,[379] nor a 'hybrid' public authority, some of whose functions being of a public nature. The Church of England generally, and

372. Paragraph 51.
373. App No. 7552/09, 4 March 2014.
374. ECtHR, App No. 8916/05, 30 June 2011, paras 48–54.
375. *See* para. 30.
376. *See* para. 3 of Joint Concurring Opinion. The two judges in the minority, whilst concurring in the result, would have declared the application inadmissible. They deprecated the widening of the term 'ambit', and considered that, in doing so, the majority had made 'the methodology of the Court ... even less comprehensible'.
377. [2003] UKHL 37.
378. Note that from 13 October 2013 chancel repair liability is no longer an overriding interest. In order to be enforceable, the interest must have been registered by this date. Thereafter, if the land is disposed of for valuable consideration, the liability will become unenforceable. Prior to any such case, it remains open to a parish to register the liability whereafter if becomes binding: Land Registration Act 2002 (Transitional Provisions) (No. 2) Order 2003 Art. 2.
379. Lord Nicholls held that to hold that PCCs are core public authorities and are not capable of being victims would be 'an extraordinary conclusion': para. 15.

PCCs in particular, were essentially religious rather than governmental organisations. Even if the PCC were a 'hybrid' public authority, enforcement of chancel repair liability was not a function of a public nature; rather it was a private function.

138. In *Percy*,[380] Lord President Rodger took a similar line, *obiter*, in relation to the Church of Scotland.[381] He treated the Church of Scotland simply as a voluntary organisation, stating that although the laws and the procedures of the Church had much in common with Scots law, this merely revealed 'the hand which those trained in Scots law have had in guiding such proceedings down the centuries'. Despite this, 'the laws of the Church operate only within the Church and her courts adjudicate only on matters spiritual. In other words, the formality and indeed solemnity of all these transactions and proceedings does not disclose an intention to create relationships under the civil law; rather, it reflects the serious way in which the Church regulates the matters falling within the spiritual sphere'.[382]

139. For the purposes of the legal landscape under the Human Rights Act 1998, the General Synod of the Church of England exercises a public function by way of its power to amend statute law: for example, the Worship and Doctrine Measure 1974 repealed what was left of the Act of Uniformity 1662. It is likely that the General Synod (and the General Assembly of the Church of Scotland) will be categorised as hybrid authorities, and therefore bound by Convention rights whenever exercising its public functions but not otherwise.

140. In *R (Baiai and others) v. The Secretary of State for the Home Department and others*,[383] the issue was whether a Home Office scheme which prescribed that any person who was subject to immigration control and wished to enter into a civil marriage in the United Kingdom had to apply to the Secretary of State for a certificate of approval was discriminatory in that it exempted those marrying in accordance with the rites of the Church of England, thereby constituting a breach of Article 12 (right to marry) taken in conjunction with Article 14 (non-discrimination). The High Court[384] concluded that the scheme was indeed discriminatory. In *O'Donoghue and Others v. United Kingdom,*[385] it was held that the scheme constituted a breach of Article 14 when read together with Article 9.

380. *Helen Percy v. An Order and Judgment of the Employment Appeal tribunal dated 22 Mar. 1999* 20 March 2001 Inner House 057/17/99. The substantive case found its way to the House of Lords: *Percy v. Church of Scotland Board of National Mission* [2005] UKHL 73.
381. *Aston Cantlow v. Wallbank* [2003] UKHL 37.
382. At para. 14.
383. At first instance before Silber J, initially at [2006] EWHC 823 but with two subsequent first instance judgments. An appeal on this finding was not pursued by the Secretary of State in the Court of Appeal and did not fall for consideration in the House of Lords: [2008] UKHL 53.
384. [2006] EWHC (Admin) 823.
385. ECHR Application No. 34848107.

Chapter 3. Organisational Religious Freedom

141. With the exception of section 13 of the Human Rights Act 1998, discussed above, no specific legal provision deals with the religious freedom of organisations. However, charitable status, which attaches to many religious organisations, can yield fiscal advantages, the import and extent of which is addressed in Part III below.

Part III. Legal Status of Religious Communities

Chapter 1. Formal Status of Religious Communities

§1. Registration and Charity Law

I. Registration Law

142. Unlike many European countries,[386] English law does not prescribe detailed registration schemes for religious groups.[387] However, although the concept of registration is not part of English law, a multitude of overlapping laws have been enacted to recognise religious groups and to enable them to benefit from legal and fiscal advantages, most notably in the form of exceptions from otherwise generally applicable laws.

143. There are several legal mechanisms which require religious groups to register to acquire a certain legal status, most notably in the form of charitable status, registration as a place of religious worship[388] and for the solemnisation of marriage.[389]

144. Although there is no 'universal legal definition of religion in English law', the Supreme Court has confirmed that 'the understanding of religion in today's society is broad' and 'unless there is some contextual reason for holding otherwise, religion should not be confined to religions which recognize a supreme deity'.[390] For the purposes of the Places of Worship Registration Act 1855, religion has been described 'as a spiritual or non-secular belief system, held by a group of adherents, which claims to explain mankind's place in the universe and relationship with the infinite, and to teach its adherents how to live their lives in conformity with the

386. *See Churches and Other Religious Organisations as Legal Persons* (L. Friedner ed., Peeters 2007).
387. *See* P. Cumper & P.W. Edge, *First Amongst Equals: The English State and the Anglican Church in the 21st Century?*, 83 University of Detroit Mercy Law Review 602 at 608 (2006) and T.J. Gunn, *The Complexity of Religion and the Definition of 'Religion' in International Law*, 16 Harvard Human Rights Journal (2003) fn. 14.
388. Places of Worship Registration Act 1855.
389. Marriage Act 1949, s. 41. On which *see* Part X.
390. *R (on the Application of Hodkin) v. Registrar General of Births, Deaths and Marriages* [2013] UKSC 77 paras 34, 55 and 51.

spiritual understanding associated with the belief system'.[391] The expression 'religious worship' is 'wide enough to include religious services'.[392]

145. Registration as a place of 'public religious worship' or a 'church hall, chapel hall or similar building used in connection with' such a place enables such buildings to be exempt from local council tax.[393] It has been held that the words 'place of public religious worship' could not apply to a place from which the public was excluded and that the words 'in connection with' carry an implication of ancillary use.[394]

146. Any person guilty of public disorder at a registered place of worship commits a criminal offence.[395] Certain ecclesiastical buildings used for the time being for ecclesiastical purposes are exempted from the need for listed building consent.[396] Moreover, groups may seek to register as a charity for the advancement of religion, as discussed below.

II. Charity Law

147. Although originally charity law protected only gifts for the repair of churches and not advancement of religion itself,[397] it was soon accepted that

391. *Ibid.*, para. 57. There is 'a particular reason, if it were needed, for excluding essentially secular belief systems from religion for the purposes of' the Places of Worship Registration Act 1855 in that marriages are also permitted to occur at 'approved premises' such as hotels where no religious service shall be used: para. 58.
392. *Ibid.*, para. 62. This understanding is intended to be broader than the 'unduly narrow' definition previously found at common law where 'a place of religious worship' was defined as 'a place of which the principal use is as a place where people come together as a congregation or assembly to do reverence to God'; 'worship' has been defined as having 'some, at least, of the following characteristics: submission to the object worshipped, veneration of that object, praise, thanksgiving, prayer or intercession'. *R v. Registrar General, ex parte Segerdal* [1970] 2 QB 679 at 707, 709.
393. Section 11 of Sch. 5 to the Local Government Finance Act 1988 (as amended by s. 3 of Sch. 10 to the Local Government Finance Act 1992).
394. *Church of Jesus Christ of Latter-day Saints v. Henning* [1964] AC 420, affirmed by *Gallagher (Valuation Officer) v. Church Of Jesus Christ Of Latter-Day Saints* [2008] UKHL 56. *See also Mount Pleasant Islamic Trust v. Sykes (Valuation Officer)* [2019] 5 WLUK 697 where the Valuation Tribunal concluded that teaching areas within a madrassa were not exempt from rating, although the prayer rooms were.
395. Ecclesiastical Courts Jurisdiction Act 1860. Prosecutions under the Act are rare although *see R v. Farrant* [1973] Crim.L.R. 240 where the Court of Appeal upheld a conviction in circumstances where the Defendant was found in a churchyard at midnight *see*mingly attempting to raise the dead. The Court held that the object of the Act is 'to protect the sacred character of churches and churchyards' and that whether behaviour is indecent is a question of fact for the trial court to determine.
396. Planning (Listed Buildings and Conservation Areas) Act 1990, s. 60(1); Ecclesiastical Exemption (Listed Buildings and Conservation Areas) Order 1994, Arts 4 and 5. This applies to the Church of England, the Church in Wales, the Roman Catholic Church, the Methodist Church, the Baptist Union of Great Britain, the Baptist Union of Wales and the United Reformed Church. All other places of worship (such as those for Jews, Quakers and Lutherans) are subject to secular listed building controls.
397. Preamble to the Statute of Charitable Uses 1601.

trusts,[398] gifts and institutions for the 'advancement of religion' were charitable and thus entitled to legal and fiscal advantages.[399] The Charities Act 2011 has now codified the case law in respect of England and Wales;[400] section 3(1) recognises thirteen different 'descriptions of purposes', the third of which is the 'advancement of religion'.

148. Originally, a very restrictive definition of religion was used to exclude claims for charitable status: advancement of religion was seen as being synonymous with the promotion of the welfare of the Church of England as the established church;[401] other trusts failed as being 'against public policy as furthering the schisms of non-conformity, the errors of Rome or the infidelity of Judaism or heathenism'.[402]

149. However, since the long march of toleration, the concept of 'advancement of religion' widened considerably to include other faiths and denominations.[403] At common law, 'advancement of religion' has been defined as requiring 'faith in a god and worship of that god', thus excluding philosophical beliefs.[404] Advancement of non-religious beliefs may be held charitable under a different head of charity.

150. The definition of religion in the foregoing paragraph has also been relied upon by the Charity Commissioners[405] to hold that the Church of Scientology would not be registered as a charity on the basis that its 'core practices' did not constitute worship since they failed to 'display the essential characteristic of reverence or veneration for a supreme being'. A similar conclusion was reached in respect of The Temple of the Jedi Order where the Commission observed that 'despite being open to spiritual awareness, there is scope for Jediism and the Jedi Doctrine to be advanced and followed as a secular belief system. Jediism therefore lacks the necessary spiritual or non-secular element'.[406]

151. There have been a number of legal developments affecting the definition of religion in charity law.[407] The Charity Commission has recognised the 'promotion

---

398. A trust is a device whereby the ownership of property is split. The legal ownership of property is split from the equitable or beneficial ownership of the property.
399. *Pember v. Inhabitants of Kington* (1639) 1 Eq Cas Abr 95; *Special Commissioners of Income Tax v. Pemsel* [1891] AC 531, at 585.
400. The law was first consolidated in the Charities Act 2006. For Scotland, *see* para. 113 below.
401. *See* the comments of Lord Parker in *Bowman v. Secular Society Ltd* [1917] AC 406, 448.
402. F.H. Newark, *Public Benefit and Religious Trusts*, 62 Law Quarterly Review 234, 235 (1942).
403. *See* P.W. Edge, *Legal Responses to Religious Difference* 5 (Kluwer Law 2002).
404. *Re South Place Ethical Society, Barralet v. AG* [1980] 1 WLR 1565 *per* Dillon J at 1572. This relied on the definition of 'religious worship' found in *R v. Registrar General, ex parte Segerdal* [1970] 2 QB 679, which has now been superseded by that in *R (on the Application of Hodkin) v. Registrar General of Births, Deaths and Marriages* [2013] UKSC 77.
405. Church of Scientology Application to Charities Commission (17 November 1999).
406. The Temple of the Jedi Order- Application for Registration (16 December 2016). For a critique of the decision *see* T. Cheung, *Jediism: Religion at Law?*, 8(2) Oxford Journal of Law and Religion 350–377 (2019).
407. *See* R. Sandberg, *Clarifying the Definition of Religion in under English Law: The Need for a Universal Definition*, 20(2) Ecclesiastical Law Journal 132–157 (2018).

of religious harmony' as a new charitable purpose which is not restricted to 'religions' hitherto recognised under charity law but also includes 'beliefs' as recognised by the ECHR.[408] This is recognised by the Charities Act 2011.[409] That Act also provides a partial definition of religion:

> 'religion' includes–
>
> – a religion which involves belief in more than one god, and
> – a religion which does not involve belief in a god.[410]

152. This removes theoretical uncertainty surrounding whether the common law definition excluded those faiths which believe in more than one god, such as Buddhism. The decisions of the Charity Commission show that the common law definition remains operative, though the tests appear to have been broadened slightly.[411] In relation to an application by the Gnostic Society,[412] the Charity Commission relied on its own guidance[413] to state that there were 'four characteristics of a religion for the purpose of charity law':

(a) belief in a god (or gods) or goddess (or goddesses), or supreme being, or divine or transcendental being or entity or spiritual principle, which is the object or focus of the religion (referred to … as 'supreme being or entity');
(b) a relationship between the believer and the supreme being or entity by showing worship of, reverence for or veneration of the supreme being or entity;
(c) a degree of cogency, cohesion, seriousness and importance;
(d) an identifiable positive, beneficial, moral or ethical framework.[414]

153. While the first two characteristics elaborate and develop the common law definition of religion (which required belief in and worship of a God), the third characteristic brings charity law in line with the requirements found in human rights and discrimination laws requiring 'cogency, cohesion, seriousness and importance'.[415] The fourth characteristic incorporates the morality test found at common law[416] but goes further to introduce a public benefit requirement into the Charity Commission's definition of religion. The Commission held that the application was not for the advancement of religion because the fourth characteristic has not been met.

408. Three Faiths Forum Application (14 June 2002).
409. Section 3(1)h).
410. Section 3(2)a).
411. For criticism of this *see* P. Luxton & N. Evans, *Cogent and Cohesive? Two Recent Charity Commission Decisions on the Advancement of Religion*, Conveyancer & Property Law 144 (2011).
412. Application for Registration of the Gnostic Centre (16 December 2009), para. 23.
413. Charity Commission, *Analysis of the law underpinning Public Benefit and the Advancement of Religion*, February 2008.
414. Paragraph 23.
415. *See* para. 68 above.
416. *See*, *Thornton v. Howe* (1862) 31 Beavan 14 and *Re Watson* [1973] 1 WLR 1472 at 1483–1484: A. Bradney, *Religions, Rights and Laws* 122 (Leicester University Press 1993).

Although the Gnostic Society prayed for humanity and followed Christian teachings such as love thy neighbour, 'there was no evidence of consistent application of such codes on their website or in the literature'.[417] In 2010, the Druid Network for England and Wales was held to be a charity for the advancement of religion since there was belief in a 'supreme being or entity' and 'a relationship between the believer and the supreme being or entity by showing worship of, reverence for or veneration of the supreme being or entity'.[418]

154. As with the other charitable purposes, there are a number of requirements that need to be met which are codified in the Charities Act 2011. The gift or institution must be for charitable purposes only,[419] and must 'be for the public benefit'.[420] Section 4(2) of the Act provides that 'it is not to be presumed that a purpose of a particular description is for the public benefit' but the meaning of this provision remains a matter of debate: while it is commonly thought,[421] not least by the Charity Commission,[422] that this means that there now has to be evidence that the activities of the trust are for the benefit of the public, doubts have been expressed about this interpretation.[423]

155. Subsequent decisions of the Charity Commission have developed its understanding of public benefit.[424] In relation to the application by the Gnostic Society,[425] drawing on its own guidance, the Commission held that there were 'two principles of public benefit': 'There must be an identifiable benefit or benefits' and 'Benefit must be to the public, or a section of the public'.[426] The second principle had not been demonstrated: although courses, seminars and workshops were open

417. Application for Registration of the Gnostic Centre (16 December 2009), para. 44.
418. Application for Registration of the Druid Network (21 September 2010), para. 20. In relation to the fourth characteristic, the Commission referred to the Network's 'principle of honourable relationships' and the way in which the promotion of ethical codes were integrated explicitly in its objects and through its website. The Commission therefore concluded that there was 'evidence of an identifiable positive beneficial ethical framework promoted by the Druid Network that is capable of having a beneficial impact on the community at large': paras 50, 51 and 53.
419. Section 1(1).
420. Section 2(1)(b). *See*, further, F. Cranmer, *Religion and Public Benefit in United Kingdom Charity Law*, in *The Status of Religion and the Public Benefit in Charity Law* 81–100 (B. Bussey ed., Anthem Press 2020).
421. *See*, e.g., F. Quint & P. Hodkin, *The Development of Tolerance and Diversity in the Treatment of Religion in Charity Law*, 2 Charity Law & Practice Review 10, 1, 2 (2007); J. Warburton, *Charities and Public Benefit: From Confusion to Light?*, 10(3) Charity Law and Practice Review 1 (2008) and M. Harding, *Trusts for Religious Purposes and the Question of Public Benefit*, 71(2) Modern Law Review 159 (2008).
422. *See* their current guidance available at https://assets.publishing.service.gov.uk/government/uploads/system/uploads/attachment_data/file/358531/advancement-of-religion-for-the-public-benefit.pdf.
423. *See* J. Hackney, *Charities and Public Benefit*, 124 Law Quarterly Review 347 (2008); P. Luxton, *Public Benefit in the Advancement of Religion after the Charities Act 2006: Another Charity Muddle?*, in *Law and Religion: New Horizons* 117 (N. Doe & R. Sandberg eds, Peeters 2010) and P. Luxton, *Making Law? Parliament v. The Charity Commission* (Politeia 2009).
424. For criticism of this *see* P. Luxton & N. Evans, *Cogent and Cohesive? Two Recent Charity Commission Decisions on the Advancement of Religion*, Conveyancer & Property Law 144 (2011).
425. Application for Registration of the Gnostic Centre (16 December 2009), para. 23.
426. Paragraph 58.

to all to attend, 'the Chair of the Gnostic Society made the decision as to whether or not to allow someone to progress to the higher or second chamber'.[427] In relation to the application by the Druid Network,[428] the Commission returned to the two principles laid out in its decision on the Gnostic Society but now explained that these principles further broke down into sub-principles. The first principle requiring an identifiable benefit or benefits broke down into three sub-principles: principle 1a that 'It must be clear what the benefits are'; principle 1b that 'The benefits must be related to the aims' and principle 1c that 'Benefits must be balanced against any detriment or harm'.[429] The second principle requiring that the benefit must be to the public broken down into four sub-principles: principle 2a that 'The beneficiaries must be appropriate to the aims'; principle 2b that 'the opportunity to benefit must not be unreasonably restricted by geographical or other restrictions'; principle 2c that 'People in poverty must not be excluded from the opportunity to benefit'; and principle 2d that 'Any private benefits must be incidental'.[430] The Commission held that these requirements had been met. Unlike in its consideration of the Gnostic Society application, the Commission accepted that it was common within religions for there to 'be occasions when people need to have reached a certain level of attainment to participate in events'.[431] In September 2013, the Charity Commission posted revised public benefit guidance on its website. Revised supplementary guidance is to follow. However, at the time of writing, the original supplementary guidance on advancement of religion remains on the website even though the Commission states that it is 'under review in light of the revised general guidance ... and no longer forms part of our public benefit guidance'.

156. There is similar provision in Scotland, where the Charities and Trustee Investment (Scotland) Act 2005 provides that 'the advancement of religion' is a charitable purpose[432] and makes special provision for 'designated religious charities'.[433] A fuller discussion of charity law is beyond the scope of this volume.[434]

§2. Legal Status

I. Religious Communities as Unincorporated Associations

157. Religious groups are usually treated as voluntary associations. As noted above,[435] the Church of England and the Church of Scotland (and to a lesser extent

427. Paragraph 60.
428. Application for Registration of the Druid Network (21 September 2010).
429. Paragraphs 59–67.
430. Application for Registration of the Druid Network (21 September 2010), paras 68–79.
431. Paragraph 71.
432. Section 7(2).
433. Section 65.
434. *See* further, A. Iwobi, *Out with the Old, In with the New: Religion, Charitable Status and the Charities Act 2006*, 4 Legal Studies 619 (2009).
435. *See* Part I.

the Church in Wales) also have some recognition in public law. In all other religious groups, the relationship of members as between themselves is governed by quasi-contract and these voluntary organisations are treated as a matter of law as members club or unincorporated associations.[436] The position is very much like the statutory contract imposed by the Welsh Church Act 1914 on members of the Church in Wales.

158. Unincorporated associations exist where two or more people are voluntarily bound together for common purposes and undertake mutual duties and obligations. Unincorporated associations have no legal personality distinct from their members (unlike a corporation): they cannot sue or be sued and cannot hold property (though institutions within them may be legal owners of property if they have the status of corporations or trustees).[437] Religious voluntary associations seeking legal personality can form as a limited company.

II. Statutory Recognition

159. These private law facilities are occasionally buttressed by legislation. Religious groups are sometimes recognised by statute. Examples include the Trustee Appointment Act 1850 which simplified the transfer of places of religious worship from one group of trustees to another, the Sharing of Church Buildings Act 1969 which facilitates ecumenical sharing arrangements as well as more specific pieces of legislation such as the Methodist Church Act 1976, Dawar-e-Hadiyah (England) Act 1993 and United Reformed Church Act 2000. The 2000 Act, for instance, is a Private Act dealing with the unification of the Congregational Union of Scotland with the United Reformed Church and makes provision for trusts dealing with church property.

160. Statutory recognition does not give a religious body legal personality. Roman Catholicism, for instance, is recognised in many statutes such as the Roman Catholic Relief Act 1791 and the Roman Catholic Charities Act 1832. Yet it does not have legal personality in domestic law (the Holy See and the Vatican City do, however, enjoy such status in international law and are thus able to enter international treaties).

436. On which *see* Ch. 4 below.
437. *See*, generally, *Halsbury's Laws of England – Volume 13 Clubs* (5th ed., Lexis Nexis 2009).

Chapter 2. Autonomy of Religious Communities

§1. General Position

161. The autonomy of religious organisations in any legal system is achieved actively, through the express grant and preservation of rights of self-determination, self-governance and self-regulation; and passively, through non-interference on the part of organs of State such as national government, local or regional government or the secular courts.[438] In the United Kingdom there is no systematic provision made for the autonomy of religious organisations and, in the main, a self-denying ordinance of neutrality may be said to predominate.

162. There is a discernible reticence on the part of the English courts to become involved in adjudicating disputes within churches. This reticence may be elevated to a principle of non-interference. As Hoffmann J commented in 1993, 'the attitude of the English legislator to racing is much more akin to his attitude to religion … it is something to be encouraged but not the business of government'.[439] Similarly, Simon Brown J stated in 1992, courts are 'hardly in a position to regulate' religious functions; 'The court must inevitably be wary of entering so self-evidently sensitive an area, straying across the well-recognised divide between church and state'.[440] In HH Sant Baba Jeet Singh Ji Maharaj v. Eastern Media Group Limited and Hardeep Singh,[441] Eady J referred to the 'well-known principle of English law to the effect that the courts will not attempt to rule upon doctrinal issues or intervene in the regulation or governance of religious groups'.[442]

163. In the Court of Appeal in *Khaira v. Shergill*,[443] Mummery LJ had held that the principle of non-justiciability means that the courts will: 'abstain from adjudicating on the truth, merits or sincerity of differences in religious doctrine or belief and on the correctness or accuracy of religious practice, custom or tradition'. This statement was revisited upon the further appeal to the Supreme Court,[444] which affirmed that:

> the distinction between a religious belief or practice and its civil consequences underlies the way that the English and Scottish courts have always, until recently, approached issues arising out of disputes within a religious community or with a religious basis. In both jurisdictions the courts do not adjudicate on the truth of religious beliefs or on the validity of particular rites. But where a claimant asks the court to enforce private rights and obligations which depend on religious issues, the judge may have to determine such religious

438. *See* M. Hill, *Church Autonomy in the United Kingdom*, in *Church Autonomy: A Comparative Study* 267 (G. Robbers ed., Peter Lang 2001).
439. *R v. Disciplinary Committee of the Jockey Club ex parte Aga Khan* [1993] 1 WLR 909 at 932.
440. *R v. Chief Rabbi, ex parte Wachmann* [1992] 1 WLR 1036 at 1043.
441. [2010] EWHC (QB) 1294.
442. Paragraph 5. *See also Blake v. Associated Newspapers* [2003] EWHC 1960.
443. [2012] EWCA Civ 983.
444. *Shergill v. Khaira* [2014] UKSC 33.

> issues as are capable of objective ascertainment. The court addresses questions of religious belief and practice where its jurisdiction is invoked either to enforce the contractual rights of members of a community against other members or its governing body or to ensure that property held on trust is used for the purposes of the trust.[445]

164. The Supreme Court further stated that the law treats unincorporated religious communities as voluntary associations. It views the constitution of a voluntary religious association as a civil contract as it does the contract of association of a secular body. The courts will not adjudicate on the decisions of an association's governing bodies unless there is a question of infringement of a civil right or interest. An obvious example of such a civil interest is the loss of a remunerated office. But disputes about doctrine or liturgy are non-justiciable if they do not as a consequence engage civil rights or interests or reviewable questions of public law.[446] The civil court does not resolve the religious dispute. Nor does it decide the merits of disciplinary action if that action is within the contractual powers of the relevant organ of the association. Its role is more modest: it keeps the parties to their contract.[447]

165. Courts have declared themselves not competent to 'determine the truth of any religious belief'.[448] As Lord Nicholls said in *R v. Secretary of State for Education ex parte Williamson:*[449]

> When the genuineness of a claimant's professed belief is an issue in the proceedings the court will inquire into and decide this issue as a question of fact. This is a limited inquiry. The court is concerned to ensure an assertion of religious belief is made in good faith … . But, emphatically, it is not for the court to embark on an inquiry into the asserted belief and judge its 'validity' by some objective standard such as the source material upon which the claimant founds his belief or the orthodox teaching of the religion in question or the extent to which the claimant's belief conforms to or differs from the views of others professing the same religion. Freedom of religion protects the subjective belief of an individual. In other words, while courts may be concerned with whether the claim of religious belief was made in good faith, they are not concerned with whether the religious belief professed is a good faith in terms of judging the validity of that faith.[450]

166. Courts have also declared themselves to be neutral in matters of religion. In the context of charity law, it has been pronounced that as a result of toleration, 'the court does not prefer one religion to another and it does not prefer one sect to

445. *Ibid.*, para. 45.
446. *Ibid.*, para. 46.
447. *Ibid.*, para. 47.
448. Lord Reid, *Gilmour v. Coats* [1949] AC 426.
449. [2005] UKHL 15, at para. 22.
450. R. Sandberg, *Controversial Recent Claims to Religious Liberty*, 124 Law Quarterly Review 213, 214 (2008).

another'.[451] In *Gilmour v. Coats,*[452] it was held that the Court 'assumes that it is good for man to have and to practise a religion but where a particular belief is accepted by one religion and rejected by another the law can neither accept nor reject it'. Courts have, in the past, declared that 'any religion is at least likely to be better than none',[453] on the basis that religion operates to take a person 'outside his own petty cares and lead him to think of others'.[454] Quite whether a court would express that view now is open to doubt.

167. The following sections examine the exceptional circumstances where courts have intervened. Although the rules and structures of religious groups are generally not imposed by the State, they may be enforced by courts in certain circumstances. The analysis that follows distinguishes between private and public law.

§2. Private Law

168. It has long been accepted that, although generally a religious group is regarded as being a 'private and voluntary religious society resting only upon a consensual basis', courts are nevertheless 'still bound, when due complaint is made that a member of the society has been injured as to his rights, in any matter of a mixed spiritual and temporal character, to inquire into the laws or rules of the tribunal or authority which has inflicted the alleged injury'.[455] This will occur where action is required 'to protect some civil right or interest which is said to be infringed by their operation'.[456] This practice, which may be styled the *Forbes v. Eden* principle, means that courts will not 'enter into questions of disputed doctrine, when not necessary to do so in reference to civil interests'.[457]

169. In practice, this means that a court will intervene in two circumstances. First, a court will intervene where there is a financial interest. As Lord Cranworth noted in *Forbes v. Eden*:

> If funds are settled to be disposed of amongst members of a voluntary association according to their rules and regulations, the Court must necessarily take cognizance of those rules and regulations for the purpose of satisfying itself as to who is entitled to the funds.

170. This means that courts will intervene, for example, to give effect to a contract between members upon which financial rights such as stipends depend and will

451. Plowman J, *Re Watson* [1973] 1 WLR 1472 at 1483. *See also McFarlane v. Relate Avon Ltd* [2010] EWCA (Civ) 880.
452. [1949] AC 426 at 458–459.
453. *Neville Estates v. Madden* [1962] Ch. 832.
454. *Holmes v. AG* (1981) unreported.
455. Sir Robert Phillimore, *Brown v. Curé of Montréal* (1874) LR 6 PC 157.
456. Lord Colonsay *Forbes v. Eden* (1867) LR 1 Sc & Div 568.
457. *Ibid.*

decide whether a party fits the criterion under internal rules if it is for the purpose of becoming the beneficiary of a trust: As Lord Cranworth noted:

> There is no direct power in the Courts to decide whether A. or B. holds a particular station according to the rules of a voluntary association. But if a fund held in trust has to be paid over to the person who, according to the rules of the society, fills that character, then the Court must make itself master of the questions necessary to enable it to decide whether A. or B. is the party so entitled.

171. Second, courts will intervene with regard to the disposal and administration of property. As Lord Cranworth noted, a court 'must necessarily take cognizance of … the rules of a religious association [which] prescribe who shall be entitled to occupy a house, or to have the use of a chapel or other building'.

172. In *Shergill v. Khaira,*[458] the Supreme Court approved what had been said in *General Assembly of the Free Church of Scotland v. Overtoun,*[459] namely that the civil courts do not have the right 'to discuss the truth or reasonableness of any of the doctrines of [a] religious association'. He stated: 'The more humble, but not useless, function of the civil Court is to determine whether the trusts imposed upon property by the founders of the trust are being duly observed.'[460] In charity law, the *cy-près* scheme operates allowing property to be divided where the original charitable purpose had ceased to provide a suitable and effective method of using the property given.[461]

173. The case of *General Assembly of the Free Church of Scotland v. Overtoun*[462] involved a dispute between the majority of the Free Church of Scotland who in 1900 had entered a union with the United Presbyterian Church, and a minority who argued that, in so doing, the majority had acted in breach of the doctrines of the Free Church and, therefore, contrary to the terms of the trusts on which the Church's property was held. The House of Lords found for the minority. Halsbury C concluded that 'when men subscribe money for a particular object and leave it behind them for the promotion of that object, their successors have no right to change the object endowed'.[463] Moreover, 'there is nothing in calling an associated body a Church that exempts it from the legal obligations of insisting that money given for one purpose shall not be devoted to another. Any other view, it appears to me, would be fatal to the existence of every Nonconformist body throughout the country'.[464]

---

458. [2014] UKSC 33.
459. [1904] AC 515 at pp 644–645.
460. *Ibid.*
461. *See Dean v. Burne* [2009] EWHC (Ch) 1250, discussed by J. Rivers, *How Not to Change a Patriarch: A Discussion of Dean v. Byrne*, 12 Ecclesiastical Law Journal 71 (2010).
462. [1904] AC 515. *See* F. Cranmer, *Christian Doctrine and Judicial Review: The Free Church Case Revisited*, 6 Ecclesiastical Law Journal 318 (2002).
463. [1904] AC 626.
464. [1904] AC 627.

174. Another instance where the court may intervene is in relation to cases of defamation. In *Frank Kofi Otuo v. The Watch Tower Bible and Tract Society of Britain*[465] Warby J observed that 'It is not suggested, nor could it be, that the English authorities afford religious bodies a privilege akin to Parliamentary Privilege, such that whatever is said within the context of an official meeting or ceremony of a church or other religious institution is absolutely immune from suit in defamation, or any other tort. The thrust of the domestic authorities is quite different. It is that claims to enforce civil rights should generally be entertained by the Courts, even if they involve some determination of the internal rules or practices of a religious institution, unless that process necessitates an investigation of some matter that is, by its nature, incapable of being objectively assessed.'[466]

§3. Public Law

175. As a matter of public law in England and Wales, while the decisions of the courts of the Church of England are subject to judicial review (since it is established by law), the variously styled courts and tribunals of all other religious communities are not subject to review by the courts of the State. In *R v. Chief Rabbi, ex parte Wachmann,*[467] the claimant sought a judicial review on grounds of procedural unfairness of a decision by the Chief Rabbi, following a commission of enquiry, that Wachmann was no longer morally and religiously fit to hold rabbinical office. Simon Brown J refused leave on the grounds that there was no 'governmental interest in the decision-making power in question', that the Chief Rabbi's 'functions are essentially intimate spiritual and religious functions which the government could not and would not seek to discharge in his place were he to abdicate his regulatory responsibility'.

176. Although this reasoning seems suspect on several counts, not least since the test for judicial review is the presence of 'public' functions not 'governmental',[468] the general principle that the decisions of such religious communities are not subject to judicial review has been followed in relation to decisions made, for instance, by an Imam,[469] a Jewish Beth Din[470] and the Provincial Court of the Church in Wales.[471] This does not mean, however, that there may not be a different outcome in a case where the necessary public element was present.

465. [2019] EWHC 344 (QB).
466. *Ibid.*, para. 48. In the same paragraph the judge further observed that there may be 'truly extreme cases' in which the Court might hold an internal religious practice to be unlawful, such as one relating to human sacrifice.
467. [1992] 1 WLR 1036.
468. *O'Reilly v. Mackman* [1983] 2 AC 237. *See*, however, *Clark v. University of Lincolnshire and Humberside* [2002] 1 WLR 1988.
469. *R v. Imam of Bury Park, ex parte Sulaiman Ali* [1994] COD 142.
470. *R v. London Beth Din ex parte Bloom* [1998] COD 131.
471. *R v. Provincial Court of the Church in Wales, ex parte Clifford Williams*, 5 Ecclesiastical L. J. 129 (1999).

177. The position in Scotland is quite different. Since the Court of Session does not require a contested decision to contain any public law element in order for it to be reviewable,[472] it does not hesitate to review decisions by the tribunals of voluntary bodies where a patrimonial interest is involved. In *Brentnall v. Free Presbyterian Church of Scotland,*[473] for example, the Inner House was prepared to reduce the decision of the Free Presbyterian Synod to suspend Mr Brentnall from the exercise of his ministry and to grant reparation, on the grounds that the proceedings before the Synod had been contrary to the rules of natural justice.

472. *See West v. Secretary of State for Scotland* 1992 SC 385.
473. 1986 SLT 470.

Chapter 3. Fundamental Rights and Religious Communities

178. The effect of the ECHR upon religious communities is explored in Part II, Chapter 2.

Chapter 4. Contractual Religious Freedom

179. As stated above, religious bodies other than the Church of England and their internal laws are generally regulated by private rather than by public law. However, there are exceptions to this general picture in that the rules of certain churches have received statutory recognition. Notably, the Baptist and Congregational Trusts Act 1951 recognises the 'constitution' in the Baptist 'handbook' while the Methodist Church Act 1976 gave statutory recognition to and made further provision for the internal 'constitution' of the Methodist Church and its deed of union and model trust deeds. Generally, however, the laws of other religious groups are regarded as forming a contractual bond between members in much the same way as the contractual religious freedom imposed upon the Church in Wales by the Welsh Church Act 1914.[474]

180. The rules and structures of voluntary associations are binding on assenting members. As Lord Kingsdown acknowledged in *Long v. Bishop of Cape Town*,[475] members 'may adopt rules for enforcing discipline within their body which will be binding on those who, expressly or by implication, have assented to them'. These rules and structures are also binding on the association itself; thus, for example: 'The law imposes on the church a duty not to deprive a pastor of his office which carries a stipend, save in accordance with the procedures set forth in the book of rules.'[476]

181. This contractual bond may be styled the doctrine of consensual compact. The doctrine is most fully elucidated in the Australian case of *Scandrett v. Dowling*,[477] concerning the Anglican Church in Australia where it was held that 'the binding effect of the 'voluntary consensual compact … must have come from the shared faith of the members of the Church, or … their baptism in Christ', from 'a willingness to be bound to it because of shared faith … in *foro conscientiae*' 'its binding effect does not come from the availability of the secular sanctions of State courts of law'; 'the availability of these latter sanctions when spiritual matters become mixed with property matters is an incident of the consensual compact or contract'; so: 'where property is involved the consensual compact or contract is given the same effect, in relation to property matters, as if it were a common law contract, but does not in any way alter the primary basis of that compact or contract'.

182. These principles of contractual religious freedom also apply to the courts and tribunals of religious bodies.[478] The Arbitration Act 1996 provides that 'parties

474. *See* Part I.
475. (1863) 1 Moore NS Cases 461.
476. Lord Templeman, *Davies v. Presbyterian Church of Wales* [1986] 1 WLR 323.
477. [1992] 27 NSWLR 483.
478. *See* further the findings of Cardiff University's 'Social Cohesion and Civil Law: Marriage, Divorce and Religious Courts' Research Project funded by the AHRC/ESRC Religion and Society Programme.

should be free to agree how their disputes are resolved, subject only to such safeguards as are necessary in the public interest'.[479] Section 45 of the Act enables parties to choose for disputes to be decided 'in accordance with other considerations' rather than 'in accordance with law'.[480] This allows parties to choose systems of religious law, such as sharia law, since the definition of law for these purposes has generally been understood to mean the law of a State. However, the outcome reached by applying such considerations would be overridden by the public interest. For instance, in *KC & Anor v. City of Westminster Social & Community Services Dept,*[481] a marriage by telephone link between England and Bangladesh where there was concern as to the lack of mental capacity of one party was held to be a valid marriage under sharia and Bangladeshi law by the Court of Appeal but was held not valid under English law: the marriage was 'sufficiently offensive to the conscience of the English court' that it should refuse to recognise it.[482] The laws prohibiting discrimination on grounds of religion or belief[483] do not apply to the selection, engagement or appointment of an arbitrator.[484] On these principles, parties to a dispute may take it to a religious court (for Jews, for example, the *Beth Din*) and to enter into a contract to be bound by that court's decision. Once the parties had contracted to be so bound, the secular courts would then enforce the decision of the religious court under the secular law of contract.[485]

---

479. Section 1.
480. *See* the discussion in *Sayyed Mohammed Musawi v. R.E. International (UK) Ltd* [2007] EWHC 298.
481. [2008] EWCA Civ 198.
482. At para. 101.
483. *See* Part VII, Ch. 7.
484. *Jivraj v. Hashwani* [2011] UKSC 40.
485. For an example *see Kohn v. Wagschal and Ors* [2007] EWCA Civ 1022. *See also AI v. mt* [2013] EWHC 100 (Fam) concerning religious arbitration under the supervision of the Family courts and E. Butler-Sloss & M. Hill, *Family Law: Current Conflicts and Their Resolution*, in *Islam and English Law* (R. Griffith-Jones ed., Oxford University Press 2013), 108.

Part IV. International, Transnational and Regional Effects on Religious Communities

183. This section examines how the recognition and regulation of religion is influenced by supra-national institutions and by devolved national authorities. Chapter 1 begins by examining international law affecting religion, particularly the instruments created by the United Nations. Chapter 2 examines what we will call 'transnational' law, the EU and the ECHR (the latter in outline only, having been covered in greater detail in Part II). Chapter 3 concludes by looking at regional law affecting religion, chiefly that of Scottish Parliament in Edinburgh and the Welsh Parliament (Senedd Cymru) in Cardiff.

Chapter 1. International Law Affecting Religious Communities

§1. Introduction

184. In an era of perceived globalisation, issues concerning the recognition and regulation of religion will be influenced by factors outside the nation State.[486] Domestic controversies concerning religion are shaped by and respond to the international debate. This is evident, for example, in relation to issues concerning the wearing of Islamic dress and the question of whether freedom of expression includes a right to offend religious sensibilities.

185. International law provides globally agreed standards,[487] which influence domestic legislation but also serve as a pressure for reform, providing a yardstick against which national practice may be evaluated.[488] The following looks at the ways in which international law has influenced religion law in the United Kingdom.

§2. The Recognition of International Law in the UK Legal System

186. States may take one of two approaches to the recognition of international law. A monist approach recognises the terms of international treaties and conventions as domestic law. A dualist approach recognises the terms of international treaties and conventions as obligations under international law but not as domestic law; treaties do not create rights unless embodied in domestic legislation. The United Kingdom operates a dualist approach.[489] While the government may enter into treaties by Royal Prerogative,[490] these do not alter domestic law until provisions are expressly incorporated into domestic law (by statute or delegated legislation) or find expression in the common law.[491] International treaties are ratified by the executive and require legislative enactment before they take effect as domestic law.[492]

486. *See* J. Witte, *The Right to Freedom of Religion: An Historical Perspective from the West*, in *Routledge Handbook of Freedom of Religion or Belief* (S. Ferrari, M. Hill, A. Jamal & R. Bottoni eds, Routledge 2020).
487. *See* H. Bielefeldt, N. Ghanea & M. Wiener, *Freedom of Religion or Belief: An International Law Commentary* (Oxford University Press 2016). *See* generally, S. Ferrari, M. Hill, A. Jamal & R. Bottoni, *The Routledge Handbook on Freedom of Religion or Belief* (Routledge 2020).
488. P.W. Edge, *Legal Responses to Religious Difference* 30–32 (Kluwer Law 2002).
489. But *see* below with regard to the position in Scotland in the future.
490. Note Constitutional Reform and Governance Act 2010 s. 20 concerning the laying of Treaties before Parliament prior to ratification.
491. *See*, for instance, the comments of Phillimore LJ in *McWhirter v. Attorney-General* [1972] CMLR 882 and Lord Templeman in *Rayner (Mincing Lance) Ltd v. Department for Trade* [1990] 2 AC 418.
492. *See* the comments of Lord Atkin in *A-G Canada v. A-G for Ontario* [1937] AC 326. Note the discussion of the United Kingdom Supreme Court in *R (on the application of Miller and another) v. Secretary of State for Exiting the European Union* [2017] UKSC 5 in which the majority held that an Act of Parliament is required to authorise government ministers to give notice of the decision (following a referendum) to withdraw from the European Union.

§3. THE UNITED NATIONS

187. The United Nations was formed in 1945 as the successor to the League of Nations.[493] The Commission on Human Rights, set up in 1946, was tasked with the setting of standards. This was conceived in terms of three successive steps: producing a non-binding Declaration, to be used as the basis for a legally binding Convention, to be enforced by international implementation mechanisms. The Universal Declaration of Human Rights (UDHR) 1948 achieved the goal of producing a non-binding Declaration; with the International Covenant on Civil and Political Rights (ICCPR) 1966 and the International Covenant on Economic, Social and Cultural Rights 1966 cumulatively providing a legally binding Convention. Effective implementation in the United Kingdom, however, is still pending. In cases of religious liberty, the civil courts, particularly at first instance, rarely make explicit reference to obligations under UN instruments. In a notable exception, Baroness Hale, while joining with her fellow Law Lords in refusing to sanction the corporal punishment of children as justified under Article 9 ECHR (freedom of religion) in *R (Williamson and Others) v. Secretary of State for Education and Employment*[494] placed reliance upon passages from the United Nations Convention on the Rights of the Child[495] together with observations from the United Nations Committee on the Rights of the Child.[496]

§4. THE UNIVERSAL DECLARATION OF HUMAN RIGHTS 1948 (UDHR)

188. Both UDHR 1948 and the ICCPR 1966 contain freedom of religion provisions, which are found in Article 18 of each instrument.[497]

189. Article 18 of the UDHR may be seen as a 'watershed' in that while previously religious freedom had been 'bound up with minority rights' since the 1940s, freedom of religion became 'bound up with the development of the concept of individual human rights as an object of international legal concern'.[498] The wording of Article 18 has provided the basis for subsequent human rights guarantees both global and local. It reads:

493. On which, *see*: M.D. Evans, *Religious Liberty and International Law in Europe* Chs 3–6 (Cambridge University Press 1997).
494. [2005] UKHL 15.
495. On which, *see* the discussion on Scotland below.
496. *See In the matter of an application by the Northern Ireland Human Rights Commission for Judicial Review* [2018] UKSC 27 in which direct reference was made to reports of the United Nations Committee on the Elimination of Discrimination against Women.
497. *See* generally *Facilitating Freedom of Religion or Belief: A Deskbook* (T. Lindholm, et al. eds, Brill 2004). *See also*, D. Little, *The Organic Unity of Human Rights and the Place of Freedom of Religion or Belief: Challenge and Response,* in *Routledge Handbook of Freedom of Religion or Belief* (S. Ferrari, M. Hill, A. Jamal & R. Bottoni eds, Routledge 2020).
498. M.D. Evans, *Religious Liberty and International Law in Europe* 172–173 (Cambridge University Press 1997).

> Everyone has the right to freedom of thought, conscience and religion; this right includes freedom to change his religion or belief, and freedom, either alone or in community with others and in public or private, to manifest his religion or belief in teaching, practice, worship and observance.

190. Article 18, for the first time, distinguished between the right to freedom of thought, conscience and religion (the passive right to hold certain views) and the right to manifest religion or belief in worship, teaching, practice and observance (the active right to express and live out those views). However, unlike subsequent freedom of religion clauses, Article 18 does not include any express limitation or qualification clause. Rather, the right under Article 18 is subject to the general limitation provision found in Article 29(2).

§5. The International Covenant on Civil and Political Rights 1966 (ICCPR)

191. Article 18 of the ICCPR is a freedom of religion provision which builds upon that contained in the UDHR. It reads:

> (1) Everyone shall have the right to freedom of thought, conscience and religion. This right shall include freedom to have or adopt a religion or belief of his choice, and freedom, either individually or in community with others and in public or private, to manifest his religion or belief in worship, observance, practice and teaching.
> (2) No one shall be subject to coercion which would impair his freedom to have or to adopt a religion or belief of his choice.
> (3) Freedom to manifest one's religion or belief may be subject to such limitations as are prescribed by law and necessary to protect public safety, order, health or morals or the fundamental rights and freedoms of others.
> (4) The States Parties to the present Covenant undertake to have respect for the liberty of parents and, where applicable, legal guardians to ensure the religious and moral education of their children in conformity with their own convictions.

192. This differs from Article 18 of the Universal Declaration in four main respects. The first is a modification in Article 18.1 where 'freedom to have or adopt a religion or belief of his choice' replaces 'freedom to change his religion or belief'. This was a drafting compromise intended to appease Islamic members and is considered to be of little substantive effect.[499] The second is Article 18.2 which bans 'coercion which would impair his freedom to have or to adopt a religion or belief of his choice'. This is aimed not so much at 'zealous proselytisers and missionaries' but rather at the State seeking to prohibit the use or threat of physical force, penal

499. P.M. Taylor, *Freedom of Religion: UN and European Human Rights Law and Practice* 28, 30, 31 (Cambridge University Press 2005).

sanctions or policies and practices intended to compel citizens to adhere to a specific religious belief.[500] The third is that Article 18.3 provides a limitation clause for the right to manifest:[501] the right to manifest one's religion may be restricted if the limit is (a) prescribed by law; (b) necessary; and (c) serves one of the legitimate purposes outlined in the Article.[502] The fourth is that Article 18.4 provides a right for parents or guardians to 'ensure the religious and moral education of their children in conformity with their own convictions'. This permits public school instruction in subjects such as the general history of religions and ethics only if it is given in a neutral and objective way.[503]

193. The ICCPR is also important because of the work of the Human Rights Committee which is charged with the implementation of the International Covenant, the examination of State reports and the formulation of General Comments. Its General Comment 22 on freedom of religion provides detailed elucidation of much of the terminology. However, to date, this comment, of persuasive authority only, has been underused in the interpretation of the freedom of religion provisions in the United Kingdom.

§6. The Declaration on the Elimination of All Forms of Intolerance and Discrimination Based on Religion or Belief 1981

194. A report in 1960 entitled 'Study of Discrimination in Relation to Religious Rights and Practices', which examined freedom of religion as well as religious discrimination, led to the UN General Assembly requesting in 1962 a Declaration and Convention on the Elimination of Racial Discrimination and a similar Declaration and Convention on the Elimination of Religious Intolerance.

195. Although both a Declaration and Convention regarding race were completed by 1965, such speedy progress was not achieved in respect of the religious instruments: a draft Declaration was finally adopted by the General Assembly in 1981.[504] The Declaration on the Elimination of All Forms of Intolerance and Discrimination based on Religion or Belief 1981 does not have the legal status of an international agreement but of an international legal decision.[505]

500. *Ibid.*, 25.
501. The freedom of thought, conscience and religion is absolute.
502. For interpretation *see* para. 8 of General Comment 22.
503. *See* para. 6 of General Comment 22.
504. *See* M.D. Evans, *The UN and Freedom of Religion*, in *Law and Religion* 36 (R.J. Ahdar ed., Ashgate 2000).
505. *See* H. Bielefeldt, N. Ghanea and M. Wiener, *Freedom of Religion or Belief: An International Law Commentary* (Oxford University Press 2016).

196. Since 'it proved impossible to forge a consensus around a more detailed formulation',[506] Article 1 of the 1981 Declaration sets out freedom of religion in terms very similar to the Universal Declaration and International Covenant. It reads:

(1) Everyone shall have the right to freedom of thought, conscience and religion. This right shall include freedom to have a religion or whatever belief of his choice, and freedom, either individually or in community with others and in public or private, to manifest his religion or belief in worship, observance, practice and teaching.
(2) No one shall be subject to coercion which would impair his freedom to have a religion or belief of his choice.
(3) Freedom to manifest one's religion or belief may be subject only to such limitations as are prescribed by law and are necessary to protect public safety, order, health or morals or the fundamental rights and freedoms of others.

197. This is buttressed by Article 6 which provides a list of freedoms that are included in this general right. Furthermore, unlike UN instruments, the freedom of religion clause in Article 1 is accompanied by Article 2 which prohibits discrimination on grounds of religion or belief.

198. Although the ICCPR 1966 made reference to discrimination on grounds of religion,[507] Article 2 of the 1981 Declaration is more comprehensive using language borrowed from similar UN instruments on racial discrimination. Indeed, the rest of the Covenant focuses primary upon religious discrimination.

199. Notably, Article 3 states that discrimination on grounds of religion or belief 'constitutes an affront to human dignity and a disavowal of the principles of the Charter of the United Nations'. Article 4 provides that States shall take effective measures against religious discrimination and shall make every effort to enact legislation to achieve this. However, this provision has had little effect upon the United Kingdom: until 2003 discrimination on grounds of religion was not expressly outlawed: the new laws prohibiting discrimination (now to be found in the Equality Act 2010) have their roots not in the workings of the United Nations but rather in those of the European Union.

200. The most significant effect that the UN instruments on religious freedom have had on the United Kingdom is that they provided a model for the Council of Europe in framing the ECHR. It is the ECHR that has had the most tangible influence upon religion law in the United Kingdom, especially following the Human Rights Act 1998.[508]

506. M.D. Evans, *The UN and Freedom of Religion*, in *Law and Religion* 36 (R.J. Ahdar ed., Ashgate 2000).
507. *See* Art. 26.
508. *See* Part II. The Scottish Government has announced its intention to incorporate it into Scots law https://www.gov.scot/policies/human-rights/childrens-rights/. Article 14 of which requires States Parties to respect the right of the child to freedom of thought, conscience and religion, and that of

Chapter 2. Transnational Law Affecting Religious Communities

§1. The European Convention on Human Rights

I. Overview

201. The European Convention for the Protection of Human Rights and Fundamental Freedoms, generally known as the ECHR, was signed in Rome on 4 November 1950, ratified by the United Kingdom on 18 March 1951 and came into effect on 3 September 1953. The European Court of Human Rights was set up specifically to secure compliance with the Convention by State Governments.

202. A Committee of three judges or a Chamber of seven judges considers the admissibility of each application. Prior to 1998, a Commission had been charged with the task. Chambers of seven judges or a Grand Chamber of seventeen judges decide whether or not there has been a violation of the ECHR.[509]

203. Cases may not be entertained by the Court unless the applicant has exhausted all domestic legal remedies and has brought the complaint within six months of the final decision of the domestic authorities.[510] The Court may be petitioned by an applicant, who may be a person, a non-governmental organisation or a group of individuals, provided that they are a victim of a violation of one of the rights enshrined in the Convention.[511] As noted above,[512] churches and other religious bodies may collectively exercise Convention rights. Although technically such groups are exercising the individual rights of their members,[513] it has now been accepted that such religious bodies are 'capable of possessing and exercising the rights … in its own capacity as a representative of its members',[514] provided that the body is non-governmental.[515]

204. The strict doctrine of precedent or *stare decisis* does not apply in Strasbourg, although by convention the Court generally follows statements of principle articulated in its earlier decisions. Moreover, the European Court of Human Rights exercises a margin of appreciation, affording a latitude of deference to national legislative, executive, administrative and judicial bodies where the matter is one on which individual states are entitled to take differing positions depending on local

parents and guardians to provide direction to the child in the exercise of his or her right in a manner consistent with the evolving capacities of the child. By incorporating this UN provision into Scots law, greater weight is likely to be given to children's religious views, for example, in converting to another religion against its parents' wishes.

509. Article 27.
510. Further, the application must not be anonymous or substantially the same as a matter that has already been examined by the Court: Art. 35.
511. Article 34.
512. *See* Part II, Ch. 2.
513. *Church of X v. United Kingdom* (1968) 29 CD 70. *See* R. Sandberg, *Religion and the Individual: A Socio-Legal Perspective*, in *Religion and the Individual* 157–169 (A. Day ed., Ashgate 2008).
514. *X and the Church of Scientology v. Sweden* (1979) 16 DR 68.
515. *Holy Monasteries v. Greece* (1995) 20 EHRR 1.

circumstances.[516] The Court considers the ECHR to be a 'living instrument', to be reinterpreted and applied in the light of changing social *mores*.[517]

205. Prior to the Human Rights Act 1998, the ECHR did not have direct domestic legal effect. However, it still had some influence upon domestic law,[518] typically as persuasive authority. The ECHR was used as an aid to interpretation. Where an Act of Parliament was ambiguous, an interpretation in line with the ECHR was preferred over readings that would cause the UK to violate its Convention obligations.[519] Thus, prior to the Act, judges made reference to Articles of the ECHR as an aid to interpretation and sought to ensure that their decisions conformed to them. For example, in *Ahmad v. Inner London Education Authority*,[520] an employment case brought by a Muslim school teacher who left his employment claimed unfair dismissal after the school failed to accommodate his wish to take forty-five minutes off every Friday for prayer which he had expressed after agreeing to a full-time contract of employment, the Court of Appeal made reference to, and showed differing views as to the value of, Article 9. The Court of Appeal dismissed his claim, holding that the termination of employment was consistent with domestic education and employment law. However, while Scarman LJ spoke of the changing legal background and urged use of the Convention to facilitate a policy of 'understanding' which was 'sufficiently flexible to accommodate their beliefs and their observances,'[521] Lord Denning MR seemed less enthusiastic:

> The convention is not part of our English law, but, as I have often said, we will always have regard to it … . We will do our best to see that our decisions are in conformity with it. But it is drawn in such vague terms that it can be used for all sorts of unreasonable claims and provoke all sorts of litigation. As so often happens with high-sounding principles, they have to be brought down to earth.[522]

It seems that Lord Denning was correct. In *Ahmad,* the applicant took his claim to Strasbourg on the basis that the decision meant that the UK had failed in its international obligations.[523]

206. The Human Rights Act 1998 sought to give domestic effect to the substantive rights protected by the ECHR. This is examined in depth in Part II.

---

516. It is a similar notion to the doctrine of subsidiarity. *See also* para. 64.
517. *See*, e.g., *Tyrer v. United Kingdom* [1978] ECHR 2. *See* M. Hill, *Locating Freedom of Religion Within the Qualified Rights of the European Convention on Human Rights and in the Jurisprudence of Strasbourg,* in *Freedom of Religion or Belief: Creating the Constitutional Space for Fundamental Freedoms* (P. Babie, N. Rochow & B. Scharffs eds, Edward Elgar 2020).
518. In the words of Laws LJ, such international law 'informed the common law': *R v. DDP ex p. Kebeline* [2000] 2 AC 326.
519. *See* Lord Donaldson, *R v. Home Secretary ex p. Brind* [1990] 2 WLR 787.
520. [1978] QB 36.
521. At 48.
522. At 41.
523. As noted above, this claim was unsuccessful due to the 'specific situation rule': *see* Part II.

§2. THE EUROPEAN UNION

I. The Growing Interest in Religious Matters

207. Although the traditional economic focus of the EU meant that it paid scant regard to religious matters, recent years have seen an increase in EU law on and affecting religion.[524] A declaration appended to the Treaty of Amsterdam 1997[525] (now to be found in the Lisbon Reform Treaty in Article 15b.1) provides that: 'The Union respects and does not prejudice the status under national law of churches and religious associations or communities in the Member States.' This is commonly understood as an expression of the principle of subsidiarity in religious matters: the regulation of religion is primarily a matter for the Member States and their domestic laws. Thus, Sunday trading questions, and restrictions on the free movement of goods, are matters for national law[526] and an attempt to make Sunday the Europe-wide day of rest has failed.[527] Similarly, the Working Time Directive enables States to derogate from prescribed requirements, if there is proper regard for workers' safety and health, in relation to workers officiating in religious ceremonies in churches and religious communities.[528]

208. The impact of EU law has increased over time: most notably, matters within the economic competence of the Union may have a religious dimension and an interest in matters of religion is particularly evident in instruments dealing with external relations.[529] The EU Council of Ministers adopted the following 'conclusions on freedom of religion or belief' at the General Affairs Council meeting in Brussels on 16 November 2009, stating that:

> The Council reaffirms the strong commitment of the European Union to the promotion and protection of freedom of religion or belief.[530]

Moreover, like Article 52.3 of the draft constitution 2004, the Lisbon Reform Treaty in Article 15b.3 provides that:

524. *See* N. Doe, *Law and Religion in Europe* Ch. 10 (Oxford University Press 2011); J. Rivers, *In Pursuit of Pluralism: The Ecclesiastical Policy of the European Union*, 7 Ecclesiastical Law Journal 267 (2004) and R. McCrea, *Religion and the Public Order of the European Union* (Oxford University Press 2010). *See also*, N. Doe & F. Cranmer, *Law and Religion in the European Institutions*, in *Oxford Handbook of Religion and Europe* (L. Lustean & G. Davie, eds, Oxford University Press, forthcoming).
525. Treaty of Amsterdam 1997, Appendix: Declaration on the Status of Churches and Nonconfessional Organisations.
526. *Torfaen BC v. B&Q plc* [1989] ECR 3851.
527. *UK v. Council of Ministers* [1996] ECR I-5755.
528. Directive 93/104/EC. Art. 17.
529. N. Doe, *Towards a 'Common Law' on Religion in the European Union*, Religion, State & Society 147 (2009).
530. Statement of the Council of Ministers, 16 November 2009. Press Release 15913/09 (Presse 323).

Recognising their identity and their specific contribution, the Union shall maintain an open, transparent and regular dialogue with these churches and organisations.[531]

209. Further, under Article 6 of the Lisbon Reform Treaty, the Union recognises the rights, freedoms and principles set out in the Charter of Fundamental Rights 2000, which charter shall have 'the same legal value as the Treaties'. Article 10 of the Charter contains a freedom of religion clause which is clearly derived from Article 9(1) ECHR.[532] This Charter, which has already been cited by the EU's judicial organs, has effected a shift with the EU becoming an important source of religion law within the Member States,[533] whereas formerly most of the religion law which is common to Europe derived from national religion laws and from Strasbourg.[534] The membership of the Council of Europe is larger[535] and more religiously and culturally diverse than that of the EU. It is likely, therefore, to be the more productive source of religion law.[536]

II. Influence upon the United Kingdom

210. As noted above,[537] by dint of the European Communities Act 1972, English courts gave effect to EU laws and followed decisions of the Court of Justice of the European Union (CJEU).[538] The Act provided that UK legislation must be applied or construed in such a way to be consistent with what is now called EU law.[539]

211. European Union law had an important effect upon the religion law of the United Kingdom, particularly the prohibition against discrimination on grounds of religion or belief (along with disability, age or sexual orientation) in relation to

531. *See also* EURT, Art. 136a for promoting the role of the social partners at EU level and dialogue between them; Art. 17b: the right to petition EU institutions (also, Art. 22, Charter of Fundamental Rights); and Art. 8b.
532. *See* M. Rynkowski, *The Background to the European Union Directive 2000/78/EC*, in *Religion and Discrimination Law in the European Union* 395 (M. Hill ed., Trier 2012).
533. This refinement was predicted in M Hill, *Eguaglianza e non discriminazione a Strasbourt e Lussemburgo*, in *Il Diritto e il Dovere Dell'Uguaglianza* 61–75 (A. Pin ed., Napoli 2015) and M. Hill, *Freedom of Religion: Strasbourg and Luxembourg Compared*, in *Religion and Equality: Law in Conflict* 25–34 (W.C. Durham & D. Thayer eds, Routledge 2016).
534. N. Doe, *Towards a 'Common Law' on Religion in the European Union, Religion*, State & Society 147 (2009).
535. There are forty-seven members of the Council of Europe, the latest to join being Montenegro. With the departure of the United Kingdom, the EU has twenty-seven members.
536. Note, for example, some recent decisions of the CJEU on the wearing of the Islamic headscarf which are consistent with each other, and not easy to reconcile with Strasbourg jurisprudence: *see Achbita & Anor v. G4S Secure Solutions NV* [2016] CJEU C-157/15 and *Bougnaoui and ADDH* [2017] EUECJ C-188/15.
537. *See* General Introduction.
538. Section 2(1). The Act provided for the incorporation into UK law of the whole of European Community law and its *acquis communautaire*: its Treaties, Regulations and Directives, together with judgments of the European Court of Justice.
539. Section 2(4).

employment,[540] and later extended to the provision of goods and services, housing, education, social protection, social security and social advantage. The domestic law giving effect to these provisions is discussed below.[541] Also of relevance were rules on data protection and the processing of personal data,[542] and ritual slaughter provisions which allow exemptions for Muslim and Jewish practices.[543]

212. The United Kingdom left the European Union at 23.00 hrs (GMT) on 31 January 2020,[544] whereupon it entered an implementation period. The European Communities Act 1972 was repealed on 31 January 2020 (the 'exit day') by the European Union (Withdrawal) Act 2018, although its effect was preserved under the provisions of the European Union (Withdrawal Agreement) Act 2020 until the end of the implementation period on 31 December 2020.[545] The 2018 Act provides that the entire body of EU law in existence as at exit day becomes part of UK law as 'retained EU law'. In consequence those current provisions of EU religion law will remain in force in the United Kingdom until such time as they are repealed or abrogated by express provision in UK law.[546] However, section 5(4) of the European Union (Withdrawal) Act 2018 states that 'The Charter of Fundamental Rights is not part of domestic law on or after exit day'.

213. In relation to the case law of the CJEU decided after exit day, British courts 'may have regard' to it in 'so far as it is relevant'. However, under the principle of continuity, the case law of the CJEU from before exit day will continue to be binding on UK courts and tribunals.[547] According to section 5(1) of the European Union (Withdrawal) Act 2018, the 'principle of the supremacy of EU law does not apply to any enactment or rule of law passed or made on or after exit day'. How this will work in practice remains to be seen.

540. Directive 2000/78/EC, Art. 4(1).
541. *See* Part VII, Ch. 7.
542. Directive 95/46/EC, discussed in Part VII, Ch. 1, below.
543. Directive 93/119/EEC. Previously, under Directive 74/577/EEC, Art. 4, national provisions relating to ritual slaughter were exempted from the European requirement to stun before slaughter.
544. Under the provisions of the European Union Referendum Act 2015, a referendum was held in June 2016, resulting in a majority of 51.89% in favour of leaving the EU. On 29 March 2017, the UK government formally began the withdrawal process by invoking Article 50 of the Treaty on European Union, undertaken with the prior approval of parliament following the decision of the UK Supreme Court in *R (on the application of Miller and another) v. Secretary of State for Exiting the European Union* [2017] UKSC 5. The UK negotiated to leave the EU customs union and the single market. On 17 October 2019, the British government and the EU agreed the terms of a Withdrawal Agreement which was eventually ratified by the UK Parliament on 23 January and by the EU on 30 January. It came into force on 31 January 2020.
545. Calls for an extension of the implementation, in consequence *inter alia* of the COVID-19 pandemic were rejected by the British government.
546. Certain aspects of religion law, such as equality provisions in the workplace, may well be the subject of express provision in a future trade agreement between the UK and the EU.
547. European Union (Withdrawal) Act 2018, s. 6(7). The Supreme Court is not, however, bound by this obligation and can refuse to apply previous CJEU decisions in specified circumstances: s. 6(7).

Chapter 3. Regional Law Affecting Religious Communities

214. In addition to engagement with supra-national institutions such as the EU, regional and local devolution within the United Kingdom has seen the dissipation of competencies that traditionally belonged to the Westminster Parliament.[548] The ability of such bodies to enact laws and other regulatory instruments has the potential to effect religion law leading to a divergence across the United Kingdom and a phenomenon which has been styled 'regional ecclesiastical law'.[549] The following seeks briefly to examine the effect of devolution in England, Scotland and Wales upon the regulation of religion and matters affected by religion in those countries.

§1. England

215. Unlike Scotland, Wales and Northern Ireland, England has no elected institution of governance of its own. However, some executive functions are exercised at a regional level. There are regional offices of central government and Regional Development Agencies. Significant areas of responsibility are given to local government, which may affect religious individuals and groups. This is particularly true in relation to planning law and education, where local committees form Agreed Syllabus Conferences (ASCs) to draw up local Religious Education syllabuses. They are required to review the syllabuses every five years. Although there may be a cross-over of members, these committees are separate from Standing Advisory Council for Religious Education (SACREs), which are discussed in Part IX below.

216. However, there have been some moves towards a limited form of devolution in the English regions. The most noteworthy development is the elected mayor and Assembly in the London region and elected mayors elsewhere.[550] The executive powers held by the Mayor and the Greater London Assembly[551] in relation to local amenities, transport, policing, planning and housing have the potential to impact upon religious individuals and groups.

§2. Scotland

217. The Scotland Act 1998 provided for the creation of a new Scottish Parliament which has legislative competence over all matters except those set out in section 29 of and Schedule 5 to the Act.[552] The Scottish Parliament cannot, except in

548. *See also* the 'General Introduction'.
549. J.G. Oliva & D. Lambert, *Regional Ecclesiastical Law: Religion and Devolution in Spain and Wales*, in *Law & Religion: New Horizons* 219 (N. Doe & R. Sandberg eds, Peeters 2010).
550. Greater London Authority Act 1999. Provisions for directly elected Mayors outside of the Greater London Authority were introduced by the Local Government Act 2000. As of May 2013 and excluding the Mayor of London, there were fifteen directly elected Mayors in England.
551. In addition, there are now twenty-three directly elected Mayors in England with executive powers analogous to those exercised by the Mayor of London.
552. Scotland Act 1998 s. 28.

minor respects, amend the Scotland Act itself or certain other statutes such as the Act of Union.[553] It cannot override obligations under the Human Rights Act 1998[554] or alter laws which form part of a law of a country or territory other than Scotland.[555] Most importantly, the Scottish Parliament cannot legislate on 'reserved matters' which remain in the hands of Westminster Parliament.[556] These include constitutional matters (such as electoral arrangements, the registration and funding of political parties and the civil service), international relations, defence and national security, social security, employment regulation, economic policy, certain health matters and some criminal offences (such as treason and money laundering).[557]

218. The Scottish Parliament therefore has legislative competence in a wide range of areas and the separate Scottish Executive has administrative competence including the power to make subordinate legislation. The legislation produced by the Scottish Parliament and the administrative decisions and subordinate legislation made by the Scottish Executive are open to challenge in the courts. Competences include agriculture, the arts, economic development, education, the environment, health, home affairs, housing, local government, social services, sport, training and transport. Subject to the exceptions stated in the Scotland Act 1998, there is much room for a distinctively Scottish religion law to develop. Indeed, this is not novel; a separate legal system has long operated in Scotland and Scots private law is distinctly different from its English and Welsh counterpart.

219. Following the 'Edinburgh agreement' between the Scottish First Minister and the UK Prime Minister, it was agreed that a referendum for Scottish independence be held in Scotland. The UK government gave temporary powers to the Scottish Parliament under section 30 of the Scotland Act 1998 to do so. The Scottish Independence Referendum (Franchise) Act 2013 made provision for the holding of a referendum in Scotland on the question 'Should Scotland be an independent country?' The referendum took place on 18 September 2014 and was lost, with 44.7% voting in favour and 55.3% against. There are calls for a second referendum following the altered landscape of the United Kingdom exiting the EU – Scotland having voted against by 62% to 38%[558] – but these are likely to be resisted by the Westminster Parliament.

553. Section 37.
554. Sections 52, 57.
555. Section 30(3).
556. Section 30; Sch. 5.
557. *See*, e.g., J. Alder, *Constitutional and Administrative Law* 103–107 (7th ed., Palgrave Macmillan 2009).
558. The Electoral Commission, 'Results and turnout at the EU referendum' https://www.electoralcommission.org.uk/who-we-are-and-what-we-do/elections-and-referendums/past-elections-and-referendums/eu-referendum/results-and-turnout-eu-referendum.

§3. WALES

220. Devolution in Wales is an ongoing process. The Government of Wales Act 1998 created a system of executive devolution. Between 1998 and 2006, the National Assembly of Wales had executive legislative powers in devolved areas set out in Schedule 2 to the Act. The effect was that the Assembly, either on its own or jointly with Westminster, could do whatever government ministers in England could do, within the devolved Fields, which excluded much of the areas of religion law: key areas are retained by Westminster included religious charities, marriage, licensing of public places of worship, exemption from rates in relation to public places of worship, and criminal offences relating to religion.

221. The Assembly's competencies expanded over time. The Government of Wales Act 2006 separated the Assembly as a legislature from the Welsh Assembly Government as an executive,[559] and provided for an interim system of legislative devolution by way of Measure. Part 4 of the Government of Wales Act 2006 came into force in 2011, allowing the Assembly to pass primary legislation (Acts) in the twenty subject Fields. Thus three different types of legislation have been made by the Assembly since it was created: secondary legislative instruments passed between 1998 and 2006, Measures passed between 2006–2011 and since 2011, Acts.[560] By way of example, the Human Transplantation (Wales) Act 2013, which came into force on 1 December 2015, introduced a system of presumed consent for organ and tissue donation. There had been prolonged and strong opposition to the proposals from religious groups in Wales. There has been legislation changing compulsory religious education in the school curriculum to a wider topic of 'Religion, Values and Ethics',[561] and on removing the parental opt-out from these classes. At present there are no plans to discontinue compulsory acts of worship in schools.[562]

222. The Senedd and Elections (Wales) Act 2020 empowered the National Assembly of Wales to rename itself as the Welsh Parliament, which it did with effect from May 2020. With the renewed confidence that comes from increased legislative competence and the re-branding of the Assembly as a Parliament, it is likely that a distinctively Welsh religion law may develop over time.

559. Government of Wales Act 2006 ss 1 and 44.

560. The Wales Act 2017 introduced a new sub-s. 107(6) into the Government of Wales Act 2006 which reads: 'But it is recognised that the Parliament of the United Kingdom will not normally legislate with regard to devolved matters without the consent of the [Senedd].' This statutory language recognises and articulates the existence of a pre-existing Parliamentary convention common to the various devolved legislatures of the United Kingdom (commonly called 'the Sewel convention') but does not convert it into a legal rule justiciable by the courts. Thus, 'the policing of its scope and the manner of its operation does not lie within the constitutional remit of the judiciary, which is to protect the rule of law'. *See R (on the application of Miller) v. Secretary of State for Exiting the European Union* [2017] UKSC 5 at [148–149].

561. *See* Part IX Education

562. Notwithstanding a public petition to this effect, see https://business.senedd.wales/mgIssueHistoryHome.aspx?IId=18959.

Part V. Religion and Politics

223. Recent years have seen an increase in the legal regulation of religious groups and individuals which is somewhat at odds with the traditional general reluctance to intervene in matters of faith.[563] The increase has been shaped in part by international pressures.[564] As well as the EU,[565] the Council of Europe has been influential. The European Court of Human Rights has spoken of the State as 'the neutral and impartial organiser of the exercise of various religions, faiths and beliefs'.[566] The link between faith and social cohesion has been discussed in the Council's Parliamentary Assembly, notably in debates on reports about religious tolerance in democratic society,[567] on religion and democracy,[568] on freedom of expression and respect for religious beliefs,[569] and on the State, religion, secularity and human rights.[570] It was noted in 2008 by the Member State Foreign Ministers that the Council of Europe has 'frequently recognised inter-religious dialogue ... as a part of intercultural dialogue and encouraged religious communities to engage actively in promoting human rights, democracy and the rule of law in a multicultural Europe. Inter-religious dialogue can also contribute to a stronger consensus within society regarding the solutions to social problems'.[571]

224. It is therefore unsurprising that there has been an increase in dialogue between faith communities and the State in the United Kingdom in recent years. This takes several different forms: initiatives of the State; those of religious groups; and religious representation at various levels of civil governance.

563. M. Hill & R. Sandberg, *Is Nothing Sacred? Clashing Symbols in a Secular World*, Public Law 488 (2007); R. Sandberg, *Law and Religion* Ch. 10 (Cambridge University Press 2011).
564. *See* Part IV.
565. Whose laws, adopted in domestic legislation, will continue to cast a long shadow notwithstanding the United Kingdom's withdrawal from the European Union. *See* generally, N. Doe, *Law and Religion in Europe* Ch. 10 (Oxford University Press 2011).
566. *Refah Partisi v. Turkey* (2003) 37 EHRR 1, para. 91.
567. Doc 6732 (1993); Recommendation 1202 (1993).
568. Doc 8270 (1998); Recommendation 1396 (1999).
569. Doc 10970 (2006); Resolution 1510 (2006).
570. Doc 11298 (2007); Recommendation 1804 (2007). For a brief explanation of the roles of the Council of Ministers and the Parliamentary Assembly in relation to the European Court of Human Rights, *see* F. Cranmer, *Religion, Human Rights and the Council of Europe: A Note*, 162 Law & Justice 36 (2009).
571. White Paper, COM (2008) 30 final, *Living Together as Equals in Dignity*, para. 75.

Chapter 1. Religion Influence in Politics

§1. Governmental Responsibilities

225. The past twenty or so years have seen the development of several political initiatives to enable greater dialogue between religious groups and the government. Under the Labour Government (1997–2010), in 2003 the Faith Communities Unit was established within the Race, Cohesion and Faiths Directorate in the Home Office. This advised on, for example, the Racial and Religious Hatred Act 2006, Holocaust Memorial Day, forced marriages and reception of religious workers under migration law. In 2006, the Department for Communities and Local Government established a fixed-term Commission on Integration and Cohesion to consider how local areas could enhance diversity and respond to tensions that it might cause.[572] In 2007, the Department published an interfaith consultation paper which proposed a 'Framework for Partnership' to develop: the confidence and skills to 'bridge' and 'link'; shared spaces for interaction; structures and processes to support dialogue; and social action and opportunities for learning which build understanding. GBP 7.5 million was given to this programme over three years. For instance, the Regional Faith Forums and 'Faiths in Action' fund helped to support local initiatives that have a direct link to these aims.[573] In 2008, the Office of the Third Sector within the Cabinet Office launched the 'Faith in Action Initiative', a national three-year programme to facilitate development of a national database of faith-based organisations interested in or experienced in public sector delivery. During that year too, a Parliamentary Under-Secretary of State for Community Cohesion and Fire and Rescue Services was appointed, with 'Community Cohesion' for the first time appearing in the description of the ministerial role.

226. Interfaith initiatives continued under the Conservative–Liberal Democrat Coalition Government (2010–2015). In 2012, the position of Minister for Faith and Communities was set up at the Department for Communities and Local Government, and the Department funded various initiatives on faith and cohesion as well as the Church Urban Fund's Near Neighbours Programme.[574] In 2015, the Minister for Faith (Lord Pickles), stated: 'We all need to recognise that faith groups are a tremendous force for good; serving and supporting the downtrodden and marginalised in society, and bringing communities together. My mission [is] to ensure it remains at the heart of our shared national life … supporting the grassroots work of churches, mosques, synagogues, and temples.'[575]

572. *See* e.g., Commission on Integration and Cohesion: *Final Report: Our Shared* Future (London: DCLG, June 2007).
573. DCLG: *Face to Face and Side by Side: A Framework for Inter Faith Dialogue and Social Action: Consultation* (London: DCLG December 2007).
574. http://www.cuf.org.uk/near-neighbours.
575. 26 February 2015 https://www.gov.uk/government/speeches/recognising-the-role-of-faith-in-britain.

227. Today, within the Ministry of Housing, Communities and Local Government, the Minister for Faith works with religious and community leaders to promote faith, religious tolerance, and stronger communities within the UK.[576] In 2019, the Ministry appointed a Faith Engagement Adviser, to lead a review into how best the government should engage with faith groups in England. The adviser makes recommendations to the Communities Secretary about how the government may celebrate and support the contribution of faith groups, break down barriers and promote acceptance between faiths, and promote shared values while tackling cultures and practices that are harmful.[577]

228. In 2020, the Coronavirus pandemic stimulated active dialogue between religious bodies and the Ministry of Housing, Communities and Local Government, particularly in relation to the closure of places of religious worship and the conducting of funerals in accordance with religious rites.[578] Exchanges have been both constructive and critical.[579] The Ministry set up a new Places of Worship Taskforce to develop a plan to enable phased and safe reopening of places of worship. The Taskforce includes leaders and representatives from all the major faiths, such as the Archbishop of Canterbury, the Roman Catholic Cardinal Archbishop of Westminster, the Chief Rabbi, and representatives of the British Board of Scholars and Imams, the Hindu Council UK, City Sikhs, and Faith Action. Faith Action receives GBP 125,000 to consult and engage with different community groups and places of worship to ensure their views are represented at Taskforce meetings. The Faith Minister said: 'Places of worship serve such an important role in supporting and providing spiritual leadership for this country's diverse communities and in bringing communities and the generations together, but this also makes them places that are currently particularly vulnerable to … the pandemic.. The Taskforce jointly produces guidance with the Ministry to support places of worship in England to reopen safely. At the same time, Faith Action was awarded sums from the GBP 360 million funding recently announced by the Department for Digital, Culture, Media and Sport to provide support to the voluntary, community and social enterprise sector in line with agreed departmental priorities.[580]

§2. Equality and Human Rights Commission

229. The Equality Act 2006 made provision for the establishment of the Equality and Human Rights Commission, a corporate body which has the responsibility

576. *See* https://www.gov.uk/government/ministers/minister-for-faith.
577. 10 October 2019 https://www.gov.uk/government/news/faith-engagement-adviser-appointed.
578. For example, on 31 March 2020, having consulted faith leaders, Public Health England published new guidance to ensure funerals are conducted safely, consistent with social distancing principles https://www.gov.uk/government/news/new-advice-for-safe-funerals-after-discussions-with-faith-leaders.
579. *See* e.g., *The Telegraph*, 29 May 2020, G. Swerling, 'Religious Leaders Speak Out over Government's "Unlawful" Closure of Churches'.
580. *See* https://www.gov.uk/government/news/new-taskforce-developing-plan-to-reopen-places-of-worship.

to protect, enforce and promote equality across the protected grounds, which includes religion or belief.[581] In accordance with its statutory functions the Commission supports litigation.[582] Three recent Commission initiatives are notable.

230. First, there was a major review in 2015 of equality and human rights law relating to religion or belief. It found that: (1) the definition of belief, particularly in equality legislation, merits further assessment; (2) the impact on domestic law of some specific issues tested at European level remains unclear (despite the European Court of Human Rights (ECtHR) judgment in *Eweida* (*see* above)); (3) the position of the religious employer, and religious service provider, has been relatively unexplored in the case law, but has the potential to be significant (e.g., whether Equality Act exceptions are too narrow or too wide); (4) the role of the public sector equality duty could be explored to integrate religion or belief equality into the day to day practice of public sector organisations; and (5) it should be assessed whether a duty to accommodate religion or belief might benefit employees/employers.[583]

231. Second, there was the 2016 report on religion or belief: is the law working? This recommended, for example, that: (1) no change be made to the broad definition of the protected characteristic of religion or belief in the Equality Act; (2) no change be made to the current approach whereby the courts decide whether any particular religion or belief is protected under the Equality Act; (3) the definition of the protected characteristic of belief should be clarified through case law; (4) no change be made to the current occupational exceptions allowed under the Equality Act in employment for employers with an ethos based on religion or belief, or for employment for the purposes of an organised religion; (5) the Equality Act should not be amended to permit religion or belief or sexual orientation discrimination by organisations whose sole or main purpose is commercial; (6) there should be clarification of the extent of freedom of expression and freedom of thought, conscience and religion in relation to religious organisations which is required, through case law; (7) there should be no extension of harassment protections covering religion or belief to non-employment settings; (8) a duty of reasonable accommodation should not be introduced into law; and (9) individual employees should not be permitted to opt out of performing part of their contractual work duties due to religion or belief where this would have a potential detrimental or discriminatory impact on others.[584]

---

581. *See* www.equalityhumanrights.com/. The substantive law on religious discrimination is explored in Part VII.
582. *See Bull v. Hall and Preddy* [2013] UKSC 73, even though its promotion of the rights of a same-sex couple was at the expense of the religious beliefs of the other party. *See* para. 4 of Lady Hale's judgment.
583. Research Report 97. The review was conducted by Peter Edge and Lucy Vickers of Oxford Brookes University – *see* https://www.equalityhumanrights.com/sites/default/files/research-report-97-review-of-equality-and-human-rights-law-relating-to-religion-or-belief.pdf.
584. *See* https://www.equalityhumanrights.com/en/publication-download/religion-or-belief-law-working.

232. Third, in 2019, the Commission launched an investigation into allegations of antisemitism in the Labour Party. The investigation examined: whether unlawful acts have been committed by the Party, its employees or agents; steps taken by the Party to implement the recommendations in various earlier reports on this (by Baroness Royall, the Home Affairs Select Committee, and in the Chakrabarti report); whether the Rule Book and the Party's investigatory and disciplinary processes enable it to deal effectively with such complaints, including whether appropriate sanctions have been or could be applied; and whether the Party had responded to complaints of unlawful acts in a lawful, efficient and effective manner.[585]

§3. The Charity Commission for England and Wales

233. Given that faith-based charities form a significant part of the charitable sector, the Charity Commission plays an important role in the regulation of religion in the UK.[586] Its register shows over 22,000 religious charities in England and Wales. Between 2005 and 2007, the Commission ran fifteen workshops with representatives from over 800 faith-based organisations, to help strengthen their governance and effectiveness. Building on this, the Commission set up a dedicated Faith and Social Cohesion Unit to work with and support faith-based charities, and a Faith Advisory Group with representatives from various faiths to advise it. In 2008, the Commission issued specific guidance on the advancement of religion for the public benefit.[587] This was followed in 2009, with Faith and Social Cohesion guidance entitled *Faith in Good Governance*. Today, this is still 'the commission's core guidance for religious charities whose main focus is religious worship and related activities'. The purpose of this guidance is 'to help faith-based charities comply with charity law, and to equip them to work even better, whilst recognising that maintenance of their faith-identity, core aims, and mission is key'. The guidance includes case studies which describe approaches to governance adopted by different charities which themselves contributed to the design of the guidance.[588]

§4. The Office of the Scottish Charity Regulator

234. The Office of the Scottish Charity Regulator (OSCR) is a non-ministerial department of the Scottish Government responsible for charities in Scotland. The Office has not been as overtly proactive as the Charity Commission for England and Wales in its relations with faith-groups and faith-based charities. However, several charities have been assessed as part of its Rolling Review of the Register. In the case

585. *See* https://www.equalityhumanrights.com/en/inquiries-and-investigations/investigation-labour-party.
586. The substantive law effecting religious charities is explored in Part III.
587. Charity Commission for England and Wales, December 2008.
588. The Charity Commission, Faith and Social Cohesion, *Faith in Good Governance* (2009); *see* https://assets.publishing.service.gov.uk/government/uploads/system/uploads/attachment_data/file/355533/faithgovenglish.pdf.

of the Edinburgh Interfaith Association,[589] OSCR concluded that its constitution lacked any provision to ensure that the charity used its property exclusively for charitable purposes and recommended that the charity trustees should review the constitution and amend it accordingly.[590] Because the Rolling Review is an ongoing process, it is expected that other religious charities will come under OSCR's scrutiny. Churches and religious organisations are listed on the OSCR website.[591]

589. SC017622.

590. *Rolling Review – Phase 1a: OSCR's decisions on 30 charities* (OSCR, Edinburgh October 2008), para. 6a.

591. *See* https://www.oscr.org.uk/about-charities/overview-of-scottish-charities/.

Chapter 2. Political Influence in Religion

235. On the other side of the coin, there exist numerous organisations established by one or more religious groups to engage in dialogue with each other and with the State (in its various forms). This chapter outlines some of the religious initiatives and structures.[592] Chaplaincy is explored in Part XI.

§1. Churches' Legislation Advisory Service

236. The successor to the Churches' Main Committee,[593] the Churches' Legislation Advisory Service exists to: advance the charitable work, whether religious or otherwise, of certain churches[594] by furthering their common interest in secular matters relating to that work (other than educational work); to give advice to churches; to conduct negotiations relating to such matters; and to act as a liaison body between the churches and the machinery of government, such as government departments, local authorities and the Westminster Parliament; and to monitor and alert its members to developments in civil law and talks directly to government on religious issues. Its work covers subjects ranging from taxation, heritage grants and charity law to marriage law, immigration rules, planning and building regulations and water charges, with much else besides. Circulars are issued to members giving information and advice as are a series of booklets on aspects of church management.[595]

§2. Churches Together in Britain and Ireland

237. Churches Together in Britain and Ireland (CTBI) is an umbrella organisation which brings Christian churches together to promote Christian unity. It works alongside other Christian ecumenical initiatives such as Action for Churches Together in Scotland, CYTUN (Churches Together in Wales), Churches Together in England and the Irish Council of Churches. One of its aims is to offer 'a strong and effective (public) voice (in promoting justice and peace) through accompaniment of member churches and ecumenical partners through advocacy on behalf of and with them at national and international level'. In 2019, for example, it responded to the refugee crisis in Europe and beyond by 'calling on governments to take action,

592. There are also a number of religious think tanks as well as atheistic and humanistic groups who dialogue with the State such as the British Humanist Association and the National Secular Society.
593. *See* Churches Main Committee, *Wrestling with Caesar: The Role of the Churches Main Committee in Relations Between the Church and the State: 1941–2001* (London 2000).
594. Its members include the Anglican Churches in England, Scotland, Ireland, and Wales, the Church of Scotland, Roman Catholic Church, Baptist Union of Great Britain, Methodist Church, United Reformed Church, Lutheran Council of Great Britain and several smaller churches. It also has Churches Together in Britain and Ireland, Churches Together in England, Actions of Churches Together in Scotland, Churches Together in Wales and the Evangelical Alliance as corporate members – and the United Synagogue is an associate member.
595. www.churcheslegislation.org.uk/home.

encouraging donations from church members and providing support where possible, often through partner organisations'. CTBI is a registered charity and a company limited by guarantee established under the Articles of Association as from 2005.[596]

§3. Other Organisations

I. Christian Organisations

238. In addition to organisations representing more than one religious group, structures also exist within particular religious groups for dialogue with the State. For example, in the Church of England: one function of the General Synod is 'to consider and express [its] opinion on any … matter of religious or public interest';[597] the work of the Archbishops' Council includes 'transforming our society and communities more closely to reflect the Kingdom of God through loving acts of neighbourliness and service to all'; and its Mission and Public Affairs Division has dialogued with government on such matters as the criminal justice system and prisons.[598] The Church of Scotland has a Church and Society Council 'to engage on behalf of the Church in the national, political and social issues affecting Scotland and the world today', including 'human rights, asylum, ethics, science and technology, concerns about gambling, climate change and education issues'. The council is also charged with 'building, establishing and maintaining a series of networks and relationships with leaders and key people in society and engaging in longer-term dialogue and the exchange of ideas with them'. In 2019, there were plans to merge the Council with the World Mission Council as (provisionally) the 'Faith Impact Forum'.[599] Similar structures exist within other religious organisations: for instance, the Church in Wales has developed links with the Welsh Parliament in such areas as church schools.[600]

II. Muslim Council of Britain

239. The Muslim Council of Britain is an accord of mosques, Muslim associations and institutions in the UK.[601] An independent body, the Council promotes consultation, cooperation and coordination on Muslim affairs in the UK. Its Constitution speaks of the Council's task of 'preparing the case for, and advocating,

596. *See* https://ctbi.org.uk/our-work/.
597. Synodical Government Measure 1969, s. 2(1).
598. *See* https://www.churchofengland.org/about/leadership-and-governance/archbishops-council.
599. *See* https://www.churchofscotland.org.uk/about-us/councils-committees-and-departments/councils/church-and-society-council.
600. *See* N. Doe, ed., *A New History of the Church in Wales: Governance and Ministry, Theology and Society* 270–273 (Cambridge University Press 2020).
601. *See* N. Doe, *Comparative Religious Law: Judaism, Christianity, Islam* 22–24 (Cambridge University Press 2018), and, for British Muslims for Secular Democracy, 367.

the responsibilities and rights of Muslims living in Britain'. The aims and objectives of the Council include: 'to work for a more enlightened appreciation of Islam and Muslims in the wider society; to establish a position for the Muslim community within British society that is, fair and based on due rights; and to work for the eradication of disadvantages and forms of discrimination faced by Muslims.' Its General Assembly is 'the supreme policy-making and ruling body'.[602]

III. The Board of Deputies of British Jews

240. The Board of Deputies of British Jews originated in 1760, when seven Deputies appointed by elders of the Spanish and Portuguese Congregations formed a standing committee to pay homage to George III on his accession. At the same time the Ashkenazi Community appointed its own 'Secret Committee for Public Affairs' and it was agreed that the two committees should hold joint meetings from time to time.[603] Today, the Board consists of about 300 Deputies elected every three years by synagogue congregations and communal organisations. The Board is 'an independent organisation, free from outside control, and recognised as the body to make official representations on behalf of the Jewish Community of Great Britain to central and local government authorities, and other appropriate bodies'. The Board must protect, support and defend the interests, religious rights and customs of Jews, and consider and, if necessary, make representations on all national and local government proposals, decisions, orders, regulations, public and private Acts and other measures, including those of the European Union, to government bodies and other competent authorities. Next, it must defend and ensure the security, safety, well-being, and standing of British Jews, in cooperation with statutory authorities and relevant parties; take such appropriate action as lies within its power to advance the security, welfare and standing of Israel; and support and protect Jews and Jewish communities outside the United Kingdom.[604] The Deputies transact the business of the Board through Divisions working with the Honorary Officers (President, Vice-Presidents and Treasurer) and professional staff. The Board meets eight times a year to debate matters and to consider the reports from its various Divisions. There are four Divisions: Communities and Education; Defence and Interfaith Relations, International Affairs; and Finance and Organisation. Each has elected Deputies, supported by a professional Director. The Board also engages in interfaith dialogue.[605]

602. Constitution, Declaration of Intent, Arts 2 and 4.1.2; *see* www.mcb.org.uk/.
603. For further information *see* www.boardofdeputies.org.uk/.
604. BDBJ: Con. Arts 2 and 3.
605. The Board promotes relations between different faith communities in the UK as to e.g., education, equality and extremism, and works with the Inter Faith Network, Council of Christians and Jews, and Three Faiths Forum https://www.bod.org.uk/issues/interfaith-social-action/.

Chapter 3. Interaction Between Religion and State on a Political and Legal Level

241. In addition to the initiatives and strictures discussed above, religious representation exists at various levels of governance: at Westminster, the institutions of devolved government, and local councils.

§1. Religious Representation at the Westminster Parliament

I. The House of Lords

242. There are twenty-four bishops and two archbishops of the Church of England in the House of Lords (the Lords Spiritual):[606,607] they comprise the Archbishops of Canterbury and York and the bishops of London, Durham and Winchester *ex officiis* and the twenty-one most senior bishops by date of appointment as diocesan bishops.[608] Since 1847, whenever a new diocesan bishopric is created, the number of bishops sitting in the House of Lords is not increased.[609]

243. Lambeth Palace arranges for a duty bishop to be assigned for every day the Lords sit. A list is circulated for bishops to sign up for two or three weeks' duty. The Lords Spiritual are expected to wear their Episcopal robes whenever in the division lobby.[610]

244. A bishop normally reads the prayers at the commencement of business in the Lords.[611] Each bishop takes a week each in turn. In the absence of a bishop, a member of the House who is a clergyman of the Church of England may read prayers; if no such person is present the Lord Speaker reads prayers. During prayers the doors and galleries of the House of Lords are closed and visitors excluded.[612] The five senior bishops do not take part in the rota for prayers.

606. *See* A. Harlow, F. Cranmer & N. Doe, *Bishops in the House of Lords: A Critical Analysis*, Public Law 490–509 (2008).
607. The Monarch appoints these on the basis of the Appointment of Bishops Act 1533.
608. Neither the Bishop of Sodor and Man (who participates in the governance of the Isle of Man) nor the Bishop of Gibraltar in Europe (whose territorial jurisdiction is beyond the United Kingdom) may sit as Lords Spiritual. The seniority rule was abrogated by statutory provision following the decision of the Church of England to permit women to enter the episcopate. In an usual example of positive discrimination or affirmative action, the Lords Spiritual (Women) Act 2015 provides that whenever a vacancy arises among the Lords Spiritual during the ten years following the Act coming into force, the vacancy has to be filled by a woman, if one is eligible.
609. Ecclesiastical Commissioners Act 1847 s. 2; Bishoprics Act 1878 s. 5.
610. *Companion to the Standing Orders of the House of Lords* 4.27.
611. This practice has continued during the virtual sessions of the House of Lords, conducted during the COVID-19 emergency.
612. At 3.07.

245. Members of other religious traditions may be appointed to the Lords under the Life Peerages Act 1958 (provided their tradition allows members to accept positions of political authority).[613] They do not, however, sit as Lords Spiritual.

246. Unlike other life peers, the Lords Spiritual cease their Lords membership when they retire. By convention, archbishops are made life peers on retirement and some bishops may be similarly honoured.[614] In that case, the newly appointed peer sits as a Lord Temporal and is introduced to the House afresh.

247. The bishops owe no formal allegiance to any political party. While by convention they do not speak or vote on party political issues – whatever that might mean in practice – they have contributed to debate on many, often sensitive, moral and social issues, such as housing, divorce, abortion, homosexuality, embryology and human fertilisation and wider issues of defence and foreign affairs. A 2008 study interviewed fourteen of the Lords' bishops and found that: most considered diocesan duties had priority over Lords' duties; they are non-party-political and represent the Church of England, Christianity, and religion in general; they vote according to conscience; and they are the subject of lobbying by pressure-groups. The study also found examples of them: voting against the government; speaking on a wide range of matters, from family issues, through ethics, health, education to foreign policy; and being engaged in limited committee work.[615]

248. The recent reforms of the House of Lords have not affected the bishops.[616] Discussion around a draft Bill in 2011 proposed reducing the number of bishops to twelve, but this was abandoned. A YouGov poll for *The Times*, published in 2017, found that 62% of people said no religious clerics should have 'an automatic right to seats' in the legislature. Only 8% said the bishops should retain their seats. In 2019, the National Secular Society (NSS) backed a private member's bill to end the practice. Liberal Democrat peer Lord Taverne QC, an NSS honorary associate, presented the bill; he commented: 'One of the great achievements of the enlightenment was the separation of church and state. Theocracies in which religion is still part of the state – hardly shining examples of democracy and the protection of human rights – show how important this achievement was'; 'Although the bishops are liberal minded by comparison, the influence of the Church of England, despite the steep and ongoing decline in the number of Anglicans, should not be underestimated'; and: 'And the separation of church and state is far from complete in the UK. The continued presence of bishops in the Lords is an anachronism that should be addressed'. The bill failed.[617]

613. Examples include Methodist peer Lord Soper, Rabbi Lord Sacks and Sikh Lord Singh.
614. For example, the former Archbishop of Canterbury, Rowan Williams, became a life peer and took the title of Baron Williams of Oystermouth.
615. A. Harlow, F. Cranmer & N. Doe, *Bishops in the House of Lords: A Critical Analysis*, Public Law 490 (2008).
616. The House of Lords Reform Act 1999 removed most of the hereditary peers.
617. *See* https://www.secularism.org.uk/podcast/2020/01/ep-22-bishops-in-the-lords-dick-taverne-interview.

II. The House of Commons

249. Prayers are said at the beginning of sittings in the House of Commons. These are usually led by the Speaker's Chaplain while Members of Parliament stand facing the walls of the chamber, a practice thought to have developed due to the difficulty Members would historically have faced of kneeling to pray while wearing a sword. Members of the public are not allowed into the public gallery at this time. There is no religious representation as such. The previous bar on clergy becoming Members of Parliament was removed in 2001.[618] Further, a backbench Member of Parliament (traditionally from the Party in Government) is appointed by the Crown for the duration of a Parliament to serve as the Second Church Estates Commissioner and, *inter alia*, answer Parliamentary questions. The Member of Parliament is one of thirty-three Church Commissioners,[619] who manage the historic assets of the Church of England. Annual Reports are presented both to Parliament and the General Synod of the Church of England.[620]

§2. Religious Representation at the Scottish Parliament

250. The churches had a major role in the campaign to establish a Scottish Parliament. The Scottish Constitutional Convention was chaired by Canon Kenyon Wright. The *Claim of Right for Scotland*– the declaration of the sovereignty of the Scottish people – was directly influenced by the work of the Church and Nation Committee of the Church of Scotland on 'The Government of Scotland' (1989 Report) with its analysis of the Scottish constitutional tradition of shared and limited power.

251. The first item of business at the meeting of the Parliament each week is normally 'Time for Reflection', when an invited speaker addresses the meeting for up to four minutes. Invitations to do so are issued by the Presiding Officer on the advice of the Parliamentary Bureau. The pattern of speakers reflects the balance of beliefs in Scotland as indicated by Census returns.[621]

252. The Scottish Churches Parliamentary Office enables churches to engage with politicians, civil servants and others; to translate their commitment to the welfare of Scotland into parliamentary debate; and to contribute the range and depth of their experience, and their faith reflection, to the decision-making process. To that end, the Office monitors the work of Parliament, briefs churches on current issues

618. House of Commons (Removal of Clergy Disqualification) Act 2001, repealing the House of Commons (Clergy Disqualification) Act 1801.
619. *See*, further, Part VIII.
620. *See* Church Commissioners Measure 1947.
621. *See* http://www.parliament.scot/parliamentarybusiness/61711.aspx.

and, at the same time, briefs Members of the Parliament on churches' concerns. The Moderator of the Church of Scotland makes an annual visit to the Scottish Parliament.[622]

§3. Religious Representation at the Welsh Parliament/Senedd Cymru

253. Although prayers are not said at the Welsh Parliament, its growing powers have been met by a growth in structures for dialogue. Any religious body may make representations to its Committees including Subject Committees as well as Committees dealing with proposed legislation.

254. The Welsh Government has a Faith Communities Forum to improve relations between all the faiths in Wales. It comprises two representatives from each of the Baha'i, Buddhist, Hindu, Jewish, Muslim, Sikh communities, and Evangelical Alliance Wales. There is also a representative from the Church in Wales, Roman Catholic Church in Wales, Free Church Council, Churches Together in Wales (CYTUN) and Interfaith Council for Wales. The Welsh Government is represented by the First Minister who chairs the Forum. The Cabinet Secretary for Communities and Children is the Deputy Chair.

255. The Faith Communities Forum aims to facilitate dialogue between the Welsh Government and the major faith communities on any matters affecting the economic, social, and cultural life in Wales. Any matters of concern to faith communities may be raised as may any matters on which politicians might wish to consult faith communities. The Forum aims 'to create opportunities for faith communities to speak for themselves in this dialogue, it is not intended however that the Forum should represent a collective view on behalf of the faith communities'. The Forum normally meets twice yearly and other meetings may be called for by the leaders of the faith communities or the First Minister. The Secretariat is provided by Welsh Government officials from the Equality Team.[623]

§4. Religious Representation in Local Government

256. At the level of local government, religion is represented on the SACRE appointed by the local authority. In England, the SACRE comprises several representative groups: one member must represent the Church of England and the others must represent 'such Christian and other religious denominations as in the opinion of the authority will appropriately reflect the principal religious traditions in the area'.[624] The role and functions of the SACRE are discussed in Part IX.

622. See further https://www.scpo.scot/ .
623. *See* https://gov.wales/faith-communities-forum-guide.
624. Education Act 1996, ss 387, 391, 396.

257. Because the Church of England and the Roman Catholic Church are major providers of education, each is entitled to representation on local authority committees dealing with education in any area where they have maintained schools. Local authorities must establish one or more 'Overview and Scrutiny Committees' designed to hold the authority's executive to account. If these committees have any functions relating to education, then both the Diocesan Board of Education (for the Church of England) and the Diocesan Bishop (for the Roman Catholic Church) are entitled to nominate at least one voting member of that Committee. If another major provider exists in an area, the Secretary of State has the power to direct that similar arrangements be made for that body also.

258. The practice of prayers preceding meetings of local authorities was litigated in the High Court.[625] As a result, the Local Government (Religious etc. Observances) Act 2015 was enacted to make provision about the inclusion at local authority meetings of observances that are, and about powers of local authorities in relation to events that to any extent are, religious or related to a religious or philosophical belief. With regard to the powers of councils, the business at a meeting of a local authority in England may include time for prayers or other religious observance, or observance connected with a religious or philosophical belief. Moreover, such local authority may support or facilitate, or make arrangements to be represented at a religious event, an event with a religious element, an event connected with a religious or philosophical belief, or an event with an element connected with such a belief.[626]

625. *National Secular Society v. Bideford Town Council* [2012] EWHC 175 (Admin). A former councillor challenged the Town Council's practice of having prayers at the beginning of its council meetings. The challenge succeeded because of a technicality in local government law, which has subsequently been removed in England under s. 1(1) of the Localism Act 2011. *See also The Mayor, Commonality and Citizens of London v. Tammy Samede* [2012] EWHC 34 (QB) at 162, and approved at [2012] EWCA Civ 160.

626. The Act inserts in Part 7 of the Local Government Act 1972 s. 138A 'Prayer and other observance'.

Part VI. Labour Law Within Religious Communities

259. This part examines the employment status of ministers of religion. It begins by discussing the 'classic doctrine' that ministers of religion were not employees. The effect of recent cases upon this doctrine is then explored, examining in particular the significance of the decision of the House of Lords in *Percy v. Church of Scotland Board of Mission,*[627] the Court of Appeal decision in *New Testament Church of God v. Stewart,*[628] the Supreme Court in *President of the Methodist Conference v. Preston,*[629] and the judgment of the Court of Appeal in *Sharpe v. Bishop of Worcester.*[630] This part also examines how the Church of England has responded to government moves to award employment rights to atypical workers (including clergy) through the Ecclesiastical (Terms of Service) Measure 2009.

627. [2005] UKHL 73.
628. [2007] EWCA Civ 1004.
629. [2013] UKSC 29. *See* F. Cranmer, *Methodist Ministers: Employees or Office Holders?*, 15(3) Ecclesiastical Law Journal 316 (2013).
630. [2015] EWCA Civ 399.

Chapter 1. Scope of Application of Labour Law

260. Under domestic law, employees enjoy a number of legal rights. These include the right not to be dismissed unfairly or unlawfully; the right to be given reasons for dismissal; the right to be given an opportunity to put a case against dismissal; together with provision for financial redress. Employees also have legal protection from discrimination, which is discussed in the Part VII.

261. An employee is defined as a person who works under a contract of employment. The term applies to those who either work under a contract of employment or who work under any other contract where they agree to 'do or perform personally any work or services for another party'.[631] A distinction can be made between employees who have a contract of employment (also known as a contract of service) and workers who have a contract for services.[632]

262. If there is a contract, then the courts will decide whether it is a contract of employment on the basis of a number of tests,[633] such as the control test (does the employer have the right to exercise control in the selection of and over the work done by the employee and to suspend or dismiss?), the organisation or integration test (is the employee an integral part of the business, that is, part and parcel of it?) and the economic reality test (is the agreement one to provide remuneration?). Although no one test 'has won universal approval',[634] the current preferred test is the 'Economic Reality / Multiple Test',[635] which recognises, among other things, that 'all the relevant facts need to be looked at in the aggregate'.[636] As Mummery LJ put it in *Hall (Inspector of Taxes) v. Lorimer*,[637] 'the object of the exercise is to paint a picture from the accumulation of detail' and the 'details may also vary in importance from one situation to another'.

263. Historically, office-holders have not been considered to be employees: an office is 'a subsisting, permanent, substantive position which has its existence independently from the person who filled it, which went on and was filled in succession by successive holders'.[638]

631. Employment Rights Act 1996, s. 230. For a detailed discussion of the issue *see* I. Smith et al., *Smith & Wood's Employment Law (Thirteenth Edition)* Ch. 2 (Oxford University Press 2017)
632. The term worker is defined under s. 230(3).
633. *See*, e.g., *Ready Mixed Concrete v. Ministry of Pensions* [1968] 2 QB 497.
634. *Quashie v. Stringfellow Restaurant Limited* [2012] EWCA Civ 1735 at para. 6.
635. [1968] 2 QB 497 at 515.
636. *Warner Holidays Ltd v. Secretary of State for Social Services* [1983] ICR 440 at 453, 455.
637. [1992] 1 WLR 939 at 944.
638. *Great Western Railway Company v. Bater* [1920] 3 KB 256.

Chapter 2. Religious Ministers and Labour Law

§1. The Classical Doctrine

I. General Rule

264. Historically, ministers of religion have not been regarded as employees because they do not exercise ministry under a contract of employment.[639]

265. The classical doctrine of the courts proposed that there is a fundamental incompatibility between, on the one hand, vocation and the spiritual nature of ministerial functions and, on the other, the existence of a contract. There is generally no ministerial right to remuneration;[640] instead 'as [the minister] gives himself, leaving no time or energy to provide for the material needs of himself and his family, the Church undertakes the burden of their support and provides for each man according to his requirements. There is a basic stipend which is committed to his own stewardship'.[641] This is regarded as a gift from God through the Church: a stipend is paid by the Church as from God, to enable the cleric to live and to give him some measure of freedom for his service.[642]

266. Ministerial functions arise by way of a religious act (e.g., ordination), which is treated as a spiritual event and not a contractual transaction. For example, in *Rogers v. Booth*[643] the Court of Appeal held that a person who is an officer in the Salvation Army is not an employee. The relationship between the officer and the Salvation Army superior (the general) was spiritual not contractual. The Court of Appeal consulted the Salvation Army's Orders and Regulations. These provided that 'Every officer becomes such upon the distinct understanding that no salary or allowance is guaranteed to him'; '[t]he officer is pledged to his duty, with or without pay; he works from love to God and souls, whether he receives little or much'; and 'The army does not recognise the payment of salary in the ordinary sense; that is, the Army neither aims at paying nor professes to pay its officers an amount equal to the value of their work; but rather to supply them with sufficient for their actual needs, in view of the fact that, having devoted themselves to full-time Salvation service, they are thereby prevented from otherwise earning a livelihood'.

267. Ministers (especially clergy of the established Church of England)[644] have been treated legally as office-holders: their functions are not distributed or governed by contract but by ecclesiastical law. In *Re Employment of Church of England*

639. *See* N. Doe, *Ministers of Religion and Employment Law in the United Kingdom: Recent Judicial Developments*, Anuario de Derecho Eclesiâstico del Estado 349–355 (1997).
640. *Daly v. CIR* [1934] SC 444: 'The Church is under no obligation to pay him anything'; 'He has, indeed, no personal or independent right to maintenance.'
641. *Methodist Conference v. Parfitt* [1984] QB 368.
642. *Chalcroft v. Bishop of Norwich* (1995) 32040/95.
643. [1937] 2 All ER 751.
644. *Coker v. Diocese of Southwark* [1998] ICR 140: the 'legal framework for the work of a Church of England priest ... is unlike that of any secular employee'.

Curates,[645] the curate (an ordained cleric) was appointed by the bishop on the nomination of the incumbent of a parish to assist that incumbent. The curate was licensed by the bishop to what was described as an office (the office of curate). The High Court decided that a curate was not an employee. Parker J considered that the curate's functions and control over him were regulated by ecclesiastical jurisdiction and not by a contract.

268. When ministerial appointments are made, the parties do not intend to enter a contract of the type recognised in civil law (as there is deemed to be no intention to create legal relations).[646]

II. The Possibility of a Contract

269. Cases in the twentieth century challenged the classical doctrine of incompatibility to suggest that a contract was possible and that it might amount to a contract of employment.

270. In *Barthorpe v. Exeter Diocesan Board of Finance,*[647] it was held that a stipendiary reader in the Church of England (who was not ordained but a lay person licensed to minister) was an office-holder. However, the Employment Appeal Tribunal held that it was possible that a reader potentially could also hold a contract of employment. An office and a contract could coexist. Barthorpe had been given 'Terms of Reference for Employment' and was subject to regulations of the bishop. The case was remitted to the Industrial Tribunal (as it then was) but settled before determination.

271. Similarly, in *Methodist Conference v. Parfitt,*[648] the Court of Appeal held that a minister was not an employee on the basis that: no wage was paid to ministers; a minister cannot unilaterally resign from ministry; the minister was in a spiritual relationship with the Church; there was no intention to create legal relations; and at point of ordination, a minister does not undertake by contract to serve the Church as a minister. However, Dillon J noted that undertaking to perform spiritual work did not necessarily preclude the existence of a contract: a contract could be drafted setting out remuneration, holidays and functions, but this would be unusual.

272. This *obiter* comment in *Parfitt* proved influential. In *Davies v. Presbyterian Church of Wales,*[649] the House of Lords held there was no contract, repeating the principle that the spiritual nature of ministerial functions was incompatible with

645. [1912] 2 Ch. 563.
646. *Balfour v. Balfour* [1919] 2 KB 571; *J Evans & Son (Portsmouth) Ltd v. Andrea Merzario* [1976] 2 All ER 930.
647. (1979) ICR 900.
648. (1983) 3 All ER 747.
649. [1986] ICR 280.

the existence of a contract, but Lord Templeman admitted (as had Dillon in *Parfitt*) that in law it was possible for a contract to be created, but there was no evidence of one on the facts before the Court.

III. The Presumption Against a Contract

273. The late twentieth century case law therefore developed the notion that although it was possible for there to be a contract of employment, there was a presumption against there being such a contract. Indeed, the decisions reached, especially those by higher courts, seemed to suggest that this presumption was irrebuttable.

274. In *Santokh Singh v. Guru Nanak Gurdwara,*[650] there was no contract between a Sikh priest and his temple, even though the constitution of the temple called the priest an 'employee of the temple'. In *Guru Nanak Temple v. Sharry,*[651] the document which passed between the priest and the temple was entitled a 'contract'. The Industrial Tribunal held that there was sufficient evidence of intent to create legal relations but this was overturned by the Employment Appeal Tribunal: the parties had carelessly used language and there was no contractual intent. Similarly, in *Birmingham Mosque Trust v. Alavi*[652] the Industrial Tribunal held there was a contract between a khaleeb and the trust company running the mosque (since there was certainty of terms, agreed salary, hours of work and duties) but the Employment Appeal Tribunal reversed this. For Wood J, it was 'desirable that the same broad brush approach should be taken by all those faced with this issue … where religious factors are introduced'.

275. The Court of Appeal decision in *Coker v. Diocese of Southwark*[653] reinforced the classical doctrine. The case concerned a curate of the Church of England. The Industrial Tribunal held that letters exchanged between the curate and the bishop clearly indicated a contract.[654] This was overturned by the Employment Appeal Tribunal whose decision was upheld by the Court of Appeal. For Mummery LJ, there was no contract between the Church and the minister by virtue of the lack of intention to create legal relations; the legal effect of ordination is call to an office regulated by law and it is not necessary to enter a contract for the creation, definition, execution or enforcement of clerical functions. Mummery LJ held that the curate's spiritual functions were matters for ecclesiastical jurisdiction and that his

650. [1990] ICR 309.
651. (1990) EAT (145/90).
652. [1992] ICR 435.
653. [1998] ICR 140.
654. It was held that the curate was an employee because there was evidence of service, control and organisation; the bishop was a likely contracting party (along with the Diocesan Board of Finance, which paid the curate); there was no incompatibility between office and contract; the Church had chosen to use secular models and a visible organisation and therefore could not escape secular standards; and for the industrial tribunal there was a presumption in favour of a contract and this must be rebutted to oust the jurisdiction of the Court.

relationship with the bishop was regulated by canonical obedience, under 'the law of an established church which is part of the public law of England and not by a negotiated, contractual arrangement'.

§2. Subsequent Developments

276. *Coker v. Diocese of Southwark* is no longer the last word on the matter. In addition to ongoing political developments, there have been four important cases: the decision of the House of Lords in *Percy v. Church of Scotland Board of Mission,*[655] the Court of Appeal decision in *New Testament Church of God v. Stewart,*[656] the Supreme Court in *President of the Methodist Conference v. Preston,*[657] and the judgment of the Court of Appeal in *Sharpe v. Bishop of Worcester.*[658]

I. *Percy v. Church of Scotland Board of National Mission*

277. The case concerned a sex discrimination claim brought against the Church of Scotland by a former minister of the Church.[659] The two main issues were whether Percy's relationship with the Church constituted employment for the purposes of the Sex Discrimination Act 1975 and whether the claim constituted a 'spiritual matter' under the Church of Scotland Act 1921 meaning that it was within the exclusive cognisance of the Church of Scotland and its own courts.[660] Percy did not pursue her claim for wrongful dismissal at this level, accepting that she had not entered into a contract of service. Moreover, she had demitted status as a minister rather than being tried before her presbytery under the pre-2001 procedure, with the result that the matter had never come before a court of the Church. Her case was that she was employed under a contract personally to execute certain work, that is, a contract for services as distinct from a contract of service.

278. The House of Lords allowed Percy's appeal, holding that her relationship with the Church constituted employment for the purposes of the Sex Discrimination Act 1975 and was not a spiritual matter. Lord Nicholls of Birkenhead held that 'holding an office and being an employee are not inconsistent' and that the fact that Percy's status might readily be described as an ecclesiastical office led nowhere.[661]

655. [2005] UKHL 73.
656. [2007] EWCA Civ 1004. *See also MacDonald v. Free Presbyterian Church of Scotland* [2010] UKEAT S/0034/09/B1 (10 February 2010) and *Maga v. Trustees of the Birmingham Archdiocese of the Roman Catholic Church* [2010] EWCA Civ 256.
657. [2013] UKSC 29. *See* F. Cranmer, *Methodist Ministers: Employees or Office Holders?*, 15(3) Ecclesiastical Law Journal 316 (2013).
658. [2015] EWCA Civ 399.
659. *See* F. Cranmer & S. Peterson, *Employment, Sex Discrimination and the Churches: The Percy Case*, 8 Ecclesiastical Law Journal 392–405 (2006).
660. *See* Part I for further discussion of the second issue.
661. Paragraph 15.

He held that although there were 'many arrangements or happenings in church matters where, viewed objectively on ordinary principles, the parties cannot be taken to have intended to enter into a legally-binding contract',[662] this principle should not be carried too far:

> It cannot be carried into arrangements which on their face are to be expected to give rise to legally-binding obligations. The offer and acceptance of a church post for a specific period, with specific provision for the appointee's duties and remuneration and travelling expenses and holidays and accommodation, seems to me to fall firmly within this latter category.[663]

For Lord Nicholls, it was 'time to recognise that employment arrangements between a church and its ministers should not lightly be taken as intended to have no legal effect'.[664] On the facts, the documents on their face showed that Percy entered into a contract with the Board to provide services to the Church on the agreed terms and conditions. The House had been shown and told nothing to displace this prima facie impression.

279. Lord Hoffmann dissented on the application of these principles to the facts of the case. He agreed that there was plainly an intention to create legal relations. He commented that saying that a priest was a 'servant of God' or was 'not employed because her appointment was not accompanied by an intention to create legal relations' was unhelpful since it gave 'the impression that she operates entirely outside the legal system'.[665] However, on the facts, the legal relations in this case were not a contract of employment. Performance of the duties of an office which does not involve any contractual relationship can be said to be employment under a contract.

280. The House of Lords decision in *Percy* does not, in and of itself, mean that ministers of religion now have employment rights. It does, however, tend to show that the presumption against a contract is rebuttable. Indeed, the comments of their lordships concerning the intention to create legal relations suggest that the presumption has been removed. The Court of Appeal judgment in *New Testament Church of God v. Stewart* is important in indicating how *Percy* is to be interpreted.

II. *New Testament Church of God v. Stewart*

281. The case concerned a minister of religion whose pastorate had been terminated. The tribunal had held that the claimant was an employee for the purposes of section 230 of the Employment Rights Act 1996. The Church appealed citing their

662. Paragraph 23.
663. Paragraph 24.
664. Paragraph 26.
665. Paragraphs 61–62.

rights under Article 9 ECHR. The claimant submitted that the decision of the House of Lords in *Percy* involved a fundamental change and resolved the issue in his favour.

282. The Court of Appeal dismissed the appeal but considered both the importance of *Percy* and the Article 9 argument. Pill LJ held that *Percy* did not overrule the earlier cases. Instead, it established that 'the fact-finding tribunal is no longer required to approach its consideration of the nature of the relationship between a minister and his church with the presumption that there was no intention to create legal relations'.[666] *Percy* leaves it open to employment tribunals to find, 'provided of course a careful and conscientious scrutiny of the evidence justifies such a finding,' that there is an intention to create legal relations between a church and one of its ministers.

283. Pill LJ held that the statement in *Parfitt* that the spiritual nature of the work is a relevant consideration remained a principle of the law of England and Wales and reflected the principles stated in Article 9 ECHR. This requires that respect be given to the faith and doctrine of the particular church, which may run counter to there being a relationship enforceable at law between the priest, curate or minister and the Church. The law should not readily impose a legal relationship on members of a religious community which would be contrary to their religious beliefs. Employment tribunals should, therefore, carefully analyse the particular facts, which will vary from church to church, and probably from religion to religion, before reaching a conclusion.[667]

284. For Arden LJ, Article 9 was engaged in the present case since one aspect of freedom of religion is the freedom of a religious organisation to be allowed to function peacefully and free from arbitrary State intervention.[668] A religious organisation may, as one of its beliefs, consider that ministers should not have contracts of employment or that the State should not interfere in the way they conduct their organisation. Interference with that belief might be a violation of Article 9, though the interference will not constitute a violation of Article 9 if the conditions in Article 9(2) are satisfied.[669] Arden LJ rejected the submission that for Article 9 to be engaged it had to be an express tenet of the religion that no contract is formed between the minister and the religious body or some part of it.[670] She held that it was sufficient that the beliefs are found to be inconsistent with the implication of any contract or alternatively any contract of employment. Arden LJ held that the fact that in an employment dispute one party to the litigation is a religious body or that the other party is a minister of religion does not of itself engage Article 9. The implication of a contract of employment is not automatically an interference with religious beliefs. Rather, it is within the fact-finding function of the court or tribunal.

666. Paragraph 35.
667. Paragraph 55.
668. Paragraph 60.
669. Paragraph 61.
670. Paragraph 62. This argument has, however, been accepted in relation to other domestic Art. 9 claims, especially those concerning religious dress.

On the facts of this case, the tribunal came to a different conclusion looking at the evidence as a whole and was entitled so to do.

III. *President of the Methodist Conference v. Preston*

285. The case concerned a Minister in the Methodist Church who wished to prosecute a claim against the Church in an employment tribunal for unfair dismissal. The original Employment Tribunal in *Preston*[671] had held that a minister of the Methodist Church could not be an employee because it was bound by the Court of Appeal's decision in *The President of the Methodist Conference v. Parfitt.*[672] This was reversed by the Employment Appeal Tribunal[673] whose decision was upheld by the Court of Appeal[674] which had both held that Preston had served under a contract of employment. The Supreme Court reversed the decision of the Court of Appeal and declared that the claimant was not an employee.

286. However, although the Supreme Court ultimately agreed with the Employment Tribunal that Preston was not an employee, it was also made clear that the reasoning of *Parfitt* was no longer good law. As Lord Sumption noted, much of the earlier case law was 'influenced by relatively inflexible tests borne of social instincts which came more readily to judges of an earlier generation than they do in the more secular and regulated context of today'.[675] His Lordship held that the earlier cases had erred in treating ministers of religion as an 'abstract categorisation'; the 'correct approach is to examine the rules and practices of the particular church and any special arrangements made with the particular minister'.[676] The decision of the House of Lords in *Percy* meant 'the question whether a minister of religion serves under a contract of employment can no longer be answered simply by classifying the minister's occupation by type: office or employment, spiritual or secular'. There was now no presumption 'against the contractual character of the services of ministers'. Instead, the 'primary considerations are the manner in which the minister was engaged, and the character of the rules or terms governing his or her service', a task which like 'all exercises in contractual construction' needs to construe the parties' intentions 'against their factual background'. *Percy* confirmed that 'this factual background included the spiritual character of a minister's calling', but that this 'could not be conclusive'.[677]

287. The Supreme Court reversed the decision of the Court of Appeal which had held that Preston had served under a contract of employment on the basis that the judgment paid insufficient attention to the facts and the Deed of Union and the Standing Orders 'which were the foundation of Ms. Preston's relationship with the

671. The claimant's surname was Moore when proceedings began. She subsequently married.
672. [1983] 3 All ER 747.
673. [2010] UKEAT 0219101503.
674. [2011] EWCA Civ 1581.
675. [2013] UKSC 29, para. 2.
676. Paragraph 26.
677. Paragraph 8. *See also* the speech of Lord Hope at paras 30 and 34.

Methodist Church'.[678] Their broad brush approach 'would mean that almost any arrangements for the service of a minister of religion would be contractual'.[679] This underscores how cases concerning employment status will be fact-specific.

IV. *Sharpe v. Bishop of Worcester*

288. In *Sharpe v. Worcester Diocesan Board of Finance Ltd,*[680] the Employment Appeal Tribunal found that *Preston* had clarified the law and that it was 'now unnecessary to refer to all of the earlier cases'.[681] It was 'now abundantly clear that cases concerning the employment status of a minister of religion cannot be determined simply by asking whether the minister is an office holder or in employment' and 'there is no presumption against ordained ministers being engaged under contracts'.[682] Rather, each case must always be determined on its own particular facts' and 'each case will always be fact specific, and probably Church specific'.[683] This meant that, as far as the Employment Appeal Tribunal was concerned, the approach of the Employment Tribunal which had held that an ordained minister in the Church of England was neither an employee nor a worker was wrong because it had failed 'to carry out the full analysis that *Preston* now establishes is required'.[684] The Employment Appeal Tribunal held that:

> the focus should have been on whether there was an express contract between the Claimant and the Bishop, having regard to the rules and practices of the Church and the particular arrangements made with the Claimant. … The judge should therefore have conducted a careful analysis of the rules and practices of the Church, the manner in which the Claimant was engaged and the particular arrangements made with him, as revealed by all the relevant documentation, … in order to determine whether, properly analysed, they were characteristic of a contract and, if so, whether it was a contract of employment.[685]

That was not the end of the matter. The Court of Appeal overturned the judgment of the Employment Appeal Tribunal, reinstating the judgment of the Employment Tribunal at first instance which had concluded that Sharpe was not an employee. It is important to note, however, that the only real criticism of the Employment Appeal Tribunal's judgment was in relation to the way in which it had treated the Employment Tribunal's findings of fact. As Arden LJ observed 'the conclusion of the employment judge [at first instance] that there was no contract, or no contract of employment, between the parties was the result of a detailed examination of the

678. [2013] UKSC 29 para. 26.
679. Paragraph 25.
680. [2013] UKEAT 0243 12 2811.
681. Paragraphs 111–112.
682. Paragraphs 146–147.
683. Paragraphs 148, 151 In fact they are likely to be post-specific even within the same church: M. Hill, *Terms of Service*, 163 (7563) New Law Journal 10 (2013).
684. [2013] UKEAT 0243 12 2811, para. 181.
685. Paragraph 179.

facts and the law. The employment judge considered the case law concerning the nature of an ordained minister's spiritual duties with great care and at length'.[686] Recognising and reinforcing the point that whether a minister of religion is an employee will always be a fact sensitive question, Arden LJ explained that 'the facts must be looked at in the individual case and in the round'[687] and underscored the point that 'the fact that a person is an officeholder does not mean that he cannot be an employee'.[688]

289. The question of the employment status of ministers has been further affected by a series of cases concerning the vicarious liability of religious groups for torts committed by those who work for them.[689] While in some cases it has been conceded that ministers of religion should be treated as if they were employees for the purpose of vicarious liability,[690] in other cases it has been contended that the religious organisation could not be vicariously liable for the actions of ministers of religion since ministers were not employees. This argument has not found favour with the courts. In *JGE v. The Trustees of Portsmouth Roman Catholic Diocesan Trust,*[691] Ward LJ held that, although he was 'completely satisfied that there was no contract' between the priest and the bishop, the Church remained nevertheless vicariously liable for the priest's actions.[692] He considered that there was 'a need to adapt to current demands' and to consider whether a bishop could be vicariously liable on the basis that the relationship was akin to employment.[693] He concluded that 'the time has come emphatically to announce that the law of vicarious liability has moved beyond the confines of a contract of service'.[694]

290. This judgment was subsequently approved by the Supreme Court in *The Catholic Child Welfare Society v. Various Claimants.*[695] Lord Phillips affirmed the general principle that the 'relationship that gives rise to vicarious liability is in the vast majority of cases that of employer and employee under a contract of employment'.[696] However, he held that vicarious liability could also arise where the relationship between the defendant and the tortfeasor is akin to that between an employer and an employee.[697] The Supreme Court was clear that the technicalities of whether ministers of religion are employees would not inhabit the finding of

686. Paragraph 38.
687. Paragraph 92.
688. Paragraph 91.
689. Not all cases concerning vicarious liability for ministers of religion are relevant to the current issue. The litigation culminating in *Raggett v. The Society of Jesus Trust 1929 for Roman Catholic Purposes* [2012] EWHC 3132(QB) focused upon the application of the Limitation Act 1980 and the issue of causation.
690. *Maga v. Trustees of the Birmingham Archdiocese of the Roman Catholic Church* [2010] EWCA Civ 25 *See* H. Hall, *Maga and Direct Liability for Negligence*, 167 Law & Justice 11 (2011) and F. Cranmer, *Maga and Vicarious Liability for Sexual Abuse*, 167 Law & Justice 20 (2011).
691. [2012] EWCA Civ 938.
692. Paragraph 30.
693. Paragraphs 60, 31.
694. Paragraph 73.
695. [2012] UKSC 56.
696. [2012] UKSC 5, para. 35.
697. Paragraph 47.

vicarious liability. There would be vicarious liability where religious organisations had 'facilitated the commission of the abuse by placing the abusers in a position where they enjoyed both physical proximity to their victims and the influence of authority over them both as teachers and as men of god'.[698]

291. The judgment of the Supreme Court in *The Catholic Child Welfare Society* case was recently followed by the High Court in *BXB v. Watch Tower and Bible Tract Society of Pennsylvania*[699] which found that the Society was vicariously liable for the rape of one of their congregation by an 'elder', Chamberlain J observing that 'an elder is as integral to the "business" of a congregation of Jehova's Witnesses as a priest is to the "business" of the Catholic Church'.[700] His lordship further found that the commission of the rape was a risk created by the Society having assigned certain activities to the elder in question, observing that 'any organisation that confers on its leaders power over others creates the risk that they will abuse it in that way'.[701]

698. Paragraph 84.
699. [2020] EWHC 156 (QB).
700. Paragraph 158.
701. Paragraph 163.

Chapter 3. Other Church Employees and Labour Law

292. The Supreme Court has decided that neither volunteers nor religious arbitrators are to be considered as employees.[702] However, provided that there is a contract of employment, other church employees will be in the same legal position as employees generally, enjoying a number of rights under domestic labour law, as well as under discrimination law.[703] The position of teachers in both State schools and faith schools is explored in Part IX.

702. *X v. Mid Sussex Citizens Advice Bureau* [2012] UKSC 59; *Jivraj v. Hashwani* [2011] UKSC 4.

703. *See*, e.g., *Nicholson v. Aspire Trust* [2005] Employment Tribunal Case No. 2601009/004 (21 March 2005) and *Reaney v. Hereford Diocesan Board of Finance* [2007] Employment Tribunal Case No. 1602844/2006 (17 July 2007).

Part VII. Religious Communities and Protection of the Individual

293. This part examines a number of different ways in which particular laws affect both religious groups and individuals. Special attention will be given to two areas of the law (non-discrimination and penal law) since recent years have witnessed a great deal of legislation and litigation concerning them. In relation to other areas, the law has developed in a piecemeal fashion[704] and, since many provisions predate the Human Rights Act 1998, it may be speculated that the ECHR might be more significant in any future litigation concerning these provisions.

704. For a criticism of this *see* W. Menski, *Law, Religion and Culture in Multicultural Britain, in Law and Religion*, in *Multicultural Societies* 54 (R. Mehdi et al. eds, DJØF Publishing 2008).

Chapter 1. Protection of Privacy

294. There is no general privacy law in the United Kingdom.[705] However, data protection laws do exist in pursuance of European Union obligations.[706] Any individual or organisation which processes or handles personal data is a 'data controller' for the purposes of this legislation and so should be registered as such with the Information Commissioner's Office (and pay the prescribed fee) unless they are exempt.[707] The Church of England's Parish Resources website contains a summary of the requirements of the General Data Protection Regulations (GDPR) which are relevant to parishes.[708]

295. Certain requirements are imposed on all data controllers, whether registered or not, such as the requirement that personal data must be processed fairly and lawfully. These would apply to religious groups and individuals. For instance, those who do keep and process records relating to an identifiable living person (a 'data subject') must normally obtain the consent of that person.

296. 'Special category data' (which includes personal data revealing religious or philosophical beliefs)[709] is subject to heightened safeguards owing to its sensitive nature. In order to lawfully process special category data, a person or organisation must identify both a lawful basis under Article 6 of the GDPR and a separate condition for processing under Article 9. There are ten bases for processing special category data in Article 9, five of which require the person or organisation to meet additional conditions and safeguards set out in the Data Protection Act 2018, Schedule 1.

705. *Kaye v. Robertson* [1991] FSR 62. *See*, however, *Campbell v. MGN* [2004] UKHL 22 in which it was accepted that Art. 8 of the ECHR, which provides a qualified right to respect for private and family life, were now part of the cause of action for breach of confidence, providing a legal basis for a private individual to control the access to, and publication of, their private information.
706. The Data Protection Act 2018 repealed the Data Protection Act 1984 and was implemented in furtherance of the European Union's General Data Protection Regulation 2016/697 (the GDPR). In short, the GDPR sets out seven principles for the lawful processing of personal data and, in so doing, seeks to protect 'fundamental rights and freedoms of natural persons and in particular their right to the protection of personal data' (Article 1(2)).
707. *See* Data Protection (Charges and Information) Regulations 2018.
708. https://www.parishresources.org.uk/gdpr/, accessed 2 July 2020.
709. GDPR, Art. 9.

Chapter 2. Freedom to Marry

297. The law relating to marriage is explored in Part X.

Chapter 3. Freedom of Expression

298. The law relating to freedom of expression is dealt with in Part IX (under 'Religion and Art' and 'Religion and Media'). A number of criminal law provisions restrain freedom of expression for religious reasons. These are discussed in full in Chapter 8 below. In addition, there is a possibility of civil litigation against all forms of media under the law of libel.

Chapter 4. Due Process Norms and Religious Groups

§1. The Right to a Fair Trial

299. Although there is no constitutional court in the United Kingdom capable of striking down provisions in primary legislation, there are several mechanisms by which the legal system ensures that the legislative, executive and judiciary function legally and in accordance with the rule of law.

300. Judicial review, 'the High Court's power to police the legality of decisions made by public bodies',[710] provides one such mechanism. In relation to decisions made by religious groups, the general principle is that while the decisions of courts of the Church of England are subject to judicial review by State courts on grounds of administrative impropriety,[711] the variously styled courts and tribunals of all other religious communities are not subject to such review, being regarded as private rather than public bodies.[712] As we have seen,[713] this is not the case in Scotland, where no distinction is drawn between the decisions of private and public bodies for the purposes of judicial review.

301. The Human Rights Act 1998, which incorporates the right to a fair trial under Article 6, is also of considerable importance. For the purposes of the Human Rights Act 1998, all courts and tribunals of the Church of England are 'public authorities' and as such must act in a way which is compatible with Convention rights. The decision of the House of Lords in *Aston Cantlow v. Wallbank*[714] suggests that, for the most part, other organs of the established Church will not be regarded as public authorities and it is unlikely that other religious groups and their institutions will be so regarded.

302. In addition, Strasbourg jurisprudence suggests that States may be vicariously liable for the failings of religious decision-makers to follow Article 6 standards. In *Pellegrini v. Italy,*[715] Strasbourg held that Roman Catholic annulment proceedings in its ecclesiastical court where the applicant was not told the nature of proceedings beforehand and not allowed to read her husband's witness statements violated Article 6 ECHR. The Court held that the applicant's right to a fair trial was 'irremediably compromised'. Since the Vatican is not party to the ECHR, the claim was made against the Italian State because the Italian courts had made operative the church court's declaration of nullity. The Court held that the Italian court 'should

710. J. Alder & K. Syrett, *Constitutional and Administrative Law* 407 (11th ed., Palgrave Macmillan 2017).
711. Ecclesiastical Jurisdiction Measure 1963 s. 81(3). *See*, e.g., *R v. North, ex parte Oakey* [1927] 1 KB 491.
712. *R v. Chief Rabbi, ex parte Wachmann* [1992] 1 WLR 1036; *R v. Imam of Bury Park, ex parte Sulaiman Ali* [1994] COD 142; *R v. London Beth Din, ex parte Bloom* [1998] COD 131; *R v. Provincial Court of the Church in Wales, ex parte Clifford Williams* (1999) 5 Ecclesiastical L. J. 129.
713. *See* paras 157 et seq. above.
714. [2003] UKHL 37.
715. (2002) 35 EHRR 2.

have refused to confirm the outcome of such unfair proceedings' and that they had 'failed in their duty to check … that the applicant had enjoyed a fair trial in the ecclesiastical proceedings'.

§2. Oath Taking

303. Historically, oath taking in courts has been a significant issue for a number of religious believers. However, today individuals are entitled to swear their own distinctive oaths in judicial proceedings (whether as claimant, defendant, witness or juror) or to make a declaration.

304. The general rule under the Oaths Act 1978 remains that the person taking the oath should hold the New Testament, or, in the case of a Jew, the Old testament, in his uplifted hand, and shall say or repeat after the officer administering the oath the words 'I swear by Almighty God that … ', followed by the words of the oath prescribed by law.[716] Unless the person about to take the oath voluntarily objects, or is physically incapable of taking the oath, the officer shall administer the oath in the form and manner aforesaid without question.[717] In Scotland, the custom is to swear the oath 'with upraised hand'.[718]

305. However, a number of exceptions to this general rule are given on the face of the statute: 'In the case of a person who is neither a Christian nor a Jew, the oath shall be administered in any lawful manner'.[719] Any person who objects to being sworn shall be permitted to make his or her solemn affirmation instead of taking an oath.[720] This applies to those 'to whom it is not reasonably practicable without inconvenience or delay to administer an oath in the manner appropriate to his religious belief'.[721]

306. The Act also provides that: 'Where an oath has been duly administered and taken, the fact that the person to whom it was administered had, at the time of taking it, no religious belief, shall not for any purpose affect the validity of the oath'.[722]

307. Ordinarily, it is considered improper to cross-examine a person who holds a particular religious belief on their decision to affirm instead of swearing on the

716. Section 1(1). The 'words of the oath prescribed by law' were approved by a resolution of the judges of the then King's Bench Division on 11 January 1927 as 'the evidence which I shall give shall be the truth, the whole truth and nothing but the truth.' However, a failure to comply with the words will not necessarily invalidate the taking of the oath because the efficacy of the oath depends upon it being taken in a way binding, and intended to be binding, upon the conscience of the person taking it: *see R v. Chapman* [1980] Crim LR 42.
717. Section 1(2).
718. Section 3.
719. Section 1(3).
720. Section 5(1).
721. Section 5(1).
722. Section 4(2).

relevant holy book,[723] although the matter is left to the discretion of the trial judge and, in criminal cases, the issue, if it arises, should be canvassed with the judge first in the absence of the jury.[724]

723. *R v. Majid* [2009] EWCA Crim 2563.

724. *R v. Mehrban* [2001] EWCA Crim 2627.

Chapter 5. Professional Secrecy

308. Strictly speaking, communications between a priest and a penitent are not privileged under the law of the State and the matter becomes particularly controversial where the reporting of abusive behaviour or child protection issues are raised.[725] The Police and Criminal Evidence Act 1984 provides that 'a confession made by an accused person may be given in evidence against him insofar as it is relevant to any matter in issue in the proceedings'.[726] The Criminal Law Revision Committee (1972) decided not to recommend that priest-penitent communications be privileged. Whilst it has been argued that a trial judge would be likely, as a matter of discretion, to exclude evidence of a confession made to a priest,[727] there is a counterargument to the effect that this might not, generally speaking, be an appropriate exercise of discretion in accordance with the relevant legislative provisions.[728]

309. That having been said, there exists a variety of case law from the time of the Reformation through to the nineteenth century which touches upon the issue, albeit with varying, indeed often contradictory, approaches.[729] An added difficulty is that many of the case reports are unsatisfactory and, in any event, do not purport to relate to sacramental confessions.[730] By way of example, in *R v. Gilham,*[731] statements made during interviews with the prison chaplain were admitted in evidence in spite of counsel's argument that 'the state of mind induced by the chaplain's conversations and exhortations made the confession one under duress'. A contrary view was taken by Baron Alderson in *R v.* Griffin[732] who opined that such conversations 'ought not to be given in evidence'.

310. That view was not, it seems, followed in *R v. Hay*[733] where a Roman Catholic priest was committed for contempt after he declined to answer questions as to whom he had received a stolen watch from, saying that to do so would 'violate the laws of the Church, as well as the natural laws'.[734]

---

725. *See*, generally, the work of the Independent Inquiry into Child Sexual Abuse which was established 'because of serious concerns that some organisations had failed and were continuing to fail to protect children from sexual abuse' https://www.iicsa.org.uk/, accessed 2 July 2020.
726. Section 76(1).
727. M. Hill, *Ecclesiastical Law* para. 5.64 (4th ed., Oxford University Press 2018); A general discretion to exclude evidence arises under the Police and Criminal Evidence Act 1984, ss 76, 78 and 82.
728. C. Grout, *The Seal of the Confessional and the Criminal Law of England and Wales*, 22 Ecclesiastical Law Journal 138–155 (2020).
729. For a review of the case law from this period *see* R. Bursell, *The Seal of the Confessional*, 2 Ecclesiastical Law Journal 84–109 at 88 (1990).
730. *See*, for example, *R v. Sparkes* (c1790) (cited in *Du Barre v. Livette* (1791) Peake 108) and *R v. Radford* (1823) (cited in argument in *R v. Gilham* (1828) 1 Mood CC 186).
731. (1828) 1 Mood CCR 452.
732. (1853) 6 Cox 219.
733. (1860) 2 F&F 4.
734. For observations to the effect that members of the clergy should not be compelled to give evidence, *see Broad v. Pitt* (1828) 3 C&P 518.

311. Twentieth century judicial attitudes to the subject are perhaps best summed up by Lord Denning who, in *Attorney General v. Mulholland,*[735] made clear that a member of the clergy, like a banker or doctor, is not entitled to refuse to answer questions when directed to by a judge.[736] More recently, *Lancashire County Council v. E & F and Others*[737] concerned an application by two elders of a Congregation of Jehovah's Witnesses to set aside a witness summons, requiring them to provide certain information, on grounds of a religious duty of confidentiality. Lieven J was prepared to assume, without deciding, that a duty of confidentiality exists in relation to things said as part of a confession to, or spiritual counselling with, an elder.[738] However, quite apart from the fact that that was not what had happened in the present case, the judge went on to observe that any such duty of confidentiality was not absolute and that a clear overriding consideration would, for example, be to protect a child from sexual abuse.[739] That having been said, as a general rule, a person who receives information given in confidence may be restrained by injunction from disclosing that information; the duty is applicable in both the public and private spheres. Confidential communications are, generally speaking, protected as a matter of public policy.[740]

312. Clergy of the established Church of England may be in a more favoured position than those of non-established churches since the duty of confidentiality which attaches to them is part of the law of the land. The proviso to Canon 113 of the 1603/1604 Canons Ecclesiastical provides that, following a sacramental confession, a minister should 'not at any time reveal and make known to any person whatsoever any crime or offence so committed to his trust and secrecy, (except they be such crimes as by the laws of this realm his own life may be called into question for concealing the same), under pain of irregularity'. This is the sole surviving canon of the 1603/1604 Canons Ecclesiastical.[741] An Act of Convocation (1959) affirms confidentiality 'as an essential principle of Church doctrine', and provides that 'if any person confess his secret and hidden sin to a priest for the unburdening of his conscience, and to receive spiritual consolation and absolution … such priest is strictly charged that he do not at any time reveal or make known to any person whatsoever any sin so committed to his trust and secrecy'.[742] This position is reaffirmed by Article 3 of the Church's 'Guidelines for the Professional Conduct of the Clergy'.

735. [1963] 1 All ER 767.
736. *Ibid.*, at 771. Although *see* the judgment of Lord Donaldson in *X Limited v. Morgan-Grampian (Publishers) Limited* [1990] 2 WLR 421 where his lordship, having likened the relationship of priest and penitent to that of lawyer and client, opined that 'Parliament would, if necessary, confer the same immunity upon priests, albeit for different reasons, but that is unnecessary because the judges traditionally do not require priests to break the seal of the confessional', at 430–431.
737. [2020] EWHC 182 Fam.
738. *Ibid.*, para. 39.
739. *Ibid.*, para. 45.
740. *Argyll v. Argyll* [1967] Ch. 302; *AG v. Jonathan Cape* [1976] QB 752.
741. Draft Canon 66 in 1947 would have forbidden a priest 'by word, writing, sign, directly or indirectly, openly or covertly, or in any way whatsoever, at any time to reveal … any sin, crime or offence', or to make use of such information but this was not included in the revised canons.
742. *See* M. Hill, *Ecclesiastical Law* 5.63 (4th ed., Oxford University Press 2018) and N. Doe, *The Legal Framework of the Church of England* 353–355 (Clarendon Press 1996).

In March 2018, the 'Seal of the Confessional Working Party' published its report which, whilst reiterating the general position of the Church, opined that whereas a privilege may have existed in the past, 'the modern law of evidence had evolved without reference to it'.[743]

743. Church of England, 'Report of the Seal of the Confessional Working Party', March 2018, para. 3(10)(4).

Chapter 6. Medical Ethics

313. In general,[744] doctors cannot refuse to undertake a lawful procedure or operation because of their own personal beliefs,[745] nor are nurses immune from dismissal on grounds of failure to obey instructions because they have a conscientious objection to the treatment concerned.[746]

314. In England and Wales, it is a crime under section 2(1) of the Suicide Act 1961 to assist another to commit suicide. The Act does not extend to Scotland, where assisting a suicide is dealt with by common law, most likely as culpable homicide. Proceedings may only be instituted for an offence under section 2(1) of the 1961 Act by, or with the consent of, the Director of Public Prosecutions (DPP).

315. In *R (Pretty) v. DPP (Secretary of State for the Home Department Intervening)*,[747] the House of Lords held that Article 8 ECHR protected personal autonomy while a person was alive but did not confer a right to decide when or how to die. In *Pretty v. United Kingdom*,[748] however, the European Court of Human Rights disagreed, holding that the Court was 'not prepared to exclude that this constitutes an interference with her right to respect for private life as guaranteed under Article 8(1)'.

316. Subsequently, in *R (Purdy) v. DPP*,[749] it was argued that the prohibition in section 2(1) violated Article 8 and, in the absence of an offence-specific policy by the DPP setting out the factors to be taken into account when deciding whether or not it was in the public interest to prosecute, that interference was not 'in accordance with the law' as required by Article 8(2). The claimant sought judicial review of the DPP's refusal to publish detailed guidance about the circumstances in which he would or would not prosecute. In its final judgment before its transformation into the Supreme Court, the House of Lords required the DPP to publish guidance on his prosecution policy in respect of those assisting persons who commit suicide. Their Lordships agreed that to assist someone to travel to a country where assisted suicide is lawful so that that person could commit suicide was an offence. In the leading judgment, Lord Hope stated explicitly that it was not for the courts to change the law in order to decriminalise assisted suicide: if changes were to be made (as to which he expressed no opinion) that was a matter for Parliament.[750] Lord Hope took the view that Article 8 was engaged[751] and that the Convention tests of accessibility and foreseeability had not been met.[752]

744. *See* H. Payne & N. Doe, *Public Health and the Limits of Religious Freedom*, 2 Emory International Law Review 19, 539 (2005).
745. *R v. Bourne* [1939] 1 KB 687.
746. *Owen v. Coventry Health Association* (1984) Employment Appeal Tribunal 816/83.
747. [2002] 1 AC 800.
748. (2002) 35 EHRR 1.
749. [2009] UKHL 45.
750. Paragraph 26.
751. Paragraph 39.
752. Paragraph 52.

317. The DPP's interim guidance was duly published on 23 September 2009 and a consultation was launched at the same time.[753] The guidance sets out the primary public interest factors both for and against prosecution in general terms. At the same time, the Lord Advocate issued a reminder that the DPP's interim guidance does not apply in Scotland and that 'any change in the current law related to homicide is properly a matter for the Scottish Parliament'.

318. This guidance was challenged. In *R (on the application of Nicklinson and another) v. Ministry of Justice,*[754] a majority of the Supreme Court dismissed the appeal against the judgment of the Court of Appeal which had found that the blanket prohibition in section (2)(1) of the 1961 Act was compatible with Article 8. The Court held that the question as to whether the current law on assisted suicide was incompatible with Article 8 lay within the United Kingdom's margin of appreciation and was therefore a question for the United Kingdom to decide. Five of the Justices held that the Supreme Court had the constitutional authority to make a declaration that the general prohibition on assisted suicide was incompatible with Article 8. Of those five, three declined to grant such a declaration, but two would have done so. Four of the Justices considered that the issue was one for Parliament. A challenge before the European Court of Human Rights was declared inadmissible.[755] In 2018, the Supreme Court was again invited to consider the issue of whether section (2)(1) of the 1961 Act is compatible with Article 8 of the ECHR. On this occasion, although the Court accepted that the issue was one of 'transcendent public importance', permission to appeal was refused.[756]

319. Except when carried out by an approved medical practitioner in circumstances carefully delineated in statute, female genital mutilation (sometimes referred to as 'female circumcision') is a criminal offence under the Female Genital Mutilation Act 2003 and the Female Genital Mutilation (Scotland) Act 2005.[757] It is, however, the presumption at common law that non-therapeutic male circumcision is lawful provided that, in the case of a child in England and Wales,[758] both parents consent:

> The decision to circumcise a child on grounds other than medical necessity is a very important one: the operation is irreversible and should only be carried out where the parents together approve of it or, in the absence of parental agreement, where a court decides that the operation is in the best interests of the child.[759]

---

753. Available at /www.cps.gov.uk/consultations/as_policy.html.
754. [2014] UKSC 38.
755. *Nicklinson and Lamb v. United Kingdom*, Application Nos 2478/15 and 1787/15, 16 July 2015.
756. *R (on the application of Conway) v. Secretary of State for Justice* (27 November 2018).
757. Which replaced for each of the two jurisdictions the Prohibition of Female Circumcision Act 1985.
758. The current guidance of the General Medical Council suggests that this must also be the common law position in Scotland: *see Personal beliefs and medical practice – guidance for doctors* paras 12 & 13 (March 2008).
759. Dame Elizabeth Butler-Sloss P, *Re J (Child's Religious Upbringing and Circumcision)* [1999] 11 WLUK 841 at para. 32. *See also Re S (Specific Issue Order: Religion: Circumcision)* [2004] EWHC

In 1995, the Law Commission for England and Wales stated that although in its view ritual circumcision was lawful, it would be helpful to 'put the lawfulness of ritual male circumcision beyond any doubt'[760]– but that has never happened.

320. One of the best-known conscience clauses in UK law is that in section 4 of the Abortion Act 1967, which provides that 'no person shall be under any duty, whether by contract or by any statutory or other legal requirement, to participate in any treatment authorised by this Act to which he has a conscientious objection'. In any legal proceedings the burden of proof of conscientious objection shall rest on the person claiming to rely on it. This does not affect 'any duty to participate in treatment which is necessary to save the life or to prevent grave permanent injury to the physical or mental health of a pregnant woman'. There has been little discussion of section 4 in the courts. However, the clause applies only to personnel actually participating in the operation, and does not excuse a refusal by a medical secretary to type a letter about a case involving an abortion.[761] This has been followed in *Doogan v. NHS Greater Glasgow & Clyde Heath Board*[762] in which it was held that section 4(1) did not entitle the claimants to refuse to delegate to, supervise or support staff on the labour ward directly involved with patients having abortions. The word 'participate' was to be understood in its ordinary sense, not in a technical one. Further, there was no breach of Article 9 ECHR given that they had in fact consciously agreed to become Labour Ward Co-ordinators though they now objected to the content of those posts and, third, because their duties did not in fact require them to provide any treatment to terminate a pregnancy directly.[763]

321. In *SPUC Pro-life Scotland Ltd v. Scottish Ministers,*[764] the Court of Session dismissed a petition by a pro-life group for judicial review of a decision by the Scottish Ministers to issue legislation which approved a pregnant woman's home as a class of place where treatment for termination of pregnancy might be carried out, noting that the treatment would continue to be carried out by a medical practitioner.[765] In *Dulgheriu and Orthova v. The London Borough of Ealing,*[766] the Court of Appeal upheld a dismissal of a challenge to the validity of a Public Spaces Protection Order (PSPO) made by the London Borough of Ealing prohibiting anti-abortion protests in the immediate vicinity of a family planning centre. Whilst the

1282 (Fam) in which Baron J refused to allow a Muslim woman separated from a non-Muslim husband to convert her two children to Islam and have her son circumcised: the children should decide for themselves which religion, if any, they wished to follow when old enough to do so and it was not in the boy's best interests to be circumcised. Although, for the considerations in an asylum and immigration law context, *see SS (Malaysia) v. Secretary of State for the Home Department* [2013] EWCA Civ 888.

760. Law Commission: *Consent in the Criminal Law. Law Commission consultation paper no 139* at 119, 128 (HMSO 1995).
761. *Janaway v. Salford Health Authority* [1989] 1 AC 537.
762. [2012] ScotCS CSOH 32.
763. Paragraph 80.
764. [2018] CSOH 85.
765. *See* The Abortion Act 1967 (Place for Treatment for the Termination of Pregnancy) (Approval) (Scotland) (2017).
766. [2019] EWCA Civ 1490.

Court accepted, among other things, that Article 9 was engaged, it observed that 'Engagement of the article 9 rights of protesters could not have tipped the balance against the making of the PSPO if Ealing was otherwise justified in making it'[767] which, the Court concluded, Ealing was.

322. Section 38 of the Human Fertilisation and Embryology Act 1990 provides a conscience clause for persons who may otherwise be under a duty to participate in any activity governed by the Act involving scientific experiments on human foetal tissue. The ground of conscience is not limited to a religious base, but must be shown by the person claiming it.

323. In *Mackereth v. Department for Work and Pensions and Another*[768] the Employment Tribunal considered the case of a Christian Doctor who would not, owing to a conscientious objection to transgenderism, refer to transgender individuals by reference to their preferred pronouns. The Employment Tribunal considered that such a conscientious objection, though sincerely held, was 'incompatible with human dignity' and conflicted with 'the fundamental rights of others, specifically here, transgender individuals'.[769]

324. Specific conscience clauses exist for clergy of the Church of England and the Church in Wales who are commonly understood to be under a legal duty to conduct opposite sex marriage of parishioners.[770] Section 8(2) of the Matrimonial Causes Act 1965 provides that no member of the clergy is to be compelled to solemnise the marriage of any person whose former marriage has been dissolved and whose former spouse is still living or to permit the marriage of such a person to be solemnised in his or her church or chapel.[771] The Gender Recognition Act 2004[772] has amended the Marriage Act 1949 to provide a similar conscience clause to state that a cleric is not obliged to solemnise a marriage where he or she 'reasonably believes' that the bride or groom has acquired a new gender under the Act.[773] A wider conscience clause is provided in relation to clerics of the Church in Wales: a cleric is not obliged to 'permit the marriage of a person to be solemnised in the church or chapel' of which they are the minister if he 'reasonably believes' that the bride or groom has acquired a new gender under the Act.[774]

767. *Ibid.*, para. 81.
768. Case No. 1304602/2018.
769. At para. 197. *See* further A. Hambler, *Beliefs Unworthy of Respect in a Democratic Society: A View from the Employment Tribunal*, 22 Ecclesiastical Law Journal 234 (2020).
770. For same sex marriage, *see* s. 2 of the Marriage (Same Sex Couples) Act 2013. *See* further Part X for details.
771. *See* M. Hill, *Ecclesiastical Law* 5.48 and 5.49 (4th ed., Oxford University Press 2018). For discussion of the Church in Wales, *see* N. Doe, *The Law of the Church in Wales* 266–269 (University of Wales Press 2002).
772. Schedule 4.
773. Marriage Act 1949, s. 5B(1).
774. Section 5B(2). *See also* Equality Act 2010, Sch. 3 para. 24 which provides an exception from the law prohibiting discrimination on grounds of gender reassignment in the provision of goods and services. This exception is enjoyed by any person included within s. 5B of the Marriage Act 1949

Chapter 7. Non-discrimination

325. One of the most significant twentieth century developments to the way in which English law regulates religion has been the extension of discrimination law specifically to cover religion or belief. The law on religious discrimination marks something of a watershed since previously only some religious groups were protected under racial discrimination laws.[775] However, this is not the only way in which discrimination law impacts upon religious groups. A number of specific exceptions from general prohibitions are afforded to religious groups. This chapter explores the extent to which English law both prohibits discrimination on grounds of religion and permits discrimination on grounds of religion.

326. Historically, English law only prohibited discrimination on grounds of race, sex and disability. In 2000, EU Directive 2000/78/EC stated that, in addition to existing prohibitions against discrimination on grounds of sex, race and disability, discrimination on grounds of sexual orientation, age and religion or belief 'should be prohibited throughout the Community' in employment and occupation. This led to new laws prohibiting discrimination on grounds of sexual orientation,[776] age[777] and religion or belief[778] covering discrimination in relation to employment. Subsequent legislation has extended protection to cover the provision of goods and services and other related matters.[779] The law is now to be found in the Equality Act 2010, which also protects gender reassignment, marriage and civil partnership, and pregnancy and maternity as 'protected characteristics'.

327. Most of the case law has concerned discrimination in relation to employment and has been heard at the level of the Employment Tribunal and also occasionally by the Employment Appeal Tribunal. It should be noted that although the decisions of the Employment Tribunal do not serve as binding precedent for subsequent cases,[780] in practice later tribunal decisions in this area do refer to previous decisions.

328. The Commission of the European Communities published a new draft Directive which would prohibit discrimination on grounds of disability, religion or

and any other person who may 'solemnise marriages according to a form, rite or ceremony of a body of persons who meet for religious worship'.

775. *Mandla v. Dowell Lee* [1983] 2 AC 548; *Seide v. Gillette Industries Limited* [1980] IRLR 427; *J H Walker Limited v. Hussain and Others* [1996] ICR 291; *Crown Suppliers (PSA) Limited v. Dawkins* [1993] ICR 517.
776. Employment Equality (Sexual Orientation) Regulations 2003.
777. Employment Equality (Age) Regulations 2006.
778. Employment Equality (Religion or Belief) Regulations 2003.
779. Equality Act 2006, Equality Act (Sexual Orientation) Regulations 2007.
780. *Secretary of State for Trade and Industry v. Cook* [1997] ICR 288 at 292. *See Halsbury's Laws of England, vol. 16: Employment*, 4th ed. (2000), para. 684.

belief, sexual orientation and age in relation to goods and services, housing, education, social protection, social security and social advantage.[781] An amended version was then published by the Swedish Presidency. The proposal has had a first (and only) reading in the European Parliament. The fact that this Directive has not been approved means that English law currently goes beyond existing European obligations, which only prohibit discrimination in relation to employment.[782] However, the Supreme Court has held that, although domestic courts are not obliged to follow EU jurisprudence in discrimination claims not concerning employment, 'for the sake of consistency and coherence it is highly desirable that we follow the same approach'.[783]

§1. Prohibiting Discrimination on Grounds of Religion

329. Discrimination on grounds of religion or belief has been expressly forbidden since 2003 in relation to employment and since 2006 in relation to goods and services.[784] The law is now to be found in the Equality Act 2010.

I. Definitions of 'Religion or Belief'

330. One of the most contentious aspects of the new law on religious discrimination has been the vexed question of the definition of religion.[785] Although the original EU Framework Directive gave no further definition of the terms 'religion or belief', the 2003 Regulations originally defined 'religion or belief' as any 'religion, religious belief, or similar philosophical belief'.[786]

331. Early employment tribunal decisions suggested that the Regulations took a broad conception of 'religion' and a narrow conception of 'belief'. *Hussain v. Bhuller Bros*,[787] for instance, found that 'attendance at home for bereavement purposes formed part of the Claimant's religion or religious belief' and seemed to go

781. *See* M. Rynkowski, *The Background to the European Union Diresctive 2000/78/EC*, in *Religion and Discrimination Law in the European Union* 395 (M. Hill ed., Trier 2012).
782. Unlike the current law (discussed below) the Directive would have covered harassment on grounds of religion or belief in relation to goods and services.
783. *Bull v. Hall* [2013] UKSC 83, para. 29. To the extent that pre-existing EU law has been carried over following Brexit, British domestic Courts would still be entitled to look to EU jurisprudence as an aid to interpretation notwithstanding that the principle of consistency and coherence no longer applies.
784. Employment Equality (Religion or Belief) Regulations 2003 SI 2003/1660; Equality Act 2006 Part 2.
785. *See* P. Griffith, *Protecting the Absence of Religious Belief? The New Definition of Religion or Belief in Equality Legislation*, 3 Religion & Human Rights 2, 149 (2007) and R. Sandberg, *A Question of Belief*, in *Religion and Law* 51 (N. Spencer ed., *Theos* 2012).
786. Employment Equality (Religion or Belief) Regulations 2003 reg. 2(1).
787. ET, Case No. 1806638/2004 (5 July 2005).

further than current human rights principles in recognising that 'If a person genuinely believes that his faith requires a certain course of action then that is, sufficient to make it part of his religion'.[788]

332. By contrast, claims were excluded on the basis that the belief professed was not a 'similar philosophical belief'. In *Williams v. South Central Limited,*[789] loyalty to a national flag or to one's native country did not constitute 'a religious belief, or similar philosophical belief' while in *Baggs v. Fudge*[790] it was held that discrimination on the basis that someone was a member of the British National Party (BNP) was outside the scope of the Regulations. The BNP was a political party and not a 'religion, or a set of religious beliefs, or a set of similar philosophical beliefs'.

333. The Equality Act 2006[791] changed the definition explicitly to include lack of religion or belief and to remove the requirement that philosophical beliefs needed to be 'similar' to religious ones in order to be protected. The definition provided in section 10 of the Equality Act 2010 is in substance the same as in the Equality Act 2006.

334. In *Grainger PLC v. Nicholson,*[792] the Employment Appeal Tribunal concluded that an asserted belief in man-made climate change, together with the alleged resulting moral imperatives arising from it, was capable of constituting a 'philosophical belief' for the purpose of the 2003 Regulations provided that: (i) it was genuinely held; (ii) it was a belief and not merely an opinion or viewpoint based on the present state of information available; (iii) it was a belief as to a weighty and substantial aspect of human life and behaviour; (iv) it attained a certain level of cogency, seriousness, cohesion and importance; and (v) it was worthy of respect in a democratic society, was compatible with human dignity and did not conflict with the fundamental rights of others. Burton J held that ECHR jurisprudence was directly relevant.

335. Employment Tribunal Chairs have considered the *Grainger v. Nicholson* tests to be met in cases concerning: beliefs in spiritualism and psychic powers;[793] anti-fox hunting beliefs;[794] beliefs in the virtue of public service broadcasting;[795] and humanist beliefs.[796] In contrast, other Employment Tribunal Chairs have concluded that the tests have not been met in cases concerning beliefs in conspiracy theories regarding 9/11;[797] a belief that a Poppy should be worn during the week

788. Compare *Arrowsmith v. United Kingdom* (1981) 3 EHRR 218.
789. ET, Case No. 2306989/2003 (16 June 2004).
790. ET, Case No. 1400114/2005 (23 March 2005).
791. Equality Act ss 44, 77(1).
792. [2009] UKEAT 0219/09/ZT (3 November 2009).
793. *Greater Manchester Police Authority v. Power* [2009] EAT 0434/09/DA (12 November 2009).
794. *Hashman v. Milton Park (Dorset) Ltd* [2011] ET 3105555/2009 (31 January 2011).
795. *Maistry v. The BBC* [2011] ET 1213142/2010 (14 February 2011).
796. *Streatfield v. London Philharmonic Orchestra Ltd* [2012] 2390772/2011(22 May 2012).
797. *Farrell v. South Yorkshire Police Authority* [2011] ET 2803805/2010 (24 May 2011).

prior to Remembrance Sunday;[798] and Marxist / Trotskyite beliefs held by trade union members.[799] In a judgment, described by two commentators as 'muddled',[800] the Employment Tribunal concluded that a belief in vegetarianism was not capable of satisfying the *Grainger* criteria.[801] Whereas, shortly thereafter, the same Employment Judge, in a different case, concluded that 'ethical veganism' is a protected philosophical belief.[802]

336. Given the adoption of the European Court of Human Rights jurisprudence, it would appear that the decision in *Baggs v. Fudge* stating that political beliefs are unprotected is no longer good law.[803] Tribunals have suggested that some political beliefs may be protected. In *Kelly v. Unison,*[804] it was suggested that a distinction could be drawn between 'political beliefs which involve the objective of the creation of a legally binding structure by power or government regulating others', which are not protected, and the beliefs that 'are expressed by his own practice but where he has no ambition to impose his scheme on others', which may be protected.[805] However, this distinction has not found favour with subsequent Employment Tribunal decisions. In *Maistry v. The BBC,*[806] in reaching its conclusion that a belief in public service broadcasting could be a philosophical belief, the Tribunal stated that it did not accept that the claimant's belief was a political opinion or based on a political philosophy. However, it observed that 'even if it had been, the appellate courts have not yet definitely determined that question'.[807] In a judgment of the Employment Tribunal (Scotland), it was held that a belief in Scottish independence does amount to a philosophical belief for the purposes of the Equality Act 2010.[808]

II. Direct Discrimination

337. Direct discrimination occurs where A treats B less favourably (because of religion or belief) than they would treat others in circumstances which are materially the same.[809] This would apply, for instance, if A refuses to offer the job to B

798. *Lisk v. Shield Guardian Co Ltd & Others* [2011] ET 3300873/2011 (14 September 2011).
799. *Kelly v. Unison* [2009] ET 2203854/08 (22 December 2009).
800. F. Cranmer & R. Sandberg, *A Critique of the Decision in Conisbee That Vegetarianism Is Not 'a Belief'*, 22(1) Ecclesiastical Law Journal 36 (2020).
801. *Conisbee v. Crossley Farms Ltd*, unreported, 6 September 2019 (ET (Norwich)).
802. *Casamitjana Costa v. The League Against Cruel Sports*, 21 January 2020 (ET (Norwich)).
803. Given that political beliefs are considered to be protected under Art. 9 in the ECHR jurisprudence: *X v. Austria* (1963) 13 CD 42. *See* para. 67.
804. [2009] ET 2203854/08 (22 December 2009).
805. At para. 114.
806. [2011] ET 1213142/2010 (14 February 2011).
807. At para. 19. Although *see* the judgment of the ECtHR in *Redfearn v. UK* (Application No. 47335/06).
808. *See Mr C McEleney v. Ministry of Defence* [2018] ET S/4105347/2017.
809. Equality Act 2010 s. 13. Prior to the Equality Act 2010, the requirement was that direct discrimination needed to be 'on grounds of religion or belief'. The Equality Act 2010 replaces the words 'on grounds of' with 'because of', and according to the Explanatory Notes, this had the intention not of changing the meaning but of making the legislation more accessible: Equality Act 2010 Explanatory Notes para. 61.

because B is a Hindu, if A sacks B because B's wife is an atheist or if A refuses to teach B because he thinks B is a Muslim. Discrimination also occurs where A discriminates against B even if A and B are of the same religion, provided that A discriminates on the grounds of B's religion or belief and not A's own religion or belief.[810]

338. There is no general defence of justification to direct discrimination.[811] The claimant must prove facts from which the Tribunal could conclude that unlawful discrimination has occurred. If the claimant establishes a prima facie case, then the burden of proof passes to the respondent. In direct discrimination cases, the respondent can prove that there was no discrimination but cannot justify the discrimination.[812]

339. Direct discrimination claims have seldom been successful. However, *Bodi v. Teletext*[813] provides an example to the contrary. Bodi claimed that he had not been shortlisted for the job of Duty Editor for Teletext on grounds of his Asian race or Muslim religion; he compared his treatment with that of the shortlisted candidates with equivalent or lesser experience. The Employment Tribunal found that Bodi had been directly discriminated against on grounds of race and/or religion.

340. Most other direct discrimination cases fail because, unlike *Bodi,* the claimant is unable to establish a prima facie case. The Employment Appeal Tribunal has found that if the employer's objection is to an employee inappropriately promoting his religion (rather than to the employee's religion per se) then there is no direct discrimination.[814]

341. Tribunals have found that in order to establish that there has been discrimination on grounds of religion or belief, the tribunal must be satisfied that the prohibited ground is one of the significant reasons for the treatment, 'significant' meaning more than trivial.[815] For instance,[816] in *Ferri v. Key Languages Limited*[817]

810. This is not explicitly stated in the Equality Act 2010 due to the broadness of the new definition of direct discrimination: Equality Act 2010 Explanatory Notes para. 59. Under the former law, this was explicit: Employment Equality (Religion or Belief) Regulations 2003 reg. 3(1)(a); Equality Act 2006 s. 45(1). *See also* the judgment of the Employment Appeal Tribunal in *Gan Menachem Hendon Limited v. De Groen,* Appeal No. UKEAT/0059/18/00, 12 February 2019, applying the judgment of the Supreme Court in *Lee v. Ashers Baking Co Limited* [2018] UKSC 49.

811. However, the Supreme Court has held that direct discrimination can be justified in relation to the protected characteristic of disability: *Seldon v. Clarkson Wright and Jones* [2012] UKSC 16.

812. The court or tribunal must be satisfied that the explanation for the less favourable treatment was discriminatory: *see Ladele v. London Borough of Islington* [2009] EWCA (Civ) 1357 at para. 30.

813. ET, Case No. 3300497/2005 (13–14 October 2005).

814. *Chondol v. Liverpool City Council* [2009] UKEAT/0298/08 (11 February 2009). *See also Monaghan v. Leicester Young Men's Christian Association* [2004] Employment Tribunal Case No. 1901839/2004 (26 November 2004).

815. *Ladele v. London Borough of Islington* [2008] EAT Case No. UKEAT/0453/08/RN (10 December 2008).

816. *See also Mohamed v. Virgin Trains* ET, Case No. 2201814/2004 (12–14 October 2004; 20 May 2005); EAT (2006) WL 2522403 (30 August 2006).

817. ET, Case No. 2302172/2004 (12 July 2004).

a Roman Catholic was told not to wear certain necklaces at work as they were rather loud and overtly religious. She was later dismissed due to alleged poor performance. She claimed that the dismissal constituted direct discrimination. The Tribunal found that she had not made her case: she had not proved that she was sacked for her religious belief rather than her poor performance. The Court of Appeal in *Ladele v. London Borough of Islington*[818] stated that the acts of alleged discrimination must be 'motivated' by the claimant's religious beliefs.[819] A failure to accommodate religious difference rather than a complaint that the claimant had been discriminated against because of that difference will not amount to direct discrimination. Treating people in precisely the same way cannot constitute direct discrimination.[820]

342. Other cases have failed because the claimant has not couched his claim as religious discrimination as such. For instance,[821] in *Devine v. Home Office,*[822] Devine claimed that he had been rejected for a job at the Home Office due to his sympathy for underprivileged asylum seekers. He claimed that he had been discriminated against on grounds of religion or belief since his care for disadvantaged people was a demonstration of the Christian virtue of charity. The Tribunal found his claim to be 'far too vague and ill-defined to amount to a case to answer for'. Similarly, in *McClintock v. Department of Constitutional Affairs*,[823] concerning a Justice of the Peace who resigned since he could not in conscience agree to place children with same-sex couples, both the Employment Tribunal and the Employment Appeal Tribunal held that there had been no direct discrimination since McClintock had never made it plain that his objection was underscored by conscientious or religious objection.

343. The distinction between direct and indirect discrimination was discussed by the Supreme Court in *Bull v. Hall.*[824] The case concerned whether it was discrimination on grounds of sexual orientation to refuse to provide a double-bedded room in their private hotel to a couple in a civil partnership, on the grounds that as Christians they believed that sexual activity should take place only within the context of (heterosexual) marriage. The Supreme Court, though unanimous in dismissing the appeal, was divided as to whether the discrimination complained of was direct or

818. [2009] EWCA (Civ) 1357.
819. At para. 36. The Court of Appeal also stated that remarks must be taken in context. Dyson LJ rejected what he perceived to be 'a pedantically literal, unrealistic or a contextual interpretation' of a comment by a line manager's that it was wrong to 'be accommodating people's religious beliefs in the Registry Services'. He held that this did not show that she was motivated by the claimant's religious beliefs. *See* para. 35.
820. At para. 29. In *Eweida and Others v. United Kingdom* (2013) 57 EHRR 8, the Court held that the direct discrimination claim brought by Ladele was inadmissible since the applicant had failed to exhaust domestic remedies: para. 55.
821. *See also Harris v. NKL Automotive Ltd & Anor* [2007] UKEAT/0134/07/DM; 2007 WL 2817981 (3 October 2007).
822. ET Case No. 2302061/2004 (9 August 2004).
823. [2007] UKEAT/0223/07/CEA (31 October 2007).
824. [2013] UKSC 83.

indirect. Lady Hale, Lord Kerr and Lord Toulson held that the appellants' policy constituted direct discrimination on grounds of sexual orientation. As Lady Hale observed:

> when it came to denying a double bed …, which they would have given to a heterosexual married couple, [the appellants] were not only applying the criterion that they were unmarried. They were also applying a criterion that their legal relationship was not that of one man or one woman, in other words a criterion indistinguishable from sexual orientation.[825]

Lord Neuberger and Lord Hughes held that the appellants' policy constituted indirect discrimination. Lord Hughes held that the sexual orientation was not the ground for the less favourable treatment; the ground was that they were unmarried.[826]

344. In *Lee v. Ashers Baking Company Limited,*[827] the Supreme Court held that there had been no direct discrimination where a bakery had refused to provide to a gay customer a cake, iced with the message 'support gay marriage', because of the sincere religious beliefs of the bakery owners that same-sex marriage is inconsistent with Biblical teaching. Lady Hale observed that there was no less favourable treatment 'because anyone else would have been treated in the same way … the objection was to being required to promote the message on the cake'.[828]

345. In *Gan Menachem Hendon Limited v. De Groen,*[829] a teacher had been dismissed from her post in a Jewish nursery after it had come to light that she was cohabiting with her boyfriend. Both the Headteacher and the Managing Director of the nursery held the view that cohabitation outside of marriage was wrong and that the revelation relating to Ms. De Groen's private life had, among other things, damaged the nursery's reputation.[830] Whilst the Employment Appeal Tribunal dismissed appeals against findings that Ms. De Groen had been subjected to direct sex discrimination and harassment, it allowed the appeal against the finding that there had been direct discrimination against Ms. De Groen on grounds of religion or belief, observing that 'the conclusion that section 10(1) of the 2010 Act prohibits less favourable treatment by an employer on the basis of its own religion or belief is wrong. It is a conclusion that cannot survive the reasoning of Baroness Hale of Richmond PSC in her judgment in *Lee v. Ashers Baking* … '.[831]

825. Paragraph 30.
826. Paragraph 91.
827. [2018] UKSC 49.
828. *Ibid.*, para.47.
829. Appeal No. UKEAT/0059/18/00, 12 February 2019.
830. *Ibid.*, paras 3–9.
831. At para. 20.

III. Indirect Discrimination

346. Indirect discrimination occurs where A applies or would apply a provision, criterion or practice (PCP) equally: (i) which puts, or would put, persons of B's religion or belief at a particular disadvantage compared with others; (ii) which puts, or would put, B at that disadvantage; and (iii) which A cannot show to be a proportionate means of achieving a legitimate aim.[832] For example, A applies 'no headwear' policy to staff. B, an employee, is a Sikh. This rule disadvantages Sikhs in general and B in particular.

347. The key point about indirect discrimination is that it can be justified, for example, by security or health and safety concerns. Its operation is therefore similar to the analysis of the right to manifest under Article 9, where the focus is on interference then justification. Indirect discrimination is more common than direct discrimination and there have been some successful cases, including the first case argued under the goods and services provisions of the Equality Act 2006, *R (on the application of Watkins-Singh) v. The Governing Body of Aberdare Girls' High School.*[833]

348. *Watkins-Singh* concerned a 14 year old girl of Punjabi-Welsh heritage, who was told to remove her Kara bangle[834] at school. While the school saw the case as concerning Article 9, Watkins-Singh's legal team argued that the refusal to allow Watkins-Singh to wear the Kara at school was unlawful as indirect unjustified race and religious discrimination contrary to the Race Relations Act 1976 and the Equality Act 2006.

349. In relation to the indirect discrimination claim, Silber J noted that it was not disputed that Sikhs were both a racial and religious group[835] and that the school's uniform policy constituted a provision, criterion or practice which had a disparate impact upon pupils who shared Watkins-Singh's race and religion compared with those 'pupils whose religious beliefs or racial beliefs were not compromised by the uniform code on the issue of the Kara or any other similar item of jewellery'.[836] Silber J rejected the defendant's contention that there would only be a 'particular disadvantage' where a member of the group is prevented from wearing something that they are required to wear.[837] Rather, the judge concluded that a 'particular disadvantage' would occur – but would not only occur – where a pupil is forbidden from wearing an item where 'that person genuinely believed for reasonable grounds that wearing this item was a matter of exceptional importance to this or her racial identity or his or her religious belief' and where 'the wearing of the item can be shown objectively to be of exceptional importance to his or her religion or race,

832. Equality Act 2010, s. 19.
833. [2008] EWHC (Admin) 1865.
834. The Kara bangle is a steel bracelet worn as a matter of obligation by all initiated Sikhs and as a gesture of solidarity by many uninitiated Sikhs.
835. *Mandla v. Dowell Lee* [1983] 2 AC 548; Equality Act 2006 s. 44(a).
836. Paragraph 46.
837. Paragraphs 51–55.

even if the wearing of the article is not an actual requirement of that person's religion or race'.[838] He concluded that both these subjective and objective elements were satisfied on the facts of the case: nothing had been suggested to undermine the truthfulness of Watkins-Singh's comments[839] and the wearing of the item could be shown to be of exceptional importance to her religion and race as a Sikh even if not a requirement of the religion or race.[840]

350. Having decided that there was a particular disadvantage, Silber J turned to the question of justification, holding that the indirect discrimination was not justified by a legitimate aim. He held that it could not be said that allowing pupils to wear a Kara caused substantial difficulties because pupils may stand out, nor that it undermines the uniform policy's aim of fostering a community spirit because the Kara is small and is usually hidden by a long-sleeved sweater. Moreover, it could not be said that the ban was justified in that it minimised pressures resulting from wealth and style. The claim of indirect discrimination therefore succeeded. The contrast between Silber J's judgment and the much more restrictive approach taken in the Article 9 case law[841] has led commentators to question whether the litigants may be best advised to argue discrimination law claims in preference to Article 9 claims, at least in relation to the wearing of religious dress and symbols.[842]

351. A further example of a successful claim of indirect discrimination in relation to religious dress and symbols is the Employment Tribunal's decision in *Noah v. Sarah Desrosiers (Wedge).*[843] The claimant, Mrs. Noah, applied for a job as an assistant stylist at the respondent's hairdressing salon. When Noah attended the interview wearing a headscarf, the interview was terminated on the basis that the hair salon was known for 'ultra-modern' hair styles which staff were supposed to display to clients. No other person was ultimately appointed to the job. The Tribunal held the provision, criterion or practice (PCP) that an employee would be required to display their hair at work for at least some of the time put persons of the same religion as the claimant at a particular disadvantage and disadvantaged the claimant notwithstanding the fact that she would not in fact have been offered a job given that no assistant stylist was ever appointed. The 2003 regulations sought to make unlawful discrimination in relation to job applicants and did not merely make reference to whether or not they were offered a job but also covered discrimination in relation to other arrangements made as part of the recruitment process. This indirect discrimination was not justified. Although it was reasonable for the respondent to take the view that the issue posed a significant risk to her business, too much weight was accorded to that concern.

838. Paragraph 56B.
839. Paragraphs 59–62.
840. Paragraphs 63–66.
841. *See* Part II.
842. R. Sandberg, *The Changing Position of Religious Minorities in English Law: The Legacy of Begum*, in *Legal Practice and Cultural Diversity* 267 (R. Grillo et al. eds, Ashgate 2009).
843. [2008] ET, Case No. 2201867/07 (29 May 2008).

352. Another area where the law on indirect discrimination has had a significant impact is in relation to making employees work on their Holy day.[844] For instance,[845] in *Fugler v. MacMillan – London Hairstudios Limited*,[846] a new 'no Saturdays off work' rule at a hairdressers was held to constitute indirect discrimination since this put Jews at a disadvantage and actually put the Jewish claimant at a disadvantage on a particular Saturday. Although serving clients on a Saturday was a legitimate aim, the employers should have considered how or if they could rearrange Fugler's duties and customers for that Saturday.

353. However, many indirect discrimination claims fail because the respondent can justify the discrimination. For instance, in *Azmi v. Kirklees Metropolitan Council*,[847] concerning a teaching assistant who was suspended for insisting on wearing a full-face veil when male members of staff were present contrary to a school instruction not to wear the full-face veil when teaching children, both the Employment Tribunal and the Employment Appeal Tribunal held that the indirect discrimination was justified. Although the 'no face-veil when teaching rule' put Muslims at a disadvantage and actually put Azmi at a disadvantage, it could be justified as a proportionate means of achieving the legitimate aim of children being taught properly.

354. In *Ladele v. London Borough of Islington*,[848] in respect of a registrar who refused on grounds of conscience to register civil partnership ceremonies, the Court of Appeal held that although there was no doubt that the Council's policy decision to designate all registrars as civil partnership registrars put a person like Ladele at a disadvantage, this was justified.[849] The 'only way' in which the Council could have achieved its aim of promoting equal opportunities and requiring its employees to act in a non-discriminatory way was to require all registrars to conduct civil partnerships.[850] For Dyson LJ, the aim of the Council's equality policy 'was of general, indeed overarching, policy significance [having] fundamental human rights, equality and diversity implications, whereas the effect on Ms Ladele of implementing the policy did not impinge on her religious beliefs: she remained free to hold those beliefs, and free to worship as she wished'.[851]

355. *Ladele* was followed in *McFarlane v. Relate*[852] concerning a counsellor who refused on grounds of his Christian beliefs to counsel same-sex couples on sexual matters. He originally worked in couples counselling but volunteered to

844. However, *see* the litigation culminating in *Mba v. Mayor and Burgress of the London Borough of Merton* [2013] EWCA Civ 1562, discussed below at para. 290.
845. *See also Williams-Drabble v. Pathway Care Solutions* ET, Case No. 2601718/2004 (2 December 2004).
846. ET, Case No. 2205090/2004 (21–23 June 2005).
847. ET, Case No. 1801450/06 (6 October 2006); [2007] UKEAT 0009 07 30003 (30 March 2007).
848. [2009] EWCA (Civ) 1357.
849. At para. 43.
850. At paras 45, 46 and 50.
851. At para. 51. Dyson LJ held that this conclusion was reinforced by Art. 9 of the ECHR: *see* paras 54–61.
852. [2010] EWCA Civ 880.

undertake a diploma course in psycho-sexual therapy. When he asked to be exempt from advising same-sex couples on sexual matters, he was told that he had to comply with Relate's equal opportunities policy and was later dismissed. In terms of indirect discrimination, the Court of Appeal found *Ladele* to be definitive on this point.[853] It was held that, although McFarlane had been disadvantaged, the employer's actions had had a legitimate aim (the provision of counselling services to all sections of the community regardless of their sexual orientation) and was proportionate.

356. The decisions in *Ladele* and *McFarlane* were both taken to the European Court of Human Rights in *Eweida and Others v. United Kingdom*[854] contending that the United Kingdom had breached Article 9 because domestic law had failed adequately to protect their right to manifest their religion.[855] In respect of *Ladele*, the Strasbourg Court held that any discrimination on grounds of religion had been justified. The Council's actions had a legitimate aim and the means pursued was proportionate.[856] It was noted that the Court 'generally allows the national authorities a wide margin of appreciation when it comes to striking a balance between competing Convention rights'.[857] This wide margin of appreciation had not been exceeded in this case. In respect of *McFarlane*, the Strasbourg Court held that there had been an interference with the applicant's Article 9 rights but that this was justified due to the margin of appreciation.[858]

357. Other indirect discrimination claims, however, have failed on the interference point rather than the justification point. For instance,[859] in *Eweida v. British Airways*,[860] a member of check-in staff wore a silver cross in breach of BA's uniform policy which prohibited visible religious symbols, unless their wearing was mandatory. The tribunal held that there was no indirect discrimination: although there was a provision that personal jewellery should be concealed by the uniform unless otherwise expressly permitted, which was applied equally, it did not put Christians at a particular disadvantage and did not disadvantage the claimant. There was no evidence that practising Christians considered the visible display of the cross to be a requirement of the Christian faith and no evidence that the provision created a barrier to Christians employed at BA.

853. The application was also noteworthy because the case was supported by a witness statement by the former Archbishop of Canterbury, Lord Carey of Clifton, in which he argued for 'a specially constituted Court of Appeal of five Lords Justices who have a proven sensibility to religious issues'. *See* further R. Sandberg, *Laws and Religion: Unravelling McFarlane v. Relate Avon Ltd*, 12(3) Ecclesiastical Law Journal 361 (2010).

854. (2013) 57 EHRR 8.

855. For a discussion of the new interpretation of Art. 9 in the decision *see* M. Hill, *Religious Symbolism and Conscientious Objection in the Workplace*, 15 Ecclesiastical Law Journal 191 (2013).

856. Paragraphs 105–106.

857. Paragraph 106.

858. Paragraph 109.

859. *See also Harris v. NKL Automotive Ltd & Anor* [2007] UKEAT/0134/07/DM; 2007 WL 2817981 (3 October 2007).

860. [2010] EWCA (Civ) 880.

358. Eweida was followed in *Chaplin v. Royal Devon & Exeter NHS Foundation Trust*[861] concerning a nurse who was asked to remove the crucifix she wore around her neck at work on grounds of health and safety. Although Chaplin had been a nurse for thirty years and had always worn the crucifix, a change to a v-necked uniform had now made the crucifix visible and the concern was that there was a risk of injury when handling patients. When she refused to remove her crucifix, she was redeployed to a non-clinical role where the hospital had no objections to her wearing the crucifix when undertaking those duties. The Employment Tribunal dismissed her claims of direct and indirect discrimination. In terms of indirect discrimination, the Employment Tribunal held that the uniform policy did not 'place "persons" at a particular disadvantage'. Despite evidence that another nurse, Mrs. Babcock, had been asked to remove her cross and chain,[862] the Employment Tribunal held that Mrs. Babcock had not been put at a particular disadvantage since the word 'particular' meant that the disadvantage suffered needed to be 'noteworthy, peculiar or singular' and this criteria had not been met since Mrs. Babcock's religious views were not so strong as to lead her to refuse to comply with the policy.[863] The Employment Tribunal added that if they had needed to decide whether the disadvantage was justified they would have held that it was since health and safety concerns provided a legitimate aim and the actions by the respondent were proportionate.[864]

359. The decisions in *Eweida* and *Chaplin* were considered by the European Court of Human Rights in *Eweida and Others v. United Kingdom.*[865] In respect of Eweida, the Strasbourg Court held that her wish to wear a crucifix 'was a manifestation of her religious belief, in the form of worship, practice and observance, and as such attracted the protection of Article 9'.[866] Moreover, BA's refusal for her to remain in post whilst visibly wearing the cross 'amounted to an interference with her right to manifest her religion'.[867] The question was whether this interference was justified under Article 9(2). The Court concluded that a fair balance had not been struck.[868] Although the national courts were afforded a margin of appreciation, they had given too much weight to the employer's wish to project a certain corporate image and not enough to the applicant's desire to manifest her religious belief. This meant that the State had 'failed sufficiently to protect the first applicant's right to manifest her religion, in breach of the positive obligation under Article 9'.[869]

861. [2010] ET Case No. 17288862009 (6 April 2010).
862. Paragraph 15.
863. Paragraph 27. This was the decision of the majority. Mr Parkhouse, by contrast, held that both nurses had been placed at a disadvantage.
864. Paragraph 29.
865. (2013) 57 EHRR 8.
866. Paragraph 89.
867. Paragraph 91.
868. Paragraph 94.
869. Paragraph 95.

360. In relation to Chaplin, the Court held that her wearing of her crucifix at work was a manifestation of her religious belief and the refusal of the health authority to allow it constituted an interference with her freedom to manifest her religion.[870] However, here the Court held that there was no violation of Article 9 since this interference was justified. The Court noted that the reason for asking her to remove the crucifix and neck-chain was the protection of health and safety on a hospital ward and this 'was inherently of a greater magnitude than that which applied in respect of Ms. Eweida'.[871] This was a matter where a 'wide margin of appreciation' was allowed since the 'hospital managers were better placed to make decisions about clinical safety than a court, particularly an international court which has heard no direct evidence'.

361. In Mba v. Mayor and Burgresses of the London Borough of Merton,[872] the Court of Appeal considered the impact of *Eweida v. United Kingdom* upon the domestic law of indirect discrimination. The claim concerned whether Sunday working constituted indirect discrimination on grounds of the claimant's Christian beliefs. The original Employment Tribunal had dismissed the claim and as part of its reasoning had taken into account how the claimant's 'belief that Sunday should be a day of rest and worship upon which no paid employment was undertaken, whilst deeply held, is not a core component of the Christian faith'. The Court of Appeal dismissed the claimant's appeal because, although there had been errors of law in the Employment Tribunal's decision, their ultimate conclusion that the disadvantage had been proportionate was plainly and unarguably right.[873] For Maurice Kay LJ, the Employment Tribunal had made an error in law by stating that the belief was not a core component. The Employment Tribunal 'went wrong' in that, although for indirect discrimination it is necessary to show that 'persons' were put (or would be put) at a disadvantage, 'it is not necessary to establish that all or most Christians, or all or most conformist Christians are or would be put at a particular disadvantage'.[874] The description of the claimant's belief as 'not a core component of the Christian faith' erred in that 'it opened the door to a quantitative test on far too wide a basis'. This left open, however, 'the question whether there is a quantitative element to be considered alongside the qualitative factor of genuine belief to be considered as part of the proportionality exercise'.[875] Maurice Kay LJ expressed the view that he was 'not convinced that there is, over and above the requirement of group disadvantage'.

362. Elias LJ agreed that the question of whether the belief was a core component 'ought not to have been weighed into the balance in relation to the justification defence' but reached this conclusion for different reasons than Maurice Kay LJ.[876]

870. Paragraph 97.
871. Paragraph 99.
872. [2013] EWCA Civ 1562.
873. Paragraphs 23–24.
874. Paragraph 17.
875. Paragraph 19.
876. Paragraph 30.

For Elias J, the Employment Tribunal did not err in law by having regard to the matter 'purely in terms of establishing indirect discrimination'.[877] Rather, the error was that considering whether the belief was compulsory breached Article 9 ECHR, following *Eweida v. United Kingdom*.[878] Article 9 was directly engaged in this case since the defendant was a public body and, although Article 9 cannot be enforced directly in employment tribunals, domestic law must be read as to be consistent with Convention rights where possible.[879] It was 'the Article 9 dimension of this case which made it inappropriate for the Employment Tribunal, when assessing justification, to weigh in the employer's favour the fact that the appellant's religious belief was not a core belief or her religion so that any group impact was limited'.[880]

IV. Victimisation

363. Victimisation occurs where A subjects B to a detriment because B does a 'protected act' or because he believes that B has done or may do a 'protected act'.[881] A 'protected act' is defined as bringing proceedings under the Equality Act 2010, giving evidence or information in connection with proceedings under the Act, doing any other thing for the purposes of or in connection with the Act or making an allegation (whether or not express) that A or another person has contravened the Act. For example, B is denied promotion by A because A regards B as a 'troublemaker' after B gave evidence in support of a claim of religious discrimination by C.

364. A does not need to be the intended target of the proceedings or allegations in which B is involved. It is not victimisation where B is making or intending to make a false allegation, unless that allegation, though incorrect, was made in good faith.[882] B must establish a causal link between his act and A's alleged victimisation of him.

365. The claim of victimisation was the only successful claim in *Azmi*.[883] After the employer received a letter alleging a breach of the Regulations, there was a marked change in the way in which they dealt with Azmi. After the letter, they were no longer patient and constructive and failed to observe their own procedure. The Tribunal concluded that a person who had not made a complaint of religious discrimination would not have had their grievance ignored in this way and that the reason for such treatment was because the claimant had made an allegation of religious discrimination. Given the lack of an explanation concerning their complete failure to deal with the grievance, the complaint of victimisation succeeded.

877. Paragraph 33.
878. Paragraph 34.
879. Paragraphs 34–35.
880. Paragraph 37.
881. Equality Act 2010, s. 27.
882. Section 27(3).
883. ET, Case No. 1801450/06 (6 October 2006); [2007] UKEAT 0009 07 30003 (30 March 2007).

366. *Page v. Lord Chancellor and Others*[884] concerned, among other things, a claim for victimisation brought by a former magistrate who had been removed from the magistracy after continuing to engage with the media about certain views held by him, namely that he did not consider it in the best interests of a child to allow him or her to be adopted by a same-sex couple. The Employment Appeal Tribunal concluded that the words spoken, as part of his interviews with the media, did not amount to a 'protected act' but, even if they had, the decision to remove him from the magistracy was properly separable from that act. As the Employment Appeal Tribunal observed, 'The position can perhaps be compared to an employee who, in the course of making a relevant allegation reveals that he has, or is about to breach some other important rule imposed by the employer. An employer who takes action to deal with the breach or proposed breach would be doing so because of that breach and not necessarily because of the protected act, although obviously the Tribunal would have to be careful to ensure that action relating to the breach was genuinely and properly separable from the allegation.'[885]

367. Prior to the Equality Act 2010, there was a pre-condition that A treated B less favourably than others for a claim to succeed. Now, however, there is no longer any need for a comparator. Victimisation is no longer a form of discrimination.

V. Harassment

368. Harassment occurs where A subjects B to unwanted conduct on the grounds of religion or belief that has the purpose or effect of violating B's dignity or creating an intimidating, hostile, degrading, humiliating or offensive environment.[886] For example: A constantly teases B about his partner's religious convictions. The Employment Appeal Tribunal has confirmed that this applies not only where an employee is harassed on the grounds of his or her own religious beliefs, but also where he or she suffers harassment because of the religious beliefs of another person.[887]

369. Conduct should be regarded as constituting harassment only if having regard to all the circumstances, including in particular the perception of B, it should reasonably be considered as having that effect.[888] In relation to employment, harassment covers both employees and those who have applied for employment.[889] Employers are no longer liable for harassment of employees by third parties.[890]

884. Appeal No. UKEAT/0304/18/LA.
885. *Ibid.*, at para. 55. The judgment of the EAT was upheld on appeal: see *Page v (1) The Lord Chancellor and (2) The Lord Chief Justice of England and Wales* [2021] EWCA Civ 254.
886. Equality Act 2010, s. 26(1).
887. *Saini v. All Saints Haque Centre & Ors* [2008] UKEAT/00227/08 (24 October 2008).
888. Equality Act 2010 s. 26(4).
889. Section 40(1).
890. Section 40(2)–(4) were repealed in 2013 on the basis that they placed an unfair risk on the employer and there were already legal remedies for the employee in such scenarios.

370. The case law to date reveals that most harassment claims fail since they are not borne out by the evidence.[891] In *Azmi*,[892] for instance,[893] the tribunal found that the claimant had not established that the school had become an intimidating, hostile, degrading, humiliating or offensive environment for her on the grounds of her religion or belief. The Tribunal noted that none of the remarks came within the category of 'comments or abuse' at which the Regulations are aimed such as sectarian jokes, verbal abuse, name-calling, teasing or tormenting. Similarly, the use of bad language in a newsroom whilst asking about the progress of a news story concerning the Pope was held to be merely an expression of ill-temper which was not intended to express hostility to the Pope or to Roman Catholicism and did not constitute harassment.[894]

371. Harassment is only outlawed in relation to employment. A clause in what was to become the Equality Act 2006 outlawing religious harassment was removed by the House of Lords. Their Lordships considered that the clause could have been used by religious groups to obtain an injunction to stop other religions staging events that they considered offensive. Under the Equality Act 2010 harassment does not apply to religion or belief or sexual orientation discrimination in the provision of goods and services.[895]

§2. Permitting Discrimination on Grounds of Religion

372. While the broad thrust of discrimination law is the outlawing of the practice of discrimination, the law exceptionally permits discrimination on grounds of religion in certain limited and specified circumstances. These religious exceptions[896] exist in addition to other exceptions such as those that apply where there is a general occupational requirement. The beneficiary and terms of the exception vary significantly but a broad distinction can be made between exceptions that apply in relation to employment and those which apply in relation to goods and services. In

891. This was true of the case of *Reaney v. Hereford Diocesan Board of Finance* [2007] Employment Tribunal, Case No. 1602844/2006 (17 July 2007), discussed below. *See also Pemberton v. Inwood* [2018] EWCA Civ 564. For a successful case in relation to sexual orientation *see English v. Thomas Sanderson Ltd* [2008] EWCA Civ 1421.

892. ET, Case No. 1801450/06 (6 October 2006); [2007] UKEAT 0009 07 30003 (30 March 2007).

893. *See also McClintock v. Department of Constitutional Affairs* [2007] UKEAT/0223/07/CEA (31 October 2007).

894. *Heafield v. Times Newspaper Ltd* [2013] UKEAT 1305 12 1701 (17 January 2013).

895. Section 29(8). However, the proposed EC directive does outlaw such harassment, which suggests that the law may be extended at some point in the future.

896. The provisions are also sometimes referred to as 'exemptions' or 'statutory defences'. The Equality Act 2010, however, uses the term 'exception' and so we follow that usage.

all cases, the exceptions are narrowly drawn and apply only to 'religious organisations, as opposed to individuals'.[897] As the Explanatory Memorandum on the EU Directive makes plain,[898] a 'double test of a justified aim and proportionate means of reaching it … is required'.

373. The exceptions can now be found in the Equality Act 2010.[899] Although originally there were plans to alter the scope of some of the exceptions in the new Act, during the parliamentary passage of the Equality Act a number of these changes were rejected as the Government sought to get the Act onto the statute books before the dissolution of the 2005–2010 Parliament. The overall effect of this is that the exceptions found in the Equality Act 2010 are generally similar to those found in the old law. In November 2009, the European Commission sent a reasoned opinion to the UK Government asserting that exceptions for religious employers under UK law were broader than those permitted under the EU Directive. Although the Government responded by saying that it was studying this reasoned opinion, the defeat of the reconfigured exceptions in the Equality Act 2010 raises the question of whether the exceptions could now be subject to challenge under EU law. The following begins by examining the exceptions in relation to employment before examining the exceptions in relation to goods and services. The exceptions found in the Marriage (Same-Sex Couples) Act 2013 are discussed separately in Part X below.

I. Employment

374. The exceptions for employment are now to be found in Schedule 9 to the Equality Act 2010. Paragraph 2 provides a separate exception from laws prohibiting discrimination on grounds of sex, marriage and sexual orientation whilst paragraph 3 provides a further exception allowing employers with an ethos based on religion or belief to discriminate on grounds of religion or belief.

A. Religious Discrimination

375. The religious exception to the prohibition of discrimination on grounds of religion or belief in relation to employment can now be found in Schedule 19 paragraph 3 of the Equality Act 2010. It provides that the law prohibiting discrimination does not apply where an employer has an 'ethos based on religion or belief' and, the following three criterion are met, having regard to that ethos and to the nature of the employment or the context in which it is carried out: (a) being of a particular

897. *Bull v. Hall* [2013] UKSC 73 at para. 8. As discussed below, the use of the term 'religious organisations' is a gloss on the legal provisions, some of which apply to 'organised religions' while others apply to 'organisations relating to religion or belief'.

898. Com (2008) 426 2008/0140, 8.

899. For discussion of the old law *see* R. Sandberg & N. Doe, *Religious Exemptions in Discrimination Law*, 2 CLJ 66, 302 (2007).

religion or belief is a genuine occupational requirement for the job, (b) it is proportionate to apply that requirement in the particular case and (c) either the person to whom the requirement is directed is not of the particular religion or belief required or the employer is not satisfied, and in all the circumstances it is reasonable for him not to be satisfied, and that he or she does satisfy the genuine occupational requirement. This exception can be seen simply as an extension of the general occupational requirement.[900]

376. Two cases concerning Prospects, a charity, which provides housing and day-care for people with learning disabilities, have concerned the application of this exception.[901] The tribunal concluded that Prospects' approach had been fatally flawed: its decision that in principle all posts should be filled by Christians and its assumption that it was sufficient to comply with the 2003 Regulations was incorrect. Rather, a job evaluation should have been carried out for every vacant post.

B. Sexual Orientation and Sex Discrimination

377. Paragraph 2 of Schedule 9 to the Equality Act 2010 provides a separate exception from laws prohibiting discrimination on grounds of sex, marriage and sexual orientation. It applies where three criteria are met.

378. First, the employment must be for the purposes of an organised religion. In *R (Amicus MSF Section) v. Secretary of State for Trade and Industry,*[902] Richards J held that the term 'organised religion' was narrower than 'religious organisation': he gave the example that 'employment as a teacher in a faith school is likely to be "for purposes of a religious organisation" but not "for purposes of an organised religion"'.[903]

379. The use of the phrase 'organised religion' seems intended to limit the ambit of the exception. The Explanatory Notes state that this is 'intended to cover a very narrow range of employment: ministers of religion and a small number of lay posts, including those that exist to promote and represent religion'.[904] This is undoubtedly the meaning which would have been given to employment for the purposes of an organised religion had the revised exceptions found in earlier drafts of the Equality Bill become law. However, given the text of the actual exception it is not obvious that the phrase has this restricted meaning. The precise scope of the phrase remains unclear. Moreover, given that Parliament in enacting section 13 of the Human Rights Act 1998 has made it clear that particular regard is to be given to the rights of a 'religious organisation', it may be asked why certain privileges have been

900. Equality Act 2010 Sch. 9 para. 1.
901. *Louise Hender v. Prospects*; *Mark Sheridan v. Prospects* [2008] ET Case Nos 2902090/2006 (Hender) & 2901366 (Sheridan) (13 May 2008).
902. [2004] EWHC 860.
903. Paragraph 116.
904. Equality Act 2010 Explanatory Notes para. 799.

afforded only to the narrower category where the beneficiary is an 'organised religion'. This may actually infringe not only section 13 but also Article 9.

380. The second requirement is that the 'compliance' or 'non-conflict' principles must be engaged. Although these terms are new to the Equality Act 2010, they are simply shorthand expressions to cover the reasons why the organised religion may discriminate (which remain largely unchanged). The compliance principle is engaged where the discrimination takes place 'so as to comply with the doctrines of the religion'.[905] The non-conflict principle is engaged where the discrimination takes place 'so as to avoid conflicting with the strongly held convictions of a significant number of the religion's followers'. In *R (Amicus MSF Section) v. Secretary of State for Trade and Industry*[906] Richards J stated that these requirements imposed 'very real additional limitations' and suggested that both tests were objective. To make use of the first basis, reference should not be made to the subjective 'motivation of the employer' but rather to 'an objective test whereby it must be shown that employment of a person not meeting the requirement would be incompatible with the doctrines of the religion'. Although Richards J conceded that the second basis is wider, he nevertheless claimed that it is 'hemmed about by restrictive language' and requires 'an objective, not subjective, test' which 'is going to be a very far from easy test to satisfy in practice'. Deciding whether a 'significant number' of followers may be offended is by no means a straightforward task. Indeed, in the case of some faiths it is further complicated by the lack of a definition of membership.[907]

381. The third requirement is that the employer can discriminate either where the employee does not meet the requirement imposed or where the employer is not satisfied and it is reasonable for him not to be satisfied that that person meets it.[908] The importance of this reasonableness requirement was stressed in *Reaney v. Hereford Diocesan Board of Finance*[909] in which the claimant had been denied the job of Diocesan Youth Officer in Hereford after the Bishop expressed his concern that since Reaney had been in a committed same-sex relationship and refused to accept Reaney's assurance that he would remain celibate. The Bishop concluded that Reaney could not at the present time make a promise not to have a same-sex relationship in future and therefore did not offer him the post. The Employment Tribunal found that the Bishop could not rely upon the exception. Though employment as a Diocesan Youth Officer was for the purposes of an organised religion and the Bishop had been permitted to apply a requirement related to sexual orientation on

905. Equality Act 2010, Sch. 9 para. 2(5).
906. [2004] EWHC 860 at para. 117.
907. *See* the findings of the Colloquium of Anglican and Roman Catholic Canon Lawyers in *Initiation, Membership and Authority in Anglican and Roman Catholic Canon Law* (J. Conn, N. Doe & J. Fox eds, Pontificial University of St Thomas Aquinas 2005) and P. Colton, *The Pursuit of a Canonical Definition of membership of the Church of Ireland*, 10(1) Ecclesiastical Law Journal 3 (2007).
908. In relation to discrimination on grounds of marriage or civil partnership, the employer can only discriminate where the employee does not meet the requirement imposed: Equality Act 2010, Sch. 9 para. 2(8).
909. [2007] Employment Tribunal, judgment 17 July 2007 (Case No. 1602844/2006).

either of the grounds laid out in the regulations, the religious exception did not apply because Reaney did meet the requirement imposed and it was not reasonable for the Bishop to conclude otherwise.

382. In *Pemberton v. Inwood,*[910] the Court of Appeal had to grapple with a situation whereby a Bishop had revoked a Canon's Permission to Officiate (PTO) and had refused to grant him an Extra Parochial Ministry Licence (EPML) after the Canon had married his same-sex partner.[911] In addition to noting the relevant Canons of the Church of England, the Court of Appeal considered the House of Bishops Pastoral Guidance on the issue.[912] The Court agreed that it 'cannot be expected to enter into a theological debate in order to determine the doctrines itself' and that, in any event, 'it ought not to do so'.[913] Having made that concession, it nevertheless found that the doctrines in relation to marriage were 'clear'[914] and were captured in Canon B30, namely that the Church considers marriage to be between one man and one woman. The Court held that the passage of the Marriage (Same Sex Couples) Act 2013 does not extend the meaning of marriage insofar as the Church is concerned and concluded that the Bishop was entitled to rely upon the Schedule 9(2) exception.[915]

383. The exception in paragraph 2 is materially the same as the old law. The main difference between them is the naming of the 'compliance' or 'non-conflict' principles. Originally, however, the exceptions in the Equality Bill would have made two significant changes. The first was to require explicitly the application of the requirement to be proportionate. The second was to provide a definition of employment for the purposes of a religious organisation as employment that 'wholly or mainly involves leading or assisting in the observation of liturgical or ritualistic practices of the religion, or promoting or expanding the doctrine of the religion'. This would have reversed the finding in *Reaney* that employment as a Diocesan Youth Officer was for the purpose of an organised religion.

384. Although these changes were rejected in Parliament, this is not fully reflected in the Explanatory Notes to the Act, which seems to impose additional requirements that are not found in the text of the exception. They state that the organised religion may only discriminate where it is 'crucial to the post' to do so and it cannot be 'merely one of several important factors'.[916] More importantly, the Explanatory Notes also state that it 'must be a proportionate way of meeting the criteria'. The text of paragraph 2 suggests that this is not the case. This raises the question of whether or not the exception is broader than that permitted under EU law.

910. [2018] EWCA Civ 564.
911. The case raised a number of issue but of importance for present purposes is the Canon's claim for discrimination pursuant to ss 15 and 53 of the 2010 Act and the Bishop's reliance upon the Sch. 9(2) exception.
912. At para. 19.
913. At para. 62.
914. *Ibid.*
915. At para. 66.
916. Equality Act 2010 Explanatory Notes para. 800.

As the Explanatory Memorandum on the EU Directive makes plain,[917] a 'double test of a justified aim and proportionate means of reaching it … is required'. Paragraph 2 does not meet these requirements since it does not on its face require proportionality.

II. Goods and Services

385. In relation to goods and services discrimination, the main religious exception is now to be found in paragraph 2 of Schedule 23 to the Equality Act 2010 which provides a general exception for 'organisations relating to religion or belief' covering discrimination in relation to goods and services. Schedule 3 provides some further exceptions in respect of goods and services. Most notably,[918] paragraph 29 provides an exception for ministers allowing them to provide a service only to persons of one sex or separate services for persons of each sex.

A. Religious Discrimination

386. Although the exceptions for both religion and sexual orientation discrimination can now be found in the same paragraph, paragraph 2 of Schedule 23 to the Equality Act 2010 is drafted so that the terms of the exception continue to differ, largely mirroring the old law. The exception applies where two criteria are met.

387. First, the discrimination must be by 'an organisation relating to religion or belief'.[919] This is defined as:

> an organisation the purpose of which is–
>
> a. to practice a religion or belief,
> b. to advance a religion or belief,
> c. to teach the practice or principles of a religion or belief,
> d. to enable persons of a religion or belief to receive any benefit, or to engage in any activity, within the framework of that religion or belief, or
> e. to improve relations, or maintain good relations, between persons of different religions or beliefs.
>
> This paragraph does not apply to an organiation whose sole or main purpose is commercial.

388. Second, the discrimination must be on certain grounds. These grounds differ between religion and belief discrimination and sexual orientation discrimination. The organisation can only discriminate on grounds of religion or belief

917. Com (2008) 426 2008/0140, 8.
918. *See also* para. 18 which provides an exception from goods and service discrimination on grounds of religion or belief where decisions are taken in accordance with immigration rules.
919. Paragraph 2(1)–(2).

'because of the purpose of the organisation' or 'to avoid causing offence, on grounds of the religion or belief to which the organisation relates, to persons of that religion or belief'.[920]

B. Sexual Orientation Discrimination

389. In relation to sexual orientation discrimination, paragraph 2 provides variations in relation to both of the requirements. In relation to the first requirement, for sexual orientation the definition of an 'organisation relating to religion or belief' is to be restricted. Part (e), to improve relations, or maintain good relations, between persons of different religions or beliefs, is to be ignored.[921] Moreover, the exception does not apply to anything done 'on behalf of a public authority' and 'under the terms of a contract between the organisation and a public authority'. This explains why the exception cannot be enjoyed by Roman Catholic adoption agencies. Although Roman Catholic adoption agencies are entitled to the exception in that they are 'organisations relating to religion or belief', they lose that exception when they contract with the State to provide their service. This proved controversial prior to the enactment of the Employment Equality (Sexual Orientation) Regulations 2007. Regulation 15 of the 2007 Regulations provided an exception that ran until 31 December 2008. Since then, discrimination by such adoption agencies on grounds of sexual orientation has been unlawful. The Charity Tribunal has held that a charity cannot seek to avoid this by changing their objects in order to rely upon an exception for charities.[922]

390. In relation to the second requirement, the organisation can only discriminate on grounds of sexual orientation 'because it is necessary to comply with the doctrine of the organisation' or 'to avoid conflict with the strongly held convictions' of a 'significant number of the religion's [or belief's] followers'.[923] Although the grounds mirror those for employment in relation to sexual orientation, the 'compliance' or 'non-conflict' labels are not used in this context.

C. Sex Discrimination

391. Paragraph 29 of Schedule 3 creates an exception for ministers, allowing them to provide a service only to persons of one sex or separate services for persons of each sex. This applies when the service is done for the purposes of an organised religion at a place used for those purposes and it is necessary in order to

920. Equality Act 2010. Sch. 23 para. 2(6).
921. Paragraph 2 (11).
922. *Catholic Care (Diocese of Leeds) v. Charity Commission for England and Wales* [2012] UKUT 395 (TCC).
923. Paragraph 2(7)–(9).

comply with the doctrines of the religion or is for the purpose of avoiding conflict with the strongly held religious convictions of a significant number of the religion's followers.

392. A minister is defined as 'a minister of religion, or other person, who performs functions in connection with the religion and holds an office or appointment in, or is accredited, approved or recognised for the purposes of, a relevant organisation in relation to the religion'. Paragraph 29 provides a definition of a 'relevant organisation in relation to a religion' which is identical to the definition of 'organisation relating to religion or belief' but for the omission of the word 'belief' on each line. This exception replaces a similar provision in section 35 of the Sex Discrimination Act 1975 but some of the requirements have been modified in order to provide consistency within the Equality Act 2010.

Chapter 8. Penal Law and Religion

393. English criminal law interacts with religion in various different ways. For example,[924] although the law occasionally allows religious exceptions from specific crimes, to fulfil religious practices,[925] there is no general defence of carrying out divine instructions[926] or special protection for religious drug use.[927] Although the common law of blasphemy in England and Wales[928] has been abolished by section 79 of the Criminal Justice and Immigration Act 2008,[929] the interaction between religion and the criminal law remains important. The category 'religious offences' is known to Parliament[930] and to academics, but not in statute.[931] There is a plethora of overlapping laws: in addition to numerous general offences that have been prosecuted in relation to religious matters, there exist numerous pieces of law designed to protect religion in particular.

§1. Offences Protecting Religious Worship

394. A number of provisions enacted in the nineteenth and early twentieth centuries protecting religious worship remain operative. Under the Offences Against the Person Act 1861, it is an offence to obstruct, by threats or force, any clergyman or other minister in or from celebrating divine service or otherwise officiating in any church, chapel, meeting house or other place of divine worship. Similarly, it is an offence to strike or offer any violence to (or to arrest pursuant to any civil process) any clergyman or other minister who is engaged in (or is, in the knowledge of the

924. For discussion of sentencing *see* C. Bakalis & P. Edge, *Taking Account of Religion in Sentencing*, 3 Legal Studies 29, 421 (2009). For discussion of clergy discipline in the Church of England *see* M. Hill, *Ecclesiastical Law* Ch. 6 (4th ed., Oxford University Press 2018).
925. Under s. 139 of the Criminal Justice Act 1988, it is a defence to the charge of having a blade in a public place if the blade is carried 'for religious reasons'.
926. *Blake v. DPP* [1993] Crim L.R 556.
927. *R v. Taylor* [2001] EWCA Crim 2263; *R v. Andrews* [2004] EWCA Crim 947; *R v. Aziz* [2012] EWCA Crim 1063.
928. The last prosecution for blasphemy in Scotland was in 1843: *Henry v. Robinson* (1843) 1 Brown 643. In any event, since (unlike in England) Scots law requires a personal interest in a matter before there can be any private prosecution and since the State is unlikely to want to prosecute for blasphemy, it has been argued that a prosecution, even if technically possible, is nowadays unlikely: *see* G. Maher, *Blasphemy in Scots Law*, Scots Law Times 257 at 260 (1977).
929. For an extended account of the development of the blasphemy law and events leading to its abolition, *see* R. Sandberg & N. Doe, *The Strange Death of Blasphemy*, 6 Modern Law Review 71, 971 (2008) and M. Hill & R. Sandberg, *Blasphemy and Human Rights: An English Experience in a European Context*, IV Derecho y Religión 145 (2009). *See also*, *The Right to Blaspheme*, in *Blasphemy and Freedom of Expression: Comparative, Theoretical and Historical Reflections after the Charlie Hebdo Massacre* 114–133 (J. Temperman & A. Koltay eds, Cambridge University Press 2017) (with R. Sandberg).
930. For example, House of Lords Select Committee on Religious Offences in England and Wales, Report 2003.
931. It would have become a statutory category had the Religious Offences Bill 2002 become law.

offender, about to engage in) any of these rites or duties (or is in the offender's knowledge, going to or returning from their performance).[932]

395. Under the Ecclesiastical Courts Jurisdiction Act 1860 it is a criminal offence to commit 'riotous, violent or indecent behaviour' in the course of lawful liturgical action.[933] The offence may be committed in any cathedral, church or chapel of the Church of England or in any chapel of any religious denomination or in any certified place of religious worship.[934] This applies not only when those acts are committed during the celebration of 'divine service' but at any time, including in any churchyard or burial ground.[935] Moreover, it is a criminal offence to molest, disturb, vex or trouble (or by any other unlawful means to disquiet or misuse) any preacher duly authorised to preach or any clergyman in holy orders ministering or celebrating any sacrament or any divine service, rite or office.[936] The offence may be committed by a clergyman acting in an indecent or violent way in his own church or churchyard.[937] A person may be removed for disturbing the congregation at the time of divine service even though no part of that service is actually proceeding at the time.[938]

396. One of the duties of churchwardens in the Church of England is to maintain order at the time of divine service but their power to apprehend or eject must be exercised 'without unnecessary violence [to] any person creating a disturbance'.[939]

397. Several offences protect the burial of the dead. It is an offence to obstruct (or attempt to obstruct), by threats or force, any clergyman or other minister in the performance of a duty in the lawful burial of the dead in any churchyard or other burial place.[940] It is an offence under the Burial Laws Amendment Act 1880 to engage in 'riotous, violent, or indecent behaviour' at any burial under the Act, or to obstruct a burial. It is also an offence to 'bring into contempt or obloquy the Christian religion, or the belief or worship of any church or denomination of Christians, or the members or any minister of any church or denomination, or any other person'.[941] It is also an offence to dig up a corpse unlawfully;[942] if the corpse is buried

932. Offences Against the Person Act 1861, s. 36; Criminal Law Act 1967, s. 1.
933. Section 2. Prosecutions under the Act are rare although *see R v. Farrant* [1973] Crim.L.R. 240 where the Court of Appeal upheld a conviction in circumstances where the defendant was found in a churchyard at midnight seemingly attempting to raise the dead. The Court held that the object of the Act is 'to protect the sacred character of churches and churchyards' and that whether behaviour is indecent is a question of fact for the trial court to determine. *See also Worth v. Terrington* (1845) 13 M&W 761 at 795; *Abrahams v Cavey* [1968] 1 QB 479 and *Jones v. Catterrall* (1902) 18 TLR 367.
934. Places of Worship Registration Act 1855.
935. *See also* Burial Laws Amendment Act 1880, ss 7 and 8.
936. Ecclesiastical Courts Jurisdiction Act 1860, s. 2; *Cope v. Barber* (1872) LR 7 CP 393.
937. *Vallancey v. Fletcher* [1897] 1 QB 265.
938. *Williams v. Glenister* (1824) 2 B&C 699.
939. Canon F15(3); Opinions of the Legal Advisory Commission, 48.
940. Offences Against the Person Act 1861, s. 36; Criminal Law Act 1967, s. 1.
941. Section 7.

in consecrated ground (of the Church of England), a faculty is required from the Consistory Court, and if reburial is to be in unconsecrated ground, a licence from the Secretary of State for Justice is also required.[943] Under the Local Authorities' Cemeteries Order 1977, section 18, it is an offence wilfully to interfere with any grave, vault, tombstone or other memorial or any flowers or plants or any such matter or to play any game or sport therein.

398. It is an offence if a person knowingly and wilfully solemnises a marriage according to the rites of the Church of England or Church in Wales[944] falsely pretending to be in Holy Orders.[945] Such persons are liable to imprisonment for a term not exceeding fourteen years. It is unlawful (but no longer a crime) under the Ecclesiastical Titles Act 1851 for a minister to assume the name, style or title of archbishop of any province, bishop of any diocese or dean of any deanery already settled as titles operative in the Church of England.[946] The Anti-social Behaviour, Crime and Policing Act 2014 created three offences in connection with forced or non-consensual marriage. The first relates to breach of a forced marriage protection order made under the Family Law Act 1996. The second concerns the use of violence, threats or other coercion for the purposes of forcing another person into a marriage, and the third relates to those who practice any form of deception with the intention of causing another person to leave the United Kingdom to enter into a forced marriage abroad.

399. In evidence to the House of Lords Select Committee on Religious Offences in England and Wales, the Law Society of Scotland stated that though the offence of riotous behaviour under section 2 of the Ecclesiastical Courts Jurisdiction Act does not extend to Scotland, the common law offence of breach of the peace (which is a much wider offence in Scotland than in England and Wales) provides the necessary protection to religious services.[947]

§2. Public Order Offences

400. The growth in public order offences in the last quarter of the twentieth century provides a number of general offences that have been used to control both religious speech and speech that may offend religious believers.[948] The general provisions of the Public Order Act 1986 have been used to prosecute successfully

942. *R v. Sharpe* (1857) Dears & B 160.
943. Burial Act 1857, s. 25. *See R (on the Application of HM Coroner for East London) v. Secretary of State for Justice* [2009] EWHC (Admin) 1974.
944. Marriage Act 1949, s. 78.
945. *Ibid.*, s. 75(1)(d).
946. The criminal offence was repealed by the Ecclesiastical Titles Act 1871.
947. Select Committee on Religious Offences in England and Wales: First Report of Session 2002– 03 (HL 95–I) para. 27: *see also Dougall v. Dykes* (1861) 4 Irvine 101: Dougall was found guilty of behaviour by which 'the mind of the ... minister and congregation were discomposed, their devotions interrupted, and they were otherwise disturbed and annoyed, all in breach of the peace'.
948. For an earlier example, *see Wise v. Dunning* [1902] 1 KB 167.

the display of a poster in a window showing events of 9/11 and the words 'Islam out of Britain'[949] and the holding of a sign by an elderly evangelical protester saying 'Stop Immorality. Stop Homosexuality. Stop Lesbianism. Jesus is Lord'.[950] Unsuccessful prosecutions have been brought in respect of the publication of *The Satanic Verses*[951] and a notice denouncing a president of a Gurdwara as a hypocrite, a liar and a 'mad dog'.[952]

401. The Protection from Harassment Act 1997 has been used to grant an injunction against an individual because of his continual harassment of members of the Mormon Church[953] and against a Sikh mother-in-law for badly treating her daughter-in-law following an arranged marriage.[954]

402. Under the International Criminal Court Act 2001 and the International Criminal Court (Scotland) Act 2001 it is an offence for a person to commit genocide which is defined as any acts committed 'with intent to destroy in whole or in part, a national, ethnical, racial or religious group'.[955] Crimes against humanity are also dealt with in the statute: a crime against humanity is any act committed as part of a widespread or systematic attack directed against any civilian population with knowledge of the attack, including persecution against any identifiable group or collectivity on religious (as well as political, racial, national, ethnic, cultural or gender) grounds.[956]

§3. Stirring up Religious Hatred

403. The Racial and Religious Hatred Act 2006 was a controversial measure which had a turbulent legislative history.[957,958] It amended the Public Order Act 1986 to create Part 3A entitled 'Hatred against Persons on Religious Grounds'. It also amended the Police and Criminal Evidence Act 1984 so that powers of citizens to arrest do not apply to the offences of stirring up religious hatred – only the police can arrest.

404. Part 3A includes numerous criminal offences protecting groups of believers from being threatened in a way that is defined by reference to religious belief or

949. *Norwood v. DDP* [2003] EWHC Admin 1564.
950. *Hammond v. DDP* [2004] EWHC Admin 69.
951. *Horseferry Road Metropolitan Stipendiary Magistrate, ex parte Siadatan* [1991] 1 QB 260
952. *Dehal v. CPS* [2005] EWHC Admin 2154.
953. *Christ of Jesus Christ of the Latter Day Saints v. Price* [2004] EWHC Admin 325.
954. *Singh v. Bhaker* [2006] Fam Law 1026.
955. International Criminal Court Act 2001 Sch. 8; International Criminal Court (Scotland) Act 2001 Sch. 1.
956. International Criminal Court Act 2001, s. 50(6), Sch. 8.
957. For a full account, *see* I. Hare, *Crosses, Crescents and Sacred Cows: Criminalising Incitement to Religious Hatred*, Public Law 521 (2006) and K. Goodall, *Incitement to Religious Hatred: All Talk and No Substance*, 1 Modern Law Review 70, 89 (2007).
958. It took four attempts to get the Act onto the statute books. *See* N. Addison, *Religious Discrimination and Hatred Law* 139–141 (Routledge 2007).

lack of religious belief. The new offences apply to the use of words or behaviour or display of written material, publishing or distributing written material, the public performance of a play, distributing, showing or playing a recording, broadcasting or including a programme in a programme service, and the possession of written materials or recordings with a view to display, publication, distribution or inclusion in a programme service.

405. For each offence the words, behaviour, written material, recordings or programmes must be threatening and intended to stir up religious hatred. Religious hatred means 'hatred against a group of persons defined by reference to religious belief or lack of religious belief'.[959] The meaning of 'religious belief or lack of religious belief' is deliberately broad.[960] The Act also deals with offences committed by corporations.[961] The maximum penalty for a conviction of stirring up religious hatred is seven years in prison.[962]

406. The requirement that only threatening behaviour is caught and that there must be an intention to stir up religious hatred were added to the Bill in Parliament contrary to Government intentions. Although this, coupled with a freedom of speech clause that was included in the final Act,[963] led to suggestions that the likelihood of a successful prosecution under the Act is slim,[964] there have been some successful cases. In *R v. Burns,*[965] the defendant had posted a series of virulently racist updates to Facebook. The defence at trial was that these posts constituted 'private banter' and that there was no intention to stir up racial hatred. Perhaps unsurprisingly, the jury rejected this.[966]

§4. Religiously Aggravated Offences

407. An increase of racial violence and harassment resulted in a new category of racially aggravated crimes under the Crime and Disorder Act 1998 and, following 9/11, the Anti-Terrorism Crime and Security Act 2001 extended these to deal with religiously aggravated offences.[967] Section 28(1) of the Crime and Disorder

959. Section 29A.
960. Explanatory Notes, para. 12.
961. Section 29M.
962. Section 29L; *see also* Explanatory Notes, para. 18.
963. Section 29J.
964. *See* generally A. Jeremy, *Practical Implications of the Enactment of the Racial and Religious Hatred Act*, 9 Ecclesiastical Law Journal 187 (2007).
965. [2017] EWCA Crim 1466.
966. *See also R v. Bitton* [2019] EWCA Crim 1372 where an individual described as a 'socially reclusive fantasist' had his sentence of two years and eight months' imprisonment upheld by the Court of Appeal in circumstances where he had posted 86 threatening, abusive or insulting social media messages with intent to stir up racial or religious hatred over a six day period in the lead up to the 2016 Brexit referendum.
967. *See* M. Idriss, *Religion and the Anti-terrorism Crime and Security Act 2001*, Criminal Law Review 890 (2002).

Act 1998 now provides two types of religious aggravation: one based on the demonstration towards the victim of religious hostility; the other based on religiously hostile motivation towards a religious group.[968]

408. First: 'An offence is religiously aggravated … if at the time of committing the offence, or immediately before or after doing so, the offender demonstrates towards the victim of the offence hostility based on the victim's membership of (or presumed membership of) a … religious group.'[969] This does not require proof that the defendant was motivated by religious hostility;[970] the test is that the defendant formed the view that the victim was a member of a religious group and that the defendant demonstrated hostility based on that membership.[971] Membership is not defined but presumed membership means presumed by the offender.[972]

409. Second, an offence is religiously aggravated if the offence is motivated (wholly or partly) by hostility towards members of a religious group based on their membership of that group.[973] This requires proof that the defendant was motivated by religious hostility. Religious aggravation may exist regardless of whether the defendant is of the same religious group as the object of the offence.[974]

410. For both types, it is immaterial whether or not the religious hostility of the offender is also based, to any extent, on any other factor.[975] Religious group means 'a group of persons defined by reference to religious belief or lack of religious belief'.[976] Religious belief is not defined.

411. The religiously aggravated crimes in the Crime and Disorder Act 1998 are based on pre-existing offences. The basic crime is aggravated by the demonstration or motivation of religious hostility. The basic crimes are the existing offences of assault, criminal damage, public order offences and offences under the Protection from Harassment Act 1997. Religiously aggravated versions of these offences carry a higher maximum punishment.

412. In Scotland, 'offences aggravated by religious prejudice' are governed by the Criminal Justice (Scotland) Act 2003. An offence is aggravated by religious prejudice if: (a) at the time of committing the offence or immediately before or after doing so, the offender evinces towards the victim (if any) of the offence malice and ill-will based on the victim's membership (or presumed membership) of a religious group, or of a social or cultural group with a perceived religious affiliation; or (b) the offence is motivated (wholly or partly) by malice and ill-will towards members

968. *R v. Rogers* [2007] 2 AC 62 *per* Baroness Hale.
969. Crime and Disorder Act 1998, s. 28(1)(a).
970. *DPP v. Green* [2004] EWHC 1125 (Admin).
971. *AG's Reference (No 4 of 2004)* [2005] 1 WLR 2810 (on racial aggravation).
972. Crime and Disorder Act 1998, s. 28(2).
973. Section 28(1)(b).
974. *White* [2001] 1 WLR 1352 (on racial aggravation).
975. Crime and Disorder Act 1998, s. 28(3).
976. Section 8(5).

of a religious group, or of a social or cultural group with a perceived religious affiliation, based on their membership of that group.[977] The court must take the aggravation into account in determining the appropriate sentence. Where the sentence in respect of the offence is different from that which the court would have imposed had the offence not been aggravated by religious prejudice, the court must state the extent of and the reasons for that difference.[978] Evidence from a single source is sufficient to prove that an offence is aggravated by religious prejudice.[979] Membership in relation to a group includes association with members of that group; and 'presumed' means presumed by the offender.[980]

413. Religious group means a group of persons defined by reference to their: (a) religious belief or lack of religious belief; (b) membership of or adherence to a church or religious organisation; (c) support for the culture and traditions of a church or religious organisation; or (d) participation in activities associated with such a culture or such traditions.[981]

977. Criminal Justice (Scotland) Act 2003 s. 74(2).
978. Section 74(3) and (4).
979. Section 74(5). This is contrary to the normal rule of evidence in Scots law that requires corroboration in criminal matters. It should be noted that 'corroboration' in this context requires two separate sources of evidence, not two different witnesses.
980. Section 74(6).
981. Section 74(7).

Part VIII. Church Financing

Chapter 1. Direct Financing of Religious Communities

§1. Historical Background

414. The mediaeval Church was financed largely by its land-holdings and by tithes (in Scotland, 'teinds') which continued, albeit in an attenuated form, until the early twentieth century.[982] At the Reformation, the monasteries were dissolved and their lands and revenues in England and Wales were, in effect, appropriated by the Crown – monastic lands were sold or else taken over by the cathedrals. 'First-fruits and tenths', previously paid to Rome, passed to the Crown. Parishes retained glebe land, but they were often poor. The clergy were poor too, and as a result were driven to holding benefices in plurality which, with the consequential non-residence, was considered a travesty until radically reformed in the nineteenth century. It was clergy poverty which prompted Queen Anne to establish 'the Governors of the Bounty of Queen Anne for the Augmentation of the Maintenance of Poor Clergy' in 1704. Governors applied funds selectively to improve poor clergy's income and, in time, to provide and repair parsonages for incumbents of small livings. The Church in Scotland was much less wealthy, and the Scottish Reformation proceeded along different lines from that in England.

415. The first efforts to put the organisation and finances of the Church of England on a more rational footing took place in 1835, when Sir Robert Peel proposed the establishment of an Ecclesiastical Commission. The Ecclesiastical Commissioners were duly established by Parliament in 1836 to reorganise dioceses, abolish surplus posts in cathedrals and to take over both the responsibility for funding bishoprics and certain cathedral costs, and the assets that had supported those responsibilities. The surplus income was to be used 'for the cure of souls in parishes where such assistance is most required'. The Commissioners had a major role in financing churches for the new population centres that grew up in the Industrial Revolution and in supporting the stipends of the clergy who worked there. In 1948 Queen Anne's Bounty and the Ecclesiastical Commissioners were merged. The primary duty of the present-day Church Commissioners is to manage their funds in

982. *See* M. Hill, *The Financing of Religious Communities in the United Kingdom*, in *The Financing of Religious Communities in the European Union* 327 (B. Basdevant-Gaudemet & S. Berlingo eds, Peeters 2009).

support of the Church's ministry; one of their principal concerns is the clergy pension fund.[983] In 2016, the investment fund of the Church of England generated an income of GBP 230.7 million.[984]

416. In Wales, the Welsh Church Act 1914 provided for the disendowment of the four Welsh dioceses of the Church of England in Wales. The Act also made arrangements for the distributing of funds to various bodies among which was the University of Wales and the National Library of Wales.[985] Today, the constitution and other rules of the Church in Wales now govern the administration of church funds, the accountability of their holders, and the regulation of income and expenditure,[986] as do the regulatory instruments of other churches, as well as Jewish and Muslim religious organisations.[987]

417. In Scotland, parishes were financed largely by teinds and glebe, while local landowners ('heritors') were responsible for the upkeep of the parish church. The financial affairs of the Church of Scotland are now the responsibility of the General Assembly and the Church of Scotland General Trustees under the provisions of the Church of Scotland (Property and Endowments) Act 1925 as amended.

§2. Current Legal Position

418. Today, direct State financial assistance for religion is very limited. Funds administered by religious organisations (and used for the religious purposes of the organisations in question) are constituted, in the main, by voluntary donations from their members. All religious organisations and faith communities in the United Kingdom, including the Church of England, are financially self-supporting.

419. The Church of England, however, retains land-holdings and other wealth accumulated in consequence of the particular nature of its historic status as the established church in England.[988] It should also be noted that religious organisations contribute in large measure to the provision of welfare services, through charitable work and social outreach, relieving central and local government of the function. A respectable argument could be maintained that many faith communities (such as the Salvation Army) are net contributors to the State.

983. *See also* Part V, Ch. 3.

984. *See* https://notesfromtheuk.com/2018/06/15/funding-the-church-of-england/ *See also*: *Harries v. The Church Commissioners for England* [1992] 1 WLR 1241: the case concerns the extent to which the Church Commissioners are under a duty to invest ethically.

985. N. Doe, ed., *A New History of the Church in Wales: Governance and Ministry, Theology and Society* 30, 33, 41, 51, 62, 65, 87, 150, 332 (Cambridge University Press 2020).

986. *See* N. Doe, *The Law of the Church in Wales* Ch. 14 (Cardiff: University of Wales Press 2002).

987. *See* N. Doe, *Comparative Religious Law: Judaism, Christianity, Islam* 335–351 (Cambridge University Press 2018).

988. *See* D. McClean, *State Financial Support for the Church: The United Kingdom*, in *Church and State in Europe: State Financial Support – Religion and the School* 77 (Proceedings of the European Consortium for Church and State Research 1992).

420. There is no direct automatic funding of religious organisations, nor any system of church tax as may be found in the European Union. The State makes no payments to religious organisations for clergy stipends or pensions.[989] However, with regard to the Church of England, the law requires clergy to conduct weddings and funerals and a fee is fixed by law;[990] no fee can be charged for baptisms (although a prescribed statutory fee is payable to the incumbent of a parish for a certificate of baptism and/or a search of the baptismal register).[991] Moreover, over recent years the government has funded various religion-related initiatives under the auspices of the Ministry of Housing, Communities and Local Government to promote faith, religious tolerance, and stronger community relations.[992] For example, in 2015 the Minister for Faith, explained how funding was available to 'create links between faith-based social action groups', such as the Together in Service volunteering initiative, the Near Neighbours initiative, and the 'Big Iftar' scheme under which 'mosques opened their doors to show non-Muslims what Ramadan is all about' and so 'help limit misunderstandings that can cause tension and distrust'.[993] In 2020, Faith Action was awarded sums from the GBP 360 million funding announced by the Department for Digital, Culture, Media and Sport to support to the voluntary, community and social enterprise sector.[994]

989. The position is different, however, in respect of Chaplains, as discussed below. *See* further Part XI.
990. Ecclesiastical Fees Measure 1986 (as amended by the Ecclesiastical Fees (Amendment) Measure 2011, the Church of England (Miscellaneous Provisions) Measure 2014, and the Parochial Fees and Scheduled Matters Amending Order 2014); *see* https://www.churchofengland.org/more/clergy-resources/national-clergy-hr/life-events-parochial-fees-and-guidance/guide-church.
991. *See* Parochial Fees Orders made (generally annually) pursuant to the Ecclesiastical Fees Measure 1986.
992. *See* https://www.gov.uk/government/ministers/minister-for-faith.
993. *See* https://www.gov.uk/government/speeches/recognising-the-role-of-faith-in-britain.
994. *See* https://www.gov.uk/government/news/new-taskforce-developing-plan-to-reopen-places-of-worship.

Chapter 2. Indirect Financing of Religious Communities

421. There is some limited indirect financial assistance for religion by the State. For instance, there is some State finance for the maintenance of historic church buildings, the very vast majority of which are owned by the Church of England. In the case of redundant church buildings, grants may be made by the State to the Churches Conservation Trust under the Redundant Churches and Other Religious Buildings Act 1969. However, since by definition, they will have ceased any spiritual purpose, the funding is of little benefit to the mission of the religious organisation; rather, it serves to care for part of the nation's heritage. Various publicly financed heritage bodies (English Heritage, Cadw in Wales,[995] and Historic Scotland) give a certain amount of grant aid for repairs and refurbishment to historic church buildings of major cultural importance – but this is because of their importance to the heritage and the built environment, not because of their religious nature. A significant amount of funding comes from the National Lottery. Even with respect to the Church of England,[996] in total the State contributes less than 10% of the Church's expenditure on its buildings. The Home Office also administers the Places of Worship Protective Security Funding Scheme under which it may award grants to instal measures such as protective alarms, security lighting and access controls.[997]

422. Registration law and charity law are explored above in Part III. Places of worship are exempt from local tax. In addition 'places of worship' that are listed by the State as being of architectural importance benefit from a temporary matching grant scheme to cover the cost of the VAT element of repairs and refurbishment.[998] Almost all religious organisations (with the exception of the Church of Scientology) are registered charities. In England and Wales charities are regulated by the Charity Commission and in Scotland by the Office of the Scottish Charity Regulator. Charities generally – whether religious or not – receive certain tax benefits not available to bodies that are not charitable. The most important of these is the Gift Aid scheme, under which the income tax that has been paid by donors on the money that they donate to charity can be reclaimed by the recipient charity from the Government.[999] Charities also benefit from exemption from rates (local property taxes) and from income and capital gains taxes, and from certain specific VAT reliefs.

995. Cadw is a Welsh word meaning 'to keep'. Cadw is the historic environment service of the Welsh Assembly Government. *See* https://gov.wales/cadw-grant-funding-or-loans.
996. ChurchCare is the Church of England's national resource, supports over 16,000 parish churches and 42 cathedrals – *see* http://www.churchcare.co.uk/churches/funding-and-grants/our-grants.
997. *See* https://www.churchofengland.org/more/church-resources/churchcare/churchcare-news/places-worship-protective-security-funding-scheme.
998. The Listed Places of Worship Grant Scheme has been extended to March 2021.
999. Thereby benefiting both the donor (if he or she is a higher-rate tax payer) and the recipient (by receiving 25% more). If the donor is a standard rate tax payer, the tax goes to the charity and the donor receives no benefit. If the donor is a higher-rate tax payer then the charity reclaim the standard rate of tax paid and the donor can reclaim the higher-rate element (therefore obtaining a 25% tax break) https://www.gov.uk/donating-to-charity/gift-aid.

423. The Government pays in various ways for chaplaincy services. Military and prison chaplains are paid for by government. Full-time hospital chaplains are usually paid for by the National Health Service (NHS).[1000] Faith schools are also subsidised from public funds.[1001] It is not clear, however, that subsidy to faith schools constitutes indirect financing of other religious activities on two grounds.[1002] First, all children have to go to school somewhere, and if the State does not provide a place at a faith school it will have to provide a place at a secular school, which means that State aid for faith schools is probably revenue-neutral. Second, Church of England schools will accept children of all faith or none – they provide an extraordinarily extensive service: approximately 1 million children attend Church of England schools; a quarter of primary schools and over 200 secondary schools are Church of England; and with 250 sponsored and over 650 converter academies, the Church is the biggest sponsor of academies in England.[1003] The Church in Wales also operates a system of church schools.[1004]

424. The Treasury and HM Revenue and Customs provide a financial regime under which it is possible for Muslims to buy property using types of mortgage that do not offend the Sharia prohibition against usury. This is the result of long and detailed negotiations between the Treasury and representatives of the Muslim faith community.[1005] For instance, the Finance Act 2005 made provision for the direct-tax treatment of certain Sharia-compliant financing vehicles: specifically, that *Murabaha* (cost-plus financing) and *Mudarabah* (participation or trust financing) would be treated for tax purposes in the same way as their traditional banking counterparts. The 'effective return' in a *Murabaha* transaction and the 'profit share return' in a *Mudarabah* transaction are now treated, for tax purposes, as payments of interest. Moreover, various Muslim bodies now provide advice on and assistance with Islamic financing.[1006] For example, the United Kingdom Islamic Finance Council, established in 2005, is a specialist advisory and developmental body focused on 'promoting and enhancing the global Islamic and ethical finance industry'; its principal service areas are: Advisory, Ethical Finance, Training and Awareness and Thought Leadership.[1007] Similarly, in order to meet the religious objections of the Exclusive Brethren to participating in collective pension funds, the Finance Act 2005 made provision for a new pension vehicle: the Alternatively Secured Pension (ASP). For the first time, ASPs allowed for tax relief on single, individually invested

1000. *See* further, Part XI.
1001. *See* further Part IX, Ch. 2.
1002. M. Hill, *The Financing of Religious Communities in the United Kingdom*, in *The Financing of Religious Communities in the European Union* 327, 331 (B. Basdevant-Gaudemet & S. Berling eds, Peeters 2009).
1003. *See* https://www.churchofengland.org/more/education-and-schools/church-schools-and-academies.
1004. For Wales, *see* N. Doe, ed., *A New History of the Church in Wales: Governance and Ministry, Theology and Society* 271 (Cambridge University Press 2020): there are 146 Church in Wales schools.
1005. This has resulted in London becoming a centre for Islamic commercial business.
1006. *See* e.g., K. Hassan, *Introduction to Islamic Banking and Finance: Principles and Practice* (Pearson Education 2013).
1007. *See* https://www.ukifc.com/.

funds; however, the Act had to be drafted in general terms and thousands of pensioners who were not Exclusive Brethren found it financially advantageous to establish ASPs.

Part IX. Education

Chapter 1. Religious Education in Public and Private Schools

§1. International and Historical Background

425. Under Article 2 of the First Protocol of the ECHR, no person shall be denied education and the State must respect the right of parents to ensure for their children education conforming to the parent's own religious convictions. This confers no right to go to any particular school. The right is infringed only if the claimant is unable to obtain education from the system as a whole.[1008] Strasbourg institutions have stressed that the rights must be read in the light of Articles 8, 9 and 10 ECHR.[1009]

426. The United Kingdom has entered a reservation in relation to the second right: the principle affirmed in the second sentence of Article 2 is accepted by the United Kingdom only insofar as it is compatible with the provision of efficient instruction and training and the avoidance of unreasonable public expenditure. It has been suggested that the effect of this 'is to qualify a right that is otherwise drafted without a qualifying subsection unlike other rights such as Articles 8–11 ECHR'.[1010]

427. Strasbourg jurisprudence on Article 2 of the First Protocol indicates that the setting and planning of curricula fall within the competence of States, who enjoy a wide margin of appreciation. However, it is forbidden to pursue an aim of indoctrination.[1011] The State 'must take care that information or knowledge included in the curriculum is conveyed in an objective, critical and pluralistic manner'.[1012]

1008. *Abdul Hakim Ali v. Head Teacher and Governors of Lord Grey School* [2006] UKHL 14.
1009. *Kjeldsen, Busk Madsen and Pederson v. Denmark* (1979) 1 EHRR 71; *Valsamis v. Greece* (1997) 24 EHRR 294.
1010. S. Knights, *Freedom of Religion, Minorities and the Law* para. 4.27 (Oxford University Press 2007).
1011. *Kjeldsen, Busk Madsen and Pedersen v. Denmark* (1979) 1 EHRR 71.
1012. *Valsamis v. Greece* (1997) 24 EHRR 294.

428. Historically, in England and Wales,[1013] primary and secondary education[1014] grew out of the work of both the established and non-established churches.[1015] However, State involvement deepened throughout the nineteenth century. Parliamentary grants for voluntary schools for the poor were available from 1833; from 1838 these were administered by a Special Committee of the Privy Council established by Order in Council.[1016]

429. The Elementary Education Act 1870 (the 'Forster Act') established local School Boards in areas where there were insufficient voluntary schools. Their function was to build and manage State schools to fill up the gaps in the system provided by the Churches. The Act contained the 'Cowper-Temple Clause' that 'no religious catechism or religious formulary distinctive of any particular denomination' was to be taught in these new schools.[1017] Education up to the age of ten became compulsory in some areas and this became universal in 1880. The Education Act 1902 passed the responsibilities of School Boards to municipal councils, which became Local Education Authorities and subsequently Local Authorities.[1018] They were also given the task of funding the voluntary schools from local taxation on an equal basis to their own 'provided' schools. Free elementary education was increasingly available, and fees were finally abolished by the Education Act 1918.

430. The Education Act 1944 (the 'Butler Act') was a watershed. It provided free secondary schooling for all, theoretically ending class inequalities. It introduced a tripartite system: pupils graded by an 'eleven-plus' exam into three intellectual groups for specific types of school: grammar, secondary modern and technical. Very few technical schools were ever established, so in reality it was a bipartite system that came into existence.

431. The Education Act 1944 also provided for compulsory Religious Instruction (RI) and worship in all schools which received state funding, though parents could withdraw children on grounds of conscience. The Act also provided for Standing Advisory Councils for Religious Education (SACREs) regulatory bodies at a local authority level – and for voluntarily aided schools which would receive some State funding but be under denominational control.

1013. For discussion of Scotland, *see* paras 491 et seq. Note that education is a devolved matter in Wales.
1014. For discussion of Higher Education, *see* paras 504 et seq.
1015. *See* A. Bradney, *Law and Faith in a Sceptical Age* 120–130 (Routledge-Cavendish 2009).
1016. C. Birchenough, *History of Elementary Education in England and Wales* 53 (University Tutorial Press 1938).
1017. Elementary Education Act 1870, s. 7, currently School Standards and Framework Act 1998, Sch. 19, para. 2(5).
1018. Under the Local Education Authorities and Children's Services Authorities (Integration of Functions) (Local and Subordinate Legislation) Order 2010, these are now known as 'Local Authorities'. The Scottish equivalent is Education Authority.

432. In 1965, a Labour Government Circular instructed local authorities to reorganise secondary education on comprehensive lines, for all children from a particular area irrespective of gender, ethnicity or social class, without any differentiation as to the type of school. While most local authorities completed this reorganisation, some only did so partially, and others did not do so at all, leading to the current patchy provision where some areas retain the bipartite system, and in others grammar schools and secondary moderns exist alongside comprehensive schools.

433. The Education Reform Act 1988 introduced the National Curriculum. A number of amendments in the House of Lords sought to secure the centrality of Christianity: collective worship was to be undertaken daily, and be 'wholly or mainly of a broadly Christian character'[1019] and Religious Education (RE), as opposed to RI, had to 'reflect the fact that the religious traditions in Great Britain are in the main Christian'.[1020] The parental right to withdraw their child was retained.[1021]

434. The Department of Education issued Circular 1/94 'Religious Education and Collective Worship' stating that: 'the relative content in the syllabus devoted to Christianity should predominate' but the 'syllabus as a whole must include all the principal religions represented in this country'. Moreover, 'the precise balance between Christianity and other religions should take account both of the national and local position'.[1022]

435. A number of documents on RE were subsequently published, all of which have also been non-statutory.[1023] These were at first developed by a number of non-departmental public bodies set up by the Department of Education: Two model syllabuses were published by the then Schools Curriculum and Assessment Authority in 1994; a National Framework for RE was published by the then Qualifications and Curriculum Authority in 2004; and *Religious Education in English Schools in 2010*, a review of RE's non-statutory guidance, was published by the then Qualification and Curriculum Development Agency. The Department of Education took back powers to determine the national curriculum from 2010 and produced non-statutory guidance. Most notably, *A Curriculum Framework for Religious Education* was published by the Religious Education Council of England and Wales in 2013 (including a foreword by the then Secretary of State).[1024]

436. These documents have gradually expanded the range of religions that can be studied. In 1994, it was stated that RE ought to include Christianity and 'other principal religions' named as Buddhism, Hinduism, Islam, Judaism and Sikhism. It also recommended that there be an opportunity to study other religious traditions

1019. Now School Standards and Framework Act 1998, Sch. 20, para. 3(2).
1020. Now Education Act 1996, s. 375(3).
1021. Originally Education Act 1870, s. 7.
1022. Paragraph 35.
1023. A. Brine & M. Chater, *How Did We Get Here? The Twin Narratives*, in *Reforming RE: Power and Knowledge in a Worldviews Curriculum* 21 (M. Chater ed., John Catt 2020).
1024. For details of their work *see* http://www.religiouseducationcouncil.org.uk.

and secularist philosophies. By 2013, the RE Council document referred to the teaching of 'religion and worldviews' to 'refer to Christianity, other principal religions represented in Britain, smaller religious communities and non-religious worldviews such as humanism'. In *R v. Secretary of State for Education ex parte R and D*,[1025] it was held that worship which 'reflected Christian sentiments' complied with the Education Reform Act 1988 even if there 'was nothing in them which was explicitly Christian'.

437. These provisions apply to all those who attend school, even to those between the ages of 16 and 18 for whom school attendance is not compulsory. Religious Studies (RS) exists as an academic subject for students to sit at the age of 16 and 18 (at GCSE and A Level). All students must study RE. Students may choose to study RS as they might any other academic subject and this might mean that there is no need to separately study RE if the RS teaching fulfils the statutory obligations for RE. The specification for RS is determined by Awarding Organisations (often known as exam boards) but this specification must conform to the Subject Content prescribed by the Secretary of State. In 2016, new GCSE Subject Content was issued for RS which placed greater emphasis upon religions. This guidance stated that the 'subject content is consistent with the requirements for the statutory provision of religious education in current legislation'. In *R (on the application of Fox) v. Secretary of State for Education*,[1026] it was held that this was 'a false and misleading statement of law' since complying with the Subject Content would not necessarily deliver the RE obligations since it might not include the study of non-religious views.

438. Today, a distinction can be made between schools whose running costs are wholly funded by the State, and independent schools that are not so funded. Most of the former are financially maintained by local authorities, follow the National Curriculum and are subject to inspection by Ofsted (a national statutory regulatory authority for schools). These schools are called 'maintained schools'. There are also a few types of State funded schools that are subject to different legal regimes, which are dealt with briefly below. Independent schools are funded by fees paid by parents and investments (and some have charitable status). They are largely free to run their own affairs, including setting their own curricula and admission policies but need to be registered with the Department for Children, Schools and Families and are subject to inspection either by Ofsted or by an inspectorate approved by the Secretary of State.

439. Although generally regarded as 'State schools', maintained schools include both those established by the State (local authorities and their predecessors) and those established by voluntary bodies (largely churches and other religious communities), the proportion of the two being approximately two-thirds/one-third. These schools are organised into five statutory categories:

1025. [1994] ELR 495 at 502.
1026. [2015] EWHC 3404 (Admin).

(a) community schools;
(b) foundation schools;
(c) voluntary schools, comprising:
  – voluntary aided schools, and
  – voluntary controlled schools.
(d) community special schools; and
(e) foundation special schools.[1027]

Community schools, community special schools and foundation special schools (the latter two catering for children with special educational needs) are exclusively State established schools. Voluntary schools, subdivided into voluntary aided and voluntary controlled categories, are almost exclusively established by a voluntary body whose successors (a charitable trust known as a 'foundation' in education law)[1028] normally own the school's land and buildings and appoint some members of the school's governing body. Foundation schools are largely State established schools – these may acquire a formal relationship with a charitable trust and become known as 'trust schools', but this category also contains a significant number of voluntarily established schools which, like voluntary schools, already have trust arrangements in place.

440. The main differences between these categories are control and financing. Community and voluntary controlled schools are run by the local authority, who employ the staff and set admission criteria. Foundation and voluntary aided schools are run by their governing body. Where a voluntary body has established a school, it will appoint 'foundation governors' whose duty is to preserve and develop the religious character of the school and to ensure that it is conducted in accordance with its trust deed. These are in the minority in voluntary controlled and foundation schools, but in the majority in the case of voluntary aided schools. In voluntary aided schools the governors, and not the local authority, are responsible for capital expenditure, but usually with the assistance of a 90% grant from central government. All types of school that have been established by religious bodies may be designated as having some form of religious character.[1029]

441. In England only, there are also Academies and Free Schools, both of which are technically independent schools, funded directly by the government rather than being run by the local authority. They do not have to follow the national curriculum. Academies are set up by a private or charitable 'sponsor' who are funded fully by central government by means of a funding agreement with the sponsor.[1030] Free Schools are run on a not-for-profit basis and can be set up by groups such as charities, community and faith groups.[1031] Technically, Free Schools are academies. Free

1027. School Standards and Framework Act 1998, s. 20.
1028. *Ibid.*, s. 21.
1029. *See* Ch. 2 below.
1030. Academies Act 2010.
1031. Education and Inspections Acct 2006 s .6A, as added by Education Act 2011 Sch. 11.

Schools are normally brand new institutions while academies are usually created by converting existing schools run by local authorities.

442. All maintained schools, both primary and secondary schools, are able to apply to the Secretary of State to become Academies.[1032] If a school which is applying to be an academy has been designated as having a religious character then the Secretary of State must consult the appropriate religious body before making an Academy Order and must also inform that religious body if he decides not to make an Academy Order.[1033] Once an Academy Order has been made by the Secretary of State, then the Local Authority must cease to maintain the school but may continue to provide financial or other assistance.[1034] Where a school is to be converted into an Academy and has been previously designated as having a particular religious character, then the Academy is to be treated as being designated as an independent school having that religious character.[1035]

443. There also exist supplementary schools, community-based initiatives that provide additional educational support in addition to attending the schools listed above. These often provide specific language, cultural and religious teaching for children from ethnic minorities.[1036]

§2. RELIGIOUS EDUCATION IN STATE SCHOOLS

444. The following focuses upon maintained schools which have not been designated as having a religious character. Those schools with a religious character and independent schools will be discussed in Chapter 2 under 'Religious Schools'.

445. The current domestic law governing religious observance in schools in England and Wales is to be found in the Education Act 1996 and the School Standards and Framework Act 1998. However, its basic provisions date back to the Butler Act. In recent years, there have been a number of calls for reform.[1037]

1032. Academies Act 2010, s. 3.

1033. The 'appropriate religious body' is defined in the case of a Church of England school or a Roman Catholic school, as 'the appropriate diocesan authority' and 'in any other case, such body or person representing the specified religion or religious denomination as is prescribed under section 88F(3)(e) of School Standards and Framework Act 1998'. 'Where there is more than one religion or religious denomination specified, references to the appropriate religious body are to be read as references to both or all of the bodies concerned': Academies Act 2010, ss 4–5, as amended by Education Act 2011 s. 55.

1034. Academies Act 2010, s. 6.

1035. Academies Act 2010, s. 6(7)–(8).

1036. *See* N. Doe, *Comparative Religious Law* 238–241 (Cambridge University Press 2018).

1037. *See* P. Cumper & A. Mawhinney, *Collective Worship in Schools: An Evaluation of Law and Policy in the UK* (AHRC Network Report 2015) and C. Clarke & L.Woodhead, *A New Settlement Revised: Religion and Belief in Schools* (Westminster Faith Debates Pamphlet 2018).

446. In England, in 2018, the Commission on RE recommended that the subject be renamed Religion and Worldviews and that a non-statutory programme of study be developed at a national level at a similar level of detail as for History and Geography in the national curriculum.[1038]

447. In Wales, the new Welsh curriculum due to be introduced from September 2022 will radically depart from the status quo. The subject is to be renamed Religion, Values and Ethics (RVE) and will be a mandatory curriculum requirement and will fall under the Humanities area of learning.[1039] It is proposed that the right to parental opt out will be removed and RVE will also 'reflect the fact that a range of non-religious philosophical convictions are held in Great Britain'.

448. The following describes the current law (i.e., prior to the Curriculum and Assessment (Wales) Bill 2020).

I. Legal Requirements

449. In relation to any community, foundation or voluntary school, the Local Authority, the governing body and the head teacher must ensure that RE is given in accordance with the local agreed syllabus.[1040] This is the syllabus agreed by the Agreed Syllabus Conference formed by the SACRE.

450. However, in exercising that power Local Authorities should 'have regard to the general principle that pupils are to be educated in accordance with the wishes of their parents, so far as that is, compatible with the provision of efficient instruction and training and the avoidance of unreasonable public expenditure'.[1041]

451. Schools must provide 'religious education in accordance with an agreed syllabus adopted for the school or for those pupils'.[1042] Such an agreed syllabus must be non-denominational.[1043]

Accordingly, if a parent requests that a pupil 'be wholly or partly excused' from receiving RE, the pupil is to be so excused until the request is withdrawn.[1044] A pupil may be withdrawn from the school to receive RE elsewhere if the pupil 'cannot with reasonable convenience' be sent to the school where religious education of that kind is provided.[1045] A pupil may not be withdrawn unless the Local Authority

1038. Commission on Religious Education, *Religion and Worldviews: The Way Forward. A National Plan for RE.* (RE Council, 2018). *See* M. Chater, ed., *Reforming RE: Power and Knowledge in a Worldviews Curriculum* (John Catt 2020).
1039. Curriculum and Assessment (Wales) Bill 2020.
1040. School Standards and Framework Act 1998, s. 69.
1041. Education Act 1996, s. 9.
1042. School Standards and Framework Act 1998, Sch. 12, para. 2(2).
1043. *Ibid.*, para. 2(5).
1044. School Standards and Framework Act 1998, s. 71.
1045. *Ibid.*, s. 71(3).

is satisfied that the arrangements proposed are such as will not interfere with the attendance of the pupil at school on any day except at the beginning or end of a school session.[1046]

II. Content

452. Each Local Authority must establish a SACRE, which consists of 'representative groups' and other 'persons co-opted as members of the council by members of the council'.[1047] The 'representative groups' required are:

(a) a group of persons to represent such Christian denominations and other religions and denominations of such religions as, in the opinion of the authority, will appropriately reflect the principal religious traditions in the area;
(b) except in the case of an area in Wales, a group of persons to represent the Church of England;
(c) a group of persons to represent such associations representing teachers as, in the opinion of the authority, ought to be represented, having regard to the circumstances of the area; and
(d) a group of persons to represent the authority.[1048]

453. Before appointing such a religious representative, 'the authority shall take all reasonable steps to assure themselves that he is representative of the religion, denomination or associations in question'.[1049] This seems to allow the Local Authority to make a value judgement as to whether someone is genuinely representative of a religious group.

454. The Local Authority is to adopt an 'agreed syllabus' for religious education after receiving the advice of a periodic conference convened for that purpose (an Agreed Syllabus Conference). The membership requirements for the Conference are the same as those for the SACRE.[1050] The resulting syllabus 'shall reflect the fact that the religious traditions in Great Britain are in the main Christian whilst taking account of the teaching and practices of the other principal religions represented in Great Britain'.[1051] The syllabus may be different for different schools, classes or pupils.

455. No agreed syllabus shall provide for religious education to be given to pupils at a school 'by means of any catechism or formulary which is distinctive of

1046. *Ibid.*, s. 71(4).
1047. Education Act 1996, s. 390.
1048. *Ibid.*, s. 390.
1049. *Ibid.*, s. 392(2).
1050. *Ibid.*, Sch. 31.
1051. *Ibid.*, s. 375(3).

a particular religious denomination (but this is not to be taken as prohibiting provision in such a syllabus for the study of such catechisms or formularies)'.[1052]

III. Rights of Teachers

456. No teacher can be required to give religious education nor is he or she to 'receive any less remuneration or be deprived of, or disqualified for, any promotion or other advantage … by reason of the fact that he does or does not give religious education'.[1053]

§3. Religious Worship in State Schools

457. The law concerning religious worship has proved controversial. The United Nations Committee on the Right of the Child has expressed its concern that pupils are required by law to take part in religious worship and has recommended that the law be changed to ensure that children themselves, as opposed to their parents, have the right to withdraw.[1054] Although reform of the law has long been mooted, no concrete proposals have been made as yet.

458. Claims have been brought in relation to whether the State is obliged to provide alternative material for those who opt out but none of these claims have reached a contested hearing.[1055]

I. Legal Requirements

459. All community, foundation or voluntary schools are required to provide a daily act of collective worship.[1056] This need not be at the beginning of the day and separate acts of worship may be provided for pupils in different ages or school groups.[1057]

460. Although normally such worship will take place on school premises, if the governing body is of the opinion that it is desirable for worship on a special occasion to take place elsewhere than on the school premises, it may make arrangements after consultation with the head teacher.[1058]

1052. Schedule 19 to the School Standards and Framework Act 1998.
1053. School Standards and Framework Act 1998 s. 59(3).
1054. *See*, e.g., United Nations Committee on the Right of the Child, *Concluding Observations on the Fifth Periodic Report of the United Kingdom of Great Britain and Northern Ireland* (2016).
1055. *See R (on the Application of Harris) v. Oxford Diocesan Schools Trust*, Claim No. CO/314/2019.
1056. School Standards and Framework Act 1998, s. 70.
1057. *Ibid.*, Sch. 20.
1058. *Ibid.*

461. Parents have a right to withdraw their children and sixth formers have a right to withdraw themselves from daily worship.[1059] If the parent of a pupil other than a sixth form pupil requests that their child may be wholly or partly excused from attendance then that pupil shall be so excused until the request is withdrawn. Likewise, if a sixth form pupil requests this then they shall be so excused. The same rules that allow pupils withdrawn from Religious Education to exceptionally receive Religious Education elsewhere also apply in relation to pupils withdrawn from religious worship.[1060]

II. Content

462. Schedule 20 to the School Standards and Framework Act 1998 states that 'the required collective worship shall be wholly or mainly of a broadly Christian character'. Collective worship is of a broadly Christian character 'if it reflects the broad traditions of Christian belief without being distinctive of any particular Christian denomination'. Not every required act of collective worship needs to be of broadly Christian character, 'provided that, taking any school term as a whole, most such acts which take place in the school do comply'.

463. One of the functions of the SACRE is to advise the Local Authority on 'such matters connected with ... religious worship in community schools or in foundation schools'.[1061] The SACRE may disapply the requirement in prescribed schools, for particular classes or for descriptions of pupils, that daily worship should be mainly Christian. On the application of the head teacher (after consulting the Governing Body, who should take appropriate steps to consult parents) the SACRE shall 'consider whether it is appropriate for the requirement' to be imposed in 'the case of the school or in the case of any class or description of pupils at the school'.[1062]

464. In determining whether it is appropriate for that requirement to apply the SACRE should 'have regard to any circumstances relating to the family backgrounds of the pupils at the school, or of the pupils of the particular class or description in question, which are relevant for determining the character of the collective worship appropriate in their case'.[1063] The SACRE is required to give the head teacher written notification of its decision on the application.[1064]

1059. *Ibid.*, ss 71, 71A.
1060. *See* para. 451 above.
1061. Education Act 1996 s. 391.
1062. *Ibid.*, s. 394(1), (5), (6).
1063. *Ibid.*, s. 394(2).
1064. *Ibid.*, s. 394(3).

465. Arrangements for worship are capable of challenge in the courts, for lacking Christian content, by parents concerned to preserve worship as part of the normal school experience.[1065]

In *R v. Secretary of State for Education ex parte R and D*,[1066] McCullough J rejected criticism of the worship in a Manchester primary school which parents argued was insufficiently Christian. The judge agreed with the Secretary of State for Education that worship 'must in some sense reflect something special or separate from ordinary school activities. [It] should be concerned with reverence or veneration paid to a being or power regarded as supernatural or divine and … the pupil at his or her level, should be capable of perceiving this'.

III. Rights of Teachers

466. No person is to be disqualified from being a teacher at a school or being employed or engaged for any other purpose at the school by reason of his or her religious opinions or for attending or omitting to attend religious worship.[1067] No teacher 'shall receive any less remuneration or be deprived of, or disqualified for, any promotion or other advantage … by reason of his religious opinions or of his attending or omitting to attend religious worship'.[1068]

467. Refusals to allow teachers time off during school hours to attend prayers have been upheld by courts as being consistent with the ECHR[1069] and the law prohibiting religious discrimination.[1070] Claims based on proselytism have also been unsuccessful. In *Powell v. Marr Corporation*[1071] a teacher suspended and subsequently sacked for expressing her views on religion and morals failed in her claim of discrimination on grounds of religion or belief.

1065. Similarly, legal challenges have been made as to the provision of materials for opt out *See R (on the Application of Harris) v. Oxford Diocesan Schools Trust*, Claim No. CO/314/2019.
1066. [1994] ELR 495 at 502.
1067. School Standards and Framework Act 1998, s. 59(2).
1068. *Ibid.*, s. 59(4).
1069. *Ahmad v. Inner London Education Authority* [1978] QB 36. *See* generally Part II.
1070. *Mayuuf v. Governing Body of Bishop Challoner Catholic Collegiate School & Anor* [2005] Employment Tribunal, Case No. 3202398/04 (21 December 2005). *See* generally Part VII, Ch. 7.
1071. [2018] UKEAT 1401951/2016.

Chapter 2. Religious Schools

468. The traditional function of the Church of England, the Roman Catholic Church and certain other religious organisations in the field of education explains in large measure the prominent role of faith communities within the current education system.[1072] The subsidising of religious schools, which began in the nineteenth century, continues to this day.[1073] Although the term 'faith schools' is now commonly used to describe all religious schools,[1074] the term is a contested one. Legally such schools are styled as schools 'with a religious character'. The two main types of such school established by religious communities are maintained and independent. The following will examine both types in turn, with reference to their legal status and the application of the rules concerning religious education and worship.

§1. State Maintained Faith Schools

I. Legal Status

469. Foundation and voluntary schools may be designated by the Secretary of State as schools having a religious character where he is satisfied that the school was established by a religious body or for religious purposes.[1075] Such an order must state the religion or religious denomination.[1076] Where more than one religion or religious denomination is so specified, this is to be construed as including a reference to any of them.

470. In relation to admissions, the general principle is that any preference made by a parent will be complied with.[1077] However, there are a number of exceptions to this rule, including where 'compliance with the preference would prejudice the provision of efficient education or the efficient use of resources'.[1078] Attendance at or abstaining from attending a Sunday school or a place of worship cannot be required as a condition of attending a maintained school.[1079]

471. Discrimination is forbidden in relation to admissions.[1080] However, schools designated as having a religious character enjoy an exception under paragraph 5(a) of Schedule 11 to the Equality Act 2010. This exception can only be relied upon if

1072. *See* P. Petchey, *Legal Issues for Faith Schools in England and Wales*, 10 Ecclesiastical Law Journal 174 (2008) and L. Vickers, *Religion and Belief Discrimination and the Employment of Teachers in Faith Schools*, 2–3 Religion & Human Rights 4, 137 (2009).
1073. M. Cruickhank, *Church and State in English Education* 3 (Macmillan 1964).
1074. Until the 1990s, the term 'church schools' was frequently used.
1075. School Standards and Framework Act 1998 s. 69(3).
1076. *Ibid.*, s. 69(4).
1077. School Standards and Framework Act 1998 s. 86.
1078. *Ibid.*, s. 86(3)(a).
1079. Education Act 1996, s. 398.
1080. Equality Act 2010, s. 85(1). This covers the refusal to admit a person as a pupil as well as the arrangements and terms concerning admissions.

the school is over-subscribed. It does not apply to other rules prohibiting discrimination by excluding pupils from school or by subjecting pupils to any other detriment.[1081] Moreover, the exception only allows schools to restrict admission on grounds of religion or belief. The exception found in paragraph 5(a) for schools with a religious character cannot discriminate on any other ground, such as on grounds of race or ethnicity. This is problematic, since often a watertight distinction cannot be drawn between race and religion.

472. In *R (on the application of E) v. JFS Governing Body,*[1082] a school's admission requirement stipulating a restricted definition of Jewishness in accordance with the teaching of the Office of the Chief Rabbi was held to be discriminatory since in effect it was a test of ethnicity which is unlawful under the Race Relations Act 1976, regardless of its religious content. The Supreme Court Justices were divided: five considered that there was direct discrimination on the grounds of race; two concluded that there was indirect discrimination; whereas two were of the view that there was no racial discrimination at all, instead a legitimate selection on the ground of religion in accordance with doctrine.

473. In *The Interim Executive Board of X School v. Chief Inspector of Education,*[1083] it was held that segregation in a faith school on grounds of sex constituted discrimination under the Equality Act 2010. The motive for the discrimination was irrelevant.

474. Admission policies are subject to the review of the Office of the Schools Adjudicator. A complaint regarding Hasmonean High School[1084] an oversubscription criterion which stated that observation of 'the laws of family purity' was one of the tests for the faith practice requirement, was upheld since because it was not reasonable, procedurally fair or objective to ask for or seek to verify this information.

475. It is generally unlawful for public authorities to discriminate on grounds of religion or belief.[1085] In *R (Diocese of Menevia) v. City and County of Swansea Council,*[1086] a policy to continue to provide free transport to pupils at Welsh medium schools but not to church schools was quashed on grounds of the Equality Act 2010. It is discrimination on grounds of religion or belief where there is discrimination against a pupil in relation to the way it provides education, affords a benefit or does not provide education or afford a benefit unless this applies to 'anything done in connection with acts of worship or other religious observance organized by or on

1081. Equality Act 2010, s. 82(2)(e)–(f).
1082. [2009] UKSC 15.
1083. [2016] EWHC (Admin) 2813.
1084. [2015] Office of the Schools Adjudicator ADA2990.
1085. Equality Act 2010, s. 29(6).
1086. [2017] EWCA Civ 1426.

behalf of a school (whether or not forming part of the curriculum)'.[1087] It is discrimination if a pupil is excluded or subject to any other detriment on grounds of religion or belief regardless of whether it is done in connection with acts of worship.[1088]

II. Religious Education and Worship

476. A distinction may be drawn between foundation and voluntary controlled schools with a religious character on the one hand and voluntary aided schools with a religious character on the other hand. The basic difference is that voluntary aided schools enjoy more freedom.[1089]

477. In a foundation or voluntary controlled school with a religious character, religious education must be in accordance with an agreed syllabus adopted for the school or for a class of pupils.[1090] Where parents request that their children receive religious education in accordance with the provisions of the trust deed relating to the school or in accordance with the tenets of the religion or religious denomination specified in relation to the school then the governors are under an obligation to 'make arrangements for securing that such religious education is given to those pupils in the school during not more than two periods in each week' unless special circumstances render it unreasonable for them to do so.[1091]

478. In voluntary aided schools with a religious character, religious education must be in accordance with the trust deed or with the tenets of the religion or religious denomination specified in relation to the school.[1092] Where parents request that their children receive religious education in accordance with any agreed syllabus and it is not reasonably convenient for the parents to send their children to a school at which that syllabus is in use then the governing body is under an obligation to 'make arrangements for religious education in accordance with that syllabus to be given to those pupils in the school' during the times set apart for the giving of religious education in the school.[1093] If the Local Authority is satisfied that the governing body is unwilling to make such arrangements, then they shall be made by the Local Authority.[1094]

479. In relation to worship, no distinction is made between foundation, voluntary aided and voluntary controlled schools with a religious character. The daily act

1087. *Ibid.,* Sch. 11, para. 6 provides this exception to s. 85(2)(a)–(d).
1088. *Ibid.,* s. 85(2)(e)–(f). Harassment and victimisation under s. 85(3)–(4) are also not covered by the exception in Sch. 11, para. 6.
1089. P. Petchey, *Legal Issues for Faith Schools in England and Wales*, 10 Ecclesiastical Law Journal 174, 177 (2008).
1090. School Standards and Framework Act 1998 Sch. 19 para. 3.
1091. *Ibid.*, para. 3(3).
1092. *Ibid.*, para. 4.
1093. *Ibid.*, para. 4(3)–(4).
1094. *Ibid.*, para. 4(5).

of collective worship must be in accordance with the trust deed or with the tenets of the religion or religious denomination specified in relation to the school.[1095]

480. The governing body of any voluntary or foundation school with a religious character must ensure that any denominational education given to pupils and the content of the school's collective worship are inspected.[1096]

III. Teachers

481. In foundation or voluntary controlled schools which have a religious character, provided that there are more than two teachers, the teaching staff will include persons (styled 'reserved' teachers) selected for their fitness and competence to give the required religious education and are specifically appointed to do so.[1097] The number of such 'reserved' teachers must not exceed one-fifth of the total number of teachers including the head teacher.[1098]

482. In the case of 'reserved' teachers, preference may be given in connection with the appointment, remuneration or promotion of teachers at the school to persons whose religious opinions are in accordance with that of the school, who attend religious worship in accordance with those tenets, and who give or are willing to give, religious education at the school in accordance with those tenets.[1099] Regard may be had, in connection with the termination of the employment or engagement of any reserved teacher at the school, to any conduct on his or her part which is incompatible with the precepts, or with the upholding of the tenets, of the specified religion or religious denomination.[1100] In relation to teachers who are not reserve teachers, the same law applies as for teachers in a school that does not have a religious character.[1101]

483. In connection with the appointment of the head teacher, where the head teacher is not to be a reserved teacher, 'regard may be had to that person's ability and fitness to preserve and develop the religious character of the school'.[1102]

484. All of the other teachers are governed by the same rules which apply to schools which do not have a religious character.[1103] No person is to be disqualified from being a teacher at the school or being employed or engaged for any other purpose at the school by reason of their religious opinions or for attending or omitting

1095. School Standards and Framework Act 1998 Sch. 20 para. 5.
1096. Education Act 2005, ss 48–50.
1097. School Standards and Framework Act 1998, s. 58(2). Similar provisions apply in relation to academies with a religious character: *see* s. 124AA, as substituted in by Education Act 2011 s. 62.
1098. *Ibid.*, s. 58(3).
1099. *Ibid.*, s. 60(3), (5)(a).
1100. *Ibid.*, s. 60(3), (5)(b).
1101. *Ibid.*, s. 59(2)–(4).
1102. *Ibid.*, s. 60(4).
1103. *Ibid.*, s. 60(2).

to attend religious worship;[1104] no teacher is to be required to give religious education;[1105] no teacher 'shall receive any less remuneration or be deprived of, or disqualified for, any promotion or other advantage by reason of the fact that he does not give religious education or by reason of his religious opinions or of his attending or omitting to attend religious worship'.[1106]

485. In voluntary aided schools which have a religious character, the rules which apply to reserved teachers may be applied to all teachers.[1107]

486. Religious schools may also be able to rely upon exceptions provided in the Equality Act 2010.[1108] These exceptions do not automatically apply to faith schools: they need to show that in the particular case the terms of the exception are met.[1109] The Employment Appeal Tribunal has suggested that education authorities cannot rely upon the exception now found in Schedule 9, paragraph 3 since they cannot have a 'religious ethos': 'The fact that it operates a statutory system under which it enables denominations to advance their ethos through schools maintained by it, does not mean that they espouse the same ethos at all'.[1110]

§2. Independent Faith Schools (Including Academies)

I. Legal Status

487. Parents may decide that their children are to be educated at home or at an independent school instead of their attending a school maintained by the Local Authority.[1111] Independent schools can be set up by any group. They must be registered and are subject to inspection,[1112] according to the Independent School Standards.[1113] Independent schools can be designated as having a religious character in the same way as a foundation or voluntary school. The order must state the religion or religious denomination in accordance with whose tenets by which education is provided at the school or by which the school is conducted.[1114] The procedure is governed by separate secondary legislation.[1115] These provisions do not apply to

1104. *Ibid.*, s. 59(2).
1105. *Ibid.*, s. 59(3).
1106. *Ibid.*, s. 59(4).
1107. School Standards and Framework Act 1998 s. 60(5).
1108. *See* Part VII, Ch. 7.
1109. *Glasgow City Council v. Mcnab* [2007] UKEAT 0037 06 1701 (17 January 2007).
1110. *Ibid.*, at para. 61.
1111. Education Act 1996 s. 463.
1112. Education and Skills Act 2008, ss 92–141. Wales remains subject to the previous legislation found in Education Act 2002, ss 156A to s. 168A.
1113. These are made by regulation under s. 94 of Education and Skills Act 2008 in England and under s. 157 of the Education Act 2002 in Wales.
1114. School Standards and Framework Act 1998, s. 124B.
1115. Designation of Schools Having a Religious Character (Independent Schools) (England) Order 2013/2162.

Academies. Where a school is to be converted into an academy and has been previously designated as having a particular religious character, then the Academy is to be treated as being designated as an independent school having that religious character.[1116]

II. Religious Education and Worship

488. Independent schools are not bound to follow the National Curriculum and requirements as to religious education and collective worship.[1117] However, the Independent School Standards must be met. These provide requirements as to the quality of education provided as well as the spiritual, moral, social and cultural development of pupils.

III. Teachers

489. Independent schools designated as having a religious character may give preference in connection with the appointment, remuneration or promotion of teachers at the school to persons whose religious opinions are in accordance with the tenets of the school, who attend religious worship in accordance with those tenets, and who give or are willing to give, religious education at the school in accordance with those tenets. Regard may be had, in connection with the termination of the employment or engagement of any teacher at the school, to any conduct on his or her part which is incompatible with the precepts, or with the upholding of the tenets, of the specified religion or religious denomination.[1118] However, schools may be liable for other discriminatory behaviour. In De *Groen v. Gan Manachem Hendon Ltd,*[1119] a teacher sacked for cohabiting did not claim unfair dismissal but successfully claimed discrimination and harassment in the context of events that led to her sacking.

490. These provisions do apply to academies. In relation to academies, unless the Secretary of State provides by order that this provision is not to apply to a specific school, the following provisions apply:[1120] Any academy with more than two teachers must include 'reserved' teachers who are specifically appointed and selected for their fitness and competence to give religious education in accordance with the tenets of the religion or the religious denomination specified in the Academy Order. The number of 'reserved' teachers in the Academy must not exceed one-fifth of the total number of teachers, including the principal. Preference may be given in connection with the appointment, promotion or remuneration of 'reserved' teachers at the Academy to persons whose religious opinions are in accordance with

1116. Academies Act 2010, s. 6(7)–(8).
1117. A. Bradney, *Law and Faith in a Sceptical Age* 131–132 (Routledge-Cavendish 2009).
1118. School Standards and Framework Act 1998 s. 124A.
1119. [2019] UKEAT 00589.
1120. School Standards and Framework Act 1998 s. 124AA, as added by Education Act 2011 s. 62.

the tenets of the religion or the religious denomination of the Academy, who attend religious worship in accordance with those tenets, or who give, or are willing to give, religious education at the Academy in accordance with those tenets. Moreover, in connection with the termination of employment or engagement of any reserved teacher at the Academy regard may be had to any conduct on the part of any 'reserved' teacher which is incompatible with the precepts, or with the upholding of the tenets, of the religion or religious denomination. These provisions do not apply to non-reserved teachers. Non-reserved teachers must not be required to give religious education and must not receive any less remuneration, or be deprived of, or disqualified for, any promotion or other advantage because they give, or do not give, religious education, or for reasons related to the teacher's religious opinions or to the teacher's attending or omitting to attend religious worship.

§3. Schools in Scotland

491. Historically, the Church of Scotland had a major part to play in the establishment of a national system of education. The Fifth Head of the *First Book of Discipline*[1121] contains a section entitled 'For the Schooles', which declares that:

> we judge it, that every several kirk have one School-master appointed, such a one at least as is able to teach Grammar and the Latina tongue if the town be of any reputation … . And furder we think it expedient that in every notable town, and especially in the town of the Superintendent, there be erected a Colledge, in which the arts, at least Logick and Rhetorick, together with the tongues, be read by sufficient masters … . And also provision for those that be poore and not able by themselves [*sic*].[1122]

This declaration was ultimately reinforced by the Education Act 1696 (An Act for founding of schools in every parish), which required that:

> there be a school founded and a schoolmaster appointed in every parish (not already provided) with the advice of the presbytery, and to this purpose that the heritors in every congregation meet amongst themselves and provide a commodious house for the school and modify a stipend to the schoolmaster, which shall not be under 100 marks nor above 200 marks, to be paid yearly at two terms.

492. Though this was very far from a system of universal free primary and secondary education in the modern sense, fees were kept low because the provision of education was partly a charge on the heritors (local landowners). Except in the very

1121. It first appeared as an MS c1560, produced at the request of the Lords of the Congregation: the first printed version (together with the *Second Book of Discipline*) was printed in 1621: *see The First Book of Discipline* (J.K. Cameron ed., The St Andrew Press 1972).

1122. *Ibid.*, 130–131.

poorest and remotest rural areas. Church of Scotland sessions appointed schoolmasters – 'dominies' – who gave the children a basic education, with the result that the general level of literacy was much higher in Scotland than in England.

493. However, demographic changes as a result of the industrial revolution put the parish school system in the new conurbations under considerable strain; and this was not finally resolved until the passing of the Education (Scotland) Act 1872. Under that Act, the State took over responsibility for schooling from the Church of Scotland and it finally became compulsory for all children aged between 5 and 13.

494. The State 'board schools' were subject to a conscience clause by which parents could remove their children from religious education; however, Roman Catholics established more than 200 'voluntary schools' outside the State system. Roman Catholic schools received some central funding but no assistance from the rates; and it was to end this disparity of provision that they were brought within the State funding system by the Education (Scotland) Act 1918.

I. The Education (Scotland) Act 1980

495. Under the provisions of the Education (Scotland) Act 1980, as amended, every public school, grant-aided school and self-governing school in Scotland shall be open to pupils of all denominations and any pupil may be withdrawn by his or her parents from any instruction in religious subjects and from any religious observance in any such school. No pupil shall be placed at any disadvantage with respect to the secular instruction given by the school either because of his or her denomination or by reason of having been withdrawn from religious instruction.[1123]

496. In the case of a pupil who boards at a public school or other educational establishment under the management of an education authority or at any self-governing school, the education authority (or, in the case of a self-governing school, the board of management) must give that pupil 'reasonable opportunities' to attend worship in accordance with the tenets of his or her religious denomination on Sundays or other days exclusively set apart for religious observance by the faith-community to which the pupil's parent belongs, or to receive religious instruction or to practise religious observance outside the school's working hours.[1124]

497. Section 16 enables trustees of a denominational school to transfer the school, its site and buildings to the education authority, 'who shall be bound to accept such transfer'. Under section 21, in a school so transferred, the education authority has the sole power to regulate the curriculum and appoint teachers; however, teachers in such schools must be approved as regards religious belief and character by representatives of the denominational body in whose interest the school has

1123. Section 9.
1124. Section 10.

been conducted.[1125] The education authority shall appoint 'a person approved as regards religious belief and character' as the unpaid supervisor of religious instruction for a transferred denominational school; the supervisor reports on the religious instruction given in the school.[1126] Where the education authority proposes to change the arrangements in respect of a denominational school under its control, the Secretary of State may not consent to such proposals unless satisfied that adequate arrangements have been made for the religious instruction of the pupils affected.[1127]

II. Religious Observance

498. Policy on religious observance is set out in Circular 1/2005: *Provision of Religious Observance in Scottish Schools.* The Circular is based on the definition and aims of religious observance proposed by the Religious Observance Review Group as 'community acts which aim to promote the spiritual development of all members of the school community and express and celebrate the shared values of the school community'.

499. Under the terms of the Circular, 'in recognition of Scotland's Christian heritage', schools are encouraged to draw on this when planning religious observance; however, the fact that many school communities contain pupils and staff from other faiths or none should be taken fully into account in supporting spiritual development. The Circular also stated that it is 'of central importance' that all pupils and staff can participate with integrity in religious observance without compromising their personal convictions.

500. As to school assemblies, there should be a clear distinction between assemblies for the purpose of religious observance and assemblies for other purposes. Religious observance needs to take place sufficiently frequently to have an impact on the spiritual development of the school community, but quality is more important than quantity. The Review Group suggested a minimum of six such assemblies in a school year, in addition to traditional celebrations. The Circular suggests, however, that many primary schools, especially, value weekly religious observance.

501. The statutory provision for parents to withdraw children from participation in religious observance should always be made known to them and their wishes respected. Where a child is withdrawn from religious observance, schools should make suitable arrangements for the child to participate in a worthwhile alternative activity. In no circumstances should a child be disadvantaged as a result of withdrawing from religious observance.

502. The Circular recognises the importance of chaplains and other faith-group leaders in such areas as acts of worship, religious and moral education and the

---

1125. Section 21(1) and (2).
1126. Section 21(3).
1127. Section 22C.

broader pastoral role and encourages head-teachers to engage and discuss religious observance with school chaplains. Chaplains' own religious stances should be respected and they should not be expected to compromise their religious beliefs.

503. As to worship, where a school, whether denominational or not, is 'continuous with a faith community', that community's faith in the 'focus of worship' may be assumed and worship may be considered to be appropriate as part of the formal activity of the school. Where there is a diversity of beliefs and practices, the appropriate context for organised acts of worship is within the informal curriculum as part of the range of activities offered by religions, groups, chaplains and other religious leaders. Consideration should be given to providing appropriate facilities in schools for acts of religious observance and worship.

§4. Higher Education

I. Historical Background

504. Both in England and in Scotland, the relationship between religion and Higher Education (HE) predates the Reformation in the sixteenth century.[1128] Oxford and Cambridge were largely religious foundations, as were St Andrew's University, Glasgow University and King's College, Aberdeen (the precursor with Marischal College of the modern University). Until the nineteenth century it was impossible for those who were not members of the Church of England to obtain a university degree in England because both Oxford and Cambridge imposed a religious test;[1129] non-Anglicans either attended the so-called Dissenting Academies or went to study in Scotland.

505. The first avowedly secular institution of higher education in England, University College, London, was established by Jeremy Bentham in 1826, partly to modernise the curriculum and partly to break the Church of England's monopoly. King's College, London, was founded in response as an avowedly Church of England establishment. The University of Durham, which was founded in 1832 under the control of the Dean and Chapter of the Cathedral, originally imposed a religious test as at Oxford and Cambridge. Religious tests were not removed until the passing of the Universities Tests Act 1871.

506. As regards the four ancient Scottish universities,[1130] the Protestant Religion and Presbyterian Church Act 1707 provided that:

1128. For a fuller discussion of the position of religion in relation to higher education in the United Kingdom, *see* F. Cranmer, *La Présence Religieuse dans l'Enseignement Supérieur au Royaume-Uni*, in *Actes de manifestations scientifiques du Centre Société, Droit et Religion en Europe* (Strasbourg University Press 2010).

1129. A. Kadish & K. Tribe, *The Market for Political Economy: The Advent of Economics in British University Culture,* 1850–1905 at 22 (Routledge 1993).

1130. St Andrews, Glasgow, Aberdeen and Edinburgh.

> in all time coming, … principals, regents, masters or others bearing office … before or at their admissions … do and shall acknowledge and profess and shall subscribe to the foresaid [Westminster] Confession of Faith as the confession of their faith, and that they will practise and conform themselves to the worship presently in use in this church, and submit themselves to the government and discipline thereof.

The generality of this provision was repealed by the Churches (Scotland) Act 1905 and its residual application to posts in theology by section 5 of the Universities (Scotland) Act 1932.

507. Recent years have seen a massive increase in the number of HE institutions empowered to award degrees in their own right and many of them have grown out of church colleges for training teachers – for example, Canterbury Christ Church University College, and the Universities of Chichester, Winchester and Gloucestershire all evolved from Church of England colleges, while Liverpool Hope University is a joint enterprise between the Roman Catholic Church and the Church of England. Traditionally, therefore, there has been a close relationship between HE and religion, both in respect of the academic study of theology and of chaplaincy to the students.

II. Legal Status

508. United Kingdom universities are public institutions funded by the various higher education funding councils and are therefore public authorities for the purposes of human rights legislation.[1131] In addition, however, in the field of religion there are several private ministerial training colleges which, though not public institutions, prepare their students for qualifications either awarded by or validated by a public university.[1132]

509. Part 6 of the Equality Act 2010 forbids discrimination on the grounds of religion or belief in education, in the provision of goods, facilities or services, the management of premises and in the exercise of public functions. More specifically, sections 91 and 92 it is unlawful for an HE institution to discriminate on grounds of religion in its admissions policy or in the way it treats its students once they are admitted to the institution, or to subject to harassment any student at the establishment or any person who has applied for admission to it.

510. There is, however, an exception under Part 2 of Schedule 12 for institutions with a religious ethos which allows them in the admission of students to a course at the institution to give preference to persons of a particular religion or

1131. The exception is the privately founded University of Buckingham. Whether or not it is a public authority for the purposes of the Human Rights Act 1998 is not clear.

1132. For example, the Free Church College in Edinburgh awards successful students a BTh which is taught within the College but validated by the University of Glasgow.

belief, if it does so to preserve the institution's religious ethos, and the course is not a course of vocational training. Colleges for the training of clergy which are associated with universities are therefore entitled to restrict entry to persons of their own denominations – though a secular university theology department would not be so entitled.

III. Teaching Religion

511. English and Scots universities have had Faculties of Theology since mediaeval times and there has never been any bar on the teaching of theology. There is certainly no parallel to the situation in France where, as a result of the rise of *laïcité*' during the nineteenth century, public universities were transformed into lay institutions everywhere. The few faculties of Catholic theology … 'could not survive and disappeared from public education'.[1133] Nor are there confessional Faculties of Theology as in Germany; theology teaching in British universities is academic rather than confessional. Though a handful of professorial chairs are annexed to cathedral canonries and therefore, in principle, open only to members of the Church of England,[1134] university teaching posts in theology are normally open to those of all faiths and none and theology/religious studies is regarded as an academic discipline like any other.

IV. Chaplaincy

512. Chaplaincy is largely a matter for the individual religious organisations and the individual universities;[1135] and its extent and nature vary widely between institutions because the institutions themselves vary so widely. In a modern provincial university, chaplaincy will most likely be provided by the churches themselves: there will probably be full- or half-time Roman Catholic, Church of England and Free Church chaplains, supplemented by unpaid chaplains from the other local churches. Some universities have 'historic' arrangements with particular denominations to provide a chaplain; and in many cases the costs for such an appointment are shared, so that the chaplain's stipend might be paid by the university and his or her housing provided by the Church in question.

1133. W. Rüegg, ed., *A History of the University in Europe Volume 3: Universities in the Nineteenth and Early Twentieth Centuries (1800–1945)* 6 (Cambridge University Press 2004). The exception is the University of Strasbourg, which teaches both Catholic and Protestant theology.

1134. Four at Oxford and one at Durham, though until recently the Oxford Chair in Ecclesiastical History and the accompanying canonry at Christ Church were held by a lay Roman Catholic, Professor Henry Mayr-Harting. In 2008 Durham established the Bede Chair in Catholic Theology, partly funded by the University and partly by various Roman Catholic trusts: its first occupant is a Roman Catholic.

1135. *See* M. Hill, *Chaplaincy Services in Public Institutions in England: History, Law and Practice*, in *Spiritual Care in Public Insituitions in Europe* (J. Tretera & Z. Horak eds, Wissenschafts-Verlag. 2019) 21.
For discussion of chaplaincy in prisons, hospitals and the armed forces, *see* Part XI, Ch. 3.

513. The major exceptions are Oxford, Cambridge and, to a lesser extent, Durham, where most of the constituent colleges either became Church of England foundations at the Reformation or were founded as Church of England institutions subsequent to it. With a handful of exceptions, religious provision is that of the Church of England under their Statutes and almost all have a college chapel and at least a half-time chaplaincy post, usually funded from the resources of the college. The other denominations appoint chaplains to the three universities as a whole.

Part X. Matrimonial and Family Law

Chapter 1. Legal Position of Religious Marriage

§1. International and Historical Background

514. The ECHR includes a number of rights that protect family life, most notably Articles 8 and 12.[1136] Article 8 provides the right to respect for private and family life, including home and correspondence. This right is qualified in much the same way as Article 9.[1137] Article 12 provides a right for men and women of marriageable age to marry and found a family according to the national laws governing the exercise of this right.

515. These Articles, buttressed by the Human Rights Act 1998, have had a major effect upon matrimonial and family law in the United Kingdom. In particular, the ECHR has 'heralded both a statutory and a judicial change towards discrimination against same-sex couples'.[1138] Strasbourg decisions have held several pieces of UK legislation discriminating against homosexuals to be unlawful.[1139] Moreover, domestic case law has recognised that the concept of family and home life has broadened (so as to include, for example, those in a same-sex relationship) and that there is a positive duty on the State to ensure that legislation is compatible with this broadened concept.[1140]

1136. *See Marriage in Anglican and Roman Catholic Canon Law* (N. Doe ed., Centre for Law and Religion 2009).

1137. *See* Part II.

1138. N. Gray & D. Brazil, *Blackstone's Guide to the Civil Partnership Act 2004* at 2 (Oxford University Press 2005).

1139. *Dudgeon v. United Kingdom* (1981) 4 EHRR 149; *Sunderland v. UK* (1997) 24 EHRR 22; *Smith and Grady v. UK* (2000) 29 EHRR 493.

1140. As Lady Hale observed in *Ghaidan v. Godin Mendoza* [2004] UKHL 30 '*Homosexual couples can have exactly the same sort of inter-dependent couple relationship as heterosexuals can. Sexual "orientation" defines the sort of person with whom one wishes to have sexual relations. It requires another person to express itself. Some people, whether heterosexual or homosexual, may be satisfied with casual or transient relationships. But most human beings eventually want more than that. They want love. And with love they often want not only the warmth but also the sense of belonging to one another which is the essence of being a couple. And many couples also come to want the stability and permanence which go with sharing a home and a life together, with or without the children who for many people go to make a family. In this, people of homosexual orientation are no different from people of heterosexual orientation*' (at para. 142).

516. Changes in social *mores* have resulted in legislative developments, chiefly the Civil Partnership Act 2004, the Marriage (Same-Sex Couples) Act 2013 and, most recently, the Civil Partnerships, Marriages and Deaths (Registrations etc.) Act 2019. Current statistics reveal that whilst married or civil partner couples remain the most common family type, representing two-thirds of families in the UK, there has been a significant increase in the number of non-married cohabitees, as well as those living alone.[1141] In 2019, there were 212,000 same-sex families in the UK, having increased by 40% since 2015. The proportion of same-sex cohabiting couples has decreased from 59.6% in 2015 to 51.6% in 2019 as a result of the growing number of same-sex married couple families.[1142] These developments have made significant changes to an area of the law which had been shaped by a strong historical Christian influence.

517. From the mid-twelfth century, the ecclesiastical courts had exclusive jurisdiction over marriage and divorce, applying Roman Canon Law. Although the Reformation in the sixteenth century had little effect in terms of the structure of the courts or the principles applied, change occurred over time with jurisdiction passing to the civil courts. In the seventeenth century, civil impediments to marriage became recognised in addition to existing canonical impediments, while the Matrimonial Causes Act 1857 transferred jurisdiction over matrimonial causes from the ecclesiastical courts of the Church of England to the High Court. Yet the import of the ecclesiastical courts did not completely disappear. For example, section 22 of the Matrimonial Causes Act 1857 provided that the proceedings and actions of the courts of the State should be 'conformable to the Principles and Rules on which the Ecclesiastical Courts have heretofore acted and given Relief'.

518. The modern law dates back to the eighteenth century. Prior to that there were various ways of solemnising marriage, religious and non-religious. In addition to a sacramental marriage church ceremony following the publication of banns or special licence,[1143] non-religious ways, such as oral declarations by the parties, were also valid. The purpose of Lord Hardwicke's Marriage Act 1753 was to regularise the performance and registration of marriages and to prescribe certain obligatory preliminaries. The Act required a public religious ceremony in the parish church of the Church of England according to authorised rites at which a clergyman would officiate; and that the marriage be preceded by banns or licence. Breach of any of these requirements, which had previously made a marriage irregular, thenceforward rendered it void.[1144]

519. The only groups excepted from these requirements were Jews and Quakers. The Marriage Act 1753 provided that their marriages could take place in accordance with their own traditions. All other religious groups, such as Roman Catholics and other Protestant denominations, had no such exception: they had to marry

1141. Families and households in the UK: 2019, Office for National Statistics.
1142. *Ibid.*
1143. *See* M. Hill, *Ecclesiastical Law* 5.36–5.42 (4th ed., Oxford University Press 2018).
1144. N. Lowe & G. Douglas, *Bromley's Family Law* 72 (11th ed., Oxford University Press 2015).

according to the rites of the Church of England.[1145] The Marriage Act 1836, some eighty years later, made such exceptional provision by its introduction of the concept of civil marriage. Together with the Births, Deaths and Registration Act 1836, the Marriage Act 1836 permitted valid marriages to take place in registry offices following a civil ceremony in the presence of a Registrar and two witnesses. Furthermore, places of worship other than those of the Church of England could be registered for the purpose of the solemnisation of marriage.[1146]

§2. Marriage Law

I. Traditional Marriage in England and Wales

520. Marriage has been traditionally defined as a voluntary and lifelong monogamous union between a man and a woman, each over the age of sixteen who are not within the prohibited degrees. The requirements for a valid marriage under English law were historically those required for a Christian marriage. This is epitomised by the classic definition of marriage in English law provided by Lord Penzance in *Hyde v. Hyde*[1147] which stated that:

> marriage, as understood in Christendom, may … be defined as the voluntary union of one man and one woman to the exclusion of all others.

Lord Penzance held that a polygamous marriage would not be recognised since it belonged 'to a system so utterly at variance with the Christian conception of marriage'. That position, however, has been somewhat modified by virtue of the Matrimonial Causes Act 1973, section 47(1), which permits a court to grant matrimonial relief and/or a declaration concerning the validity of a marriage notwithstanding the fact that a party to the marriage is, or has during the subsistence of the marriage been, married to more than one person. Section 11(d) provides that a marriage celebrated after 31 July 1971 shall be void 'in the case of a polygamous marriage entered into outside England and Wales, that either party was at the time of the marriage domiciled in England and Wales'. In *R v. Yilkyes Finok Bala and Others,*[1148] the Court of Appeal observed that the 'implicit corollary' of section 11(d) is that 'where *neither* party is domiciled in the United Kingdom at the time of the relevant polygamous marriage, valid under the law of the place of celebration, then the marriage- assuming no other incapacity- *will* be recognised as valid in English law'.[1149]

1145. C. Hamilton, *Family, Law and Religion* 43 (Sweet & Maxwell 1995).
1146. *See also* Part III.
1147. (1866) LR 1 P&D 130, 133. For a more recent analysis of the law in this area, see *NB v MI* [2021] EWHC 224 (Fam)
1148. [2016] EWCA Crim 560.
1149. [2016] EWCA Crim 560, at para. 67 (emphasis added). For an analysis of the case, *see* C Grout, *Marriage, Polygamy and the Criminal Law of Conspiracy*, 20 Ecclesiastical Law Journal 3–15 (2018).

521. Certain legal requirements for a marriage have also been modified. The Age of Marriage Act 1929 raised the minimum age formerly prescribed by the Canon Law of the Church of England and common law which had linked the minimum age to the presumed ages of puberty.[1150] Although the prohibited degrees of consanguinity[1151] and affinity[1152] have a clear religious base (with the degrees of affinity being set forth in *Leviticus*), a divergence has arisen between those of the Church and those of the State. Both the Marriage (Prohibited Degrees of Relationship) Act 1986 and the Marriage Act 1949 (Remedial) Order 2006 permit parish priests of the Church of England to refuse to marry those related by affinity whose marriage would have been void but for that Act, and to prohibit the use of the parish church accordingly. Changes made by the Gender Recognition Act 2004 do not alter the law on capacity to marry but do provide a means whereby a transgender individual may obtain a gender recognition certificate and in consequence enter into a marriage in his or her acquired gender.[1153] The conscience clause whereby a cleric can refuse to marry a divorced person[1154] extends also in the case of one who has the benefit of a gender recognition certificate.[1155]

522. The current law can be found in consolidated form in the Marriage Act 1949.[1156] The Act differentiates between marriages solemnised according to the rites of the Church of England[1157] (which for these purposes is deemed to include the Church in Wales)[1158] and marriages otherwise solemnised.[1159]

523. In relation to the Church of England, it is commonly understood that parishioners enjoy a legal right to be married in the parish church, deriving from Lord Hardwicke's Clandestine Marriage Act 1753.[1160] The case of *Argar v. Holdsworth*[1161] is usually taken as authority for the proposition that a minister of a parish commits an ecclesiastical offence if he fails to solemnise the marriage of a parishioner, there being no legal prohibition. Although doubts have been expressed on the basis that the case is authority only in relation to marriage by licence and not marriage by banns[1162] and differences between the original documents of the case and the case report,[1163] it is still widely understood that parishioners have the right

1150. That is, fourteen for boys; twelve for girls.
1151. That is, relationship by blood.
1152. That is, relationship by marriage.
1153. *See* S. Gilmore, *The Gender Recognition Act 2004*, Family Law 741 (2004).
1154. Matrimonial Causes Act 1965 s. 8(2), discussed below.
1155. Marriage Act 1949 s. 5B(1), as amended by the Gender Recognition Act 2004 s. 11, Sch. 4.
1156. N. Lowe & G. Douglas, *Bromley's Family Law* 49 (11th ed., Oxford University Press 2015).
1157. Regulated by Part II.
1158. Marriage Act 1949 s. 78(2). By virtue of the Welsh Church (Temporalities) Act 1919, nothing in the Welsh Church Act 1914 affects marriages in Wales.
1159. Regulated by Part III.
1160. M. Hill, *Ecclesiastical Law* 5.29 (4th ed., Oxford University Press 2018).
1161. (1758) 2 Lee 515.
1162. N. Doe, *The Legal Framework of the Church of England: A Critical Study in a Comparative Context* 359–360 (Clarendon Press 1996).
1163. M. Smith, *An Interpretation of Argar v. Holdsworth*, 5 Ecclesiastical Law Journal 39–41 (1998).

to have their marriages solemnised in the parish church.[1164] Indeed, in *R (Baiai, Trzcinska, Bigoku & Tilki) v. Secretary of State for the Home Department*[1165] the House of Lords acknowledged that 'the Church of England believes itself (with some Parliamentary encouragement …) required to marry for the first time anyone who lives in the parish regardless of faith or the lack of it'.[1166] This statement has been criticised on the basis that the obligation is not 'the exercise of self-belief on the part of an ecclesial community' but is rather 'part of the law of the land'.[1167] Under the provisions of the Church of England Marriage Measure 2008, the categories of persons entitled to be married in the parish church extended beyond 'parishioner' to include others having certain 'qualifying connections'.[1168]

524. The Marriage Act 1949 (as amended) provides that marriages may be solemnised according to the usages of the Society of Friends,[1169] or according to the usages of the Jews.[1170] Marriages may also take place where a housebound or detained person currently resides,[1171] in a building which is certified as a place of religious worship[1172] and registered for the solemnisation of marriage,[1173] in naval, military and air force chapels,[1174] in register offices[1175] or in approved places.[1176]

525. There exists, however, a discrete problem in relation to unregistered religious marriages, a typical example being, in the context of an Islamic marriage, where the couple participate in a nikah ceremony but subsequently fail to register the marriage under civil law. Such was the case in *Her Majesty's Attorney General v. Akhter & Anor*[1177] where the Court of Appeal concluded that such unregistered religious marriages are to be regarded as 'non-qualifying ceremonies' which are outside the scope of marriage legislation. This is significant because it means, among other things, that parties in such a position will not be able to seek financial remedy orders upon the breakdown of the relationship. The Marriage Act 1949 (Amendment) Bill, a Private Members Bill currently before Parliament, seeks to deal with the issue by making it an offence to purport to solemnise an unregistered religious marriage. This, however, assumes that the issue lies with celebrants, is unlikely to

---

1164. J. Humphreys, *The Right to Marry in the Parish Church: A Rehabilitation of Argar v. Holdsworth*, 7 Ecclesiastical Law Journal 405 (2004).
1165. [2008] UKHL 53.
1166. At para. 37 *per* Baroness Hale of Richmond.
1167. M. Hill, *Editorial*, 11 Ecclesiastical Law Journal 1, 2 (2009).
1168. *See* S. Slack, *The Right to Marry in Accordance with the Rites and Ceremonies of the Church of England*, in *Marriage in Anglican and Roman Catholic Canon Law* 6 (N. Doe ed., Centre for Law and Religion 2009). Similar legislation has been passed in respect of the Church in Wales: Marriage (Wales) Act 2010.
1169. Marriage Act 1949 s. 47.
1170. But only between two persons professing the Jewish religion: Marriage Act 1949 s. 26(1)(d).
1171. Marriage Act 1949 s. 26(1)(dd).
1172. Pursuant to the Places of Worship Registration Act 1855.
1173. Pursuant to Marriage Act 1949 ss 41–42.
1174. *Ibid.*, Part V.
1175. *Ibid.*, ss 45–46.
1176. Pursuant to Marriage Act 1949 s. 46A and B (inserted by Marriage Act 1994).
1177. [2020] EWCA Civ 122.

stop the practice and would fail to provide a remedy for those in unregistered marriages on relationship breakdown. A preferable solution would, it seems, be to deal with this in the context of cohabitation law reform.

526. In relation to civil marriages (those that occur in a register office or in approved premises) no religious service may be used.[1178] A building with a recent or continuing religious connection cannot be an approved premise.[1179] Although a religious ceremony may follow,[1180] it is the civil ceremony which is legally binding.[1181] In December 2014, the government published its response to the consultation on 'marriages by non-religious belief organisations'. The consultation sought views on whether the law should be changed to permit non-religious belief organisations (e.g., humanists) to conduct marriages in England and Wales. It also examined which organisations would be able to conduct such marriages if there was a change in the law and how such a change should be implemented. The majority of people who responded to the consultation were in favour of changing the law to allow non-religious belief ceremonies, and for those ceremonies to take place in unrestricted locations (including out of doors).[1182] In September 2020, the Law Commission published a consultation paper with provisional proposals for reform and questions for consultees. The consultation period ended in January 2021 and the Law Commission's recommendations are awaited.[1183]

II. Same-Sex Marriage

527. Prior to the introduction of same-sex marriage, the only way for a same-sex couple to formalise their relationship was by entering into a civil partnership. Civil partnerships, which have recently been extended to include opposite-sex couples, are discussed in detail in section 4 below. The options available to same-sex couples has now widened so as to include marriage. In September 2011, the Home Office announced that a public consultation to consider how to make civil marriage available to same-sex couples would begin in March 2012. The Home Office website stated that the 'consultation will cover civil marriage for same-sex

1178. Marriage Act 1949, s. 45A(4).

1179. Marriages and Civil Partnerships (Approved Premises) Regulations 2005/3168, Sch. 1.

1180. Marriage Act 1949, s. 46.

1181. *Ibid.*, s. 45(2); 46.

1182. Marriages by Non-Religious Belief Organisations: Summary of Written Responses to the Consultation and Government Response, Ministry of Justice (18 December 2014).

1183. *See* https://www.lawcom.gov.uk/project/weddings/, accessed 23 May 2020. *Getting Married: A Consultation Paper on Weddings Law* (Law Commission Consultation Paper No. 247). *See* further the judgment of the High Court in *The Queen (on the application of Harrison and Others) v. Secretary of State for Justice* [2020] EWHC 2096 (Admin) where Eady J held that the failure of English law to recognise weddings carried out in accordance with Humanist beliefs, whilst prima facie discriminatory, was justified by reference to a legitimate aim, namely the need to address differences in treatment as part of a wholesale reform of the law of marriage. Given the ongoing review by the Law Commission, the Court was satisfied that the Secretary of State had established that a fair balance was currently struck between the individual rights of the Claimants and wider community interests.

couples only – not religious marriage or opposite-sex civil partnerships'. However, the Consultation Paper included a question which asked whether respondents agreed or disagreed with the Government's proposal not to open up religious marriage to same-sex couples. The Government's response to the consultation revealed that the majority of the respondents who directly answered this question disagreed with the proposal and wanted religious marriage ceremonies to be available to same-sex couples.[1184] Those quoted in favour of same-sex religious marriage, which included campaign groups such as Stonewall and Liberty and a number of religious organisations, saw this as a question of religious freedom. Those who disagreed with same-sex religious marriage, such as the Church of England[1185] and the Muslim Council of Britain, expressed concern that they would be pressured or forced to conduct such ceremonies either under domestic law or following a ruling of the European Court of Human Rights.

528. The Government's response was to accept the argument that 'religious organisations should be permitted to conduct such ceremonies if they wish to' but that it would remain 'unlawful for a religious organisation to marry same-sex couples unless it expressly consents and opts in according to a formal process put in place by legislation'.[1186] The Government proposed a 'quadruple lock' providing four statutory provisions which would protect those religious organisations which did not wish to marry same-sex couples. The first 'lock' would be an explicit statement that no religious organisation or individual minister can be compelled to marry same-sex couples or to permit this to happen on their premises. The second 'lock' would make it unlawful for religious organisations or their ministers to marry same-sex couples unless they have expressly opted in to do so. The third 'lock' would amend the Equality Act 2010 to state that no discrimination claim could be brought against religious organisations or individual members for refusing to marry a same-sex couple or allowing their premises to be used for this purpose. The fourth 'lock' would state that the legislation did not apply to the Church of England and the Church in Wales, meaning that it would continue to be illegal for those churches to marry same-sex couples or to opt-in to do so.[1187]

529. According to the Government's Response, the fourth 'lock' recognises the 'unique position of the Church of England as the Established Church'.[1188] The Response's discussion of this focused on the fact that the legislation of same-sex marriage would lead to a conflict between the law in England and the Canon Law of the Church. Canons cannot be contrary to the customs, laws, statutes or the royal

1184. H M Government, *Equal Marriage: The Government's Response* 16 (December 2012).

1185. For an analysis of how the Church of England has grappled with the issue of same-sex marriage generally, *see* C. Smith, *The Church of England and Same-Sex Marriage: Beyond a Rights-Based Analysis*, 21 Ecclesiastical Law Journal 153–178 (2019).

1186. *Ibid.*, 17.

1187. These proposed locks marked a significant departure from Government thinking at an earlier time when the Minister assured the House of Lords that similar provisions were unnecessary during a debate on the annulment of the Marriages and Civil Partnerships (Approved Premises) Amendment Regulations 2011: HL Deb 15 December 2011, Col 1408–1447.

1188. *Ibid.*, 18.

prerogative of the realm under the Submission of the Clergy Act 1533. As the Response pointed out, such conflicts had previously been dealt with by means of conscience clauses, and here the conflict would be avoided by ensuring that 'the legislation does not interfere with the Canon Law understanding of marriage …, which we accept will be narrower than that of the civil law'. Oddly, the Response did not discuss the reason why the Church of England and the Church in Wales require special legal treatment, namely the understanding that parishioners have a legal right to be married in the Church of England (and the Church in Wales). This would mean that any extension of the legal definition of marriage to include same-sex unions would have automatically introduced a legal right to have such marriages conducted in the parish church.

530. The Marriage (Same-Sex Couples) Act 2013 largely followed the conclusions reached in the Government's Response to the consultation. The Act makes the marriage of same-sex couples lawful, creating an opt-in system for religious same-sex marriages. All parts of the 'quadruple lock' are present. No person or religious organisation is to be compelled to undertake an opt-in activity or to conduct at, consent to, be present at, carry out, or otherwise participate in a same-sex marriage where the reason for not doing that is that the relevant marriage concerns a same-sex couple.[1189] An opt-in is required before same-sex marriage can occur in places of worship and other religious ceremonies.[1190] This opt-in system does not apply to 'marriages solemnised according to the rites of the Church of England'.[1191]

531. The Equality Act 2010 was amended in two notable respects. First, the rule in section 110 (that states that an employee will remain personally liable for unlawful acts committed in the course of employment where the employer is also liable) was amended so that it does not apply in relation to refusing to conduct, consent to, be present at, carry out, or otherwise participate in a same-sex marriage where the reason for not doing so is that the relevant marriage concerns a same-sex couple.[1192] Second, a new Part 6A was added to Schedule 3 to the Equality Act to provide that it is not discrimination in relation to goods and service where a person does not conduct, consent to, be present at, carry out, or otherwise participate in a same-sex marriage where the reason for not doing so is that the relevant marriage concerns a same-sex couple.[1193]

532. Further, it is expressly provided that no Canon of the Church of England is to be considered contrary to the Submission of the Clergy Act 1533 'by virtue of its making provision about marriage being the union of one man with one woman'.[1194] Moreover, unlike the Government's response, reference is expressly made to the understanding that parishioners have a legal right to be married in their parish church: it is stated that 'Any duty of a member of the clergy to solemnize marriages

1189. Marriage (Same Sex Couples) Act 2013, s. 2.
1190. *Ibid.*, ss 3, 4 and 5.
1191. Section 4(5).
1192. Section 2(5).
1193. Section 2(6).
1194. Section 1(3).

(and any corresponding right of persons to have their marriages solemnized by members of the clergy) is not extended by this Act to marriages of same-sex couples'.[1195]

533. The Act provides that 'in the law of England and Wales, marriage has the same effect in relation to same-sex couples as it has in relation to opposite sex couples' and this applies to all 'legislation whenever passed or made'.[1196] However this does not apply to Measures and Canons of the Church of England (whenever passed), subordinate legislation (whenever passed) made under a Measure or Canon of the Church of England or 'other ecclesiastical law (whether or not contained in England and Wales legislation, and, if contained in England and Wales legislation, whenever passed or made'.[1197]

The main difference between the 'quadruple lock' in the Act as opposed to the Government's earlier response is the inclusion of a power which requires the Lord Chancellor to make an order to allow for same-sex marriage in the Church in Wales if he is satisfied that the Governing Body of the Church has resolved that the law ought to be changed.[1198] This provision enables the Church in Wales to conduct same-sex marriages in the future if it so desires. The section (introduced at the request of the Church in Wales) was thought to be necessary since if the Church of England later decides to permit same-sex marriage, it is able to put legislation before Parliament in the form of Measures; by contrast, any similar change of position by the Church in Wales would have needed primary legislation if it were not for this provision. In 2015, the Governing Body of the Church voted sixty-one in favour of same-sex marriages in church, nine in favour of blessing same-sex partnerships and fifty for making no change at all. The results were said to be too close to justify a change. However, in 2018, the Governing Body of the Church agreed, by seventy-six votes to twenty-one, that the lack of formal provision for same-sex couples was 'pastorally unsustainable'.[1199] Nevertheless, to date no changes have been made by the Church in Wales to accommodate same-sex marriages.

III. Marriage in Scotland

534. In Scotland, as in England and Wales, marriage prior to the Reformation was governed by Western Canon Law.[1200] The two systems then diverged; and marriage law in Scotland developed to include features not shared with the law of England and Wales. In addition to marriages solemnised by the Church, Scots law has traditionally recognised three classes of 'irregular' marriage as legally valid:

1195. Section 1(4).
1196. Section 11(1)–(2).
1197. Section 11(6).
1198. Section 8.
1199. *Welsh Governing Body: No Provision for Same-Sex Couples Is 'Pastorally Unsustainable and Unjust'*, Church Times, 21 September 2018.
1200. An echo of this remains in the use of the expression 'consistorial jurisdiction' to describe what in England and Wales would be called 'matrimonial causes'. Part III of the Domicile and Matrimonial Proceedings Act 1973 is headed 'Jurisdiction in consistorial causes (Scotland)'.

marriage by declaration *de praesenti*, marriage by promise *subsequente copula* and marriage by cohabitation with 'habit and repute'. The first two were abolished by the Marriage (Scotland) Act 1939 and are of historical interest only. The third, however, persisted until its abolition by section 3 of the Family Law (Scotland) Act 2006.

535. Couples are still able to rely on the principle of habit and repute provided that their cohabitation began before 4 May 2006, the date on which the Act commenced. Moreover, the commencement of the Act did not render invalid subsisting marriages by habit and repute.[1201] Such a marriage subsists where the couple have set up home together without going through any form of ceremony and, being free to marry, are generally regarded as husband and wife. There is no minimum period for cohabitation[1202] but the couple must not only behave as husband and wife but must also be so regarded by the wider community.[1203]

536. Marriages generally, whether civil or religious, are regulated by the Marriage (Scotland) Act 1977. In either case the first step is for the parties each to submit to the district registrar a notice of intention to marry, accompanied by birth certificates and, if necessary, evidence of the dissolution of any previous marriage. If there is no legal impediment, the registrar will issue a marriage schedule, normally after two weeks have elapsed from the date of application. Unlike in England and Wales, in Scotland it is the marriage schedule that provides the authority to conduct a civil marriage or to solemnise a religious one. The Church of Scotland responded to the introduction of the marriage schedule by passing Act III of 1978, repealing the Act anent Proclamation of Banns but at the same time making provision for 'any person usually resident in Scotland and requiring proclamation of banns in order to be married furth of Scotland to have banns proclaimed in any parish church within the registration district within which he or she normally resides'. Where the celebrant of a religious marriage is a minister of the Church of Scotland or of another prescribed religious body, the ceremony is conducted according to the rites of the religious body in question and Scots law recognises that as sufficient. In any other case there is a statutory requirement as to the elements which the ceremony must include in order to effect a valid marriage. At the end of the ceremony the marriage schedule is completed by the officiant, the couple and the witnesses and returned to the district registrar for registration.

537. The Marriage (Scotland) Act 1977 was amended by virtue of the Marriage and Civil Partnership (Scotland) Act 2014 which makes provision for, among other things, same-sex marriage in Scotland. In 2017, the Scottish Episcopal Church voted to allow same-sex couples to marry in its churches, making it the first major

---

1201. A valid marriage by habit and repute remains possible under s. 3(3) and (4) in relation to certain invalid marriages contracted furth of Scotland.

1202. *Kamperman v. MacIver* 1994 SLT 763, in which it was held that cohabitation for less than a year after an impediment to marriage had been removed was sufficient to establish 'habit and repute'.

1203. In *Ackerman v. Logan's Executors* 2002 SLT 37, though the wider community regarded the couple as married the close family members of the deceased did not – and the views of close family members prevailed with the court.

Christian church in the UK to do so. Its (revised) Code of Canons 2019 amended its definition of marriage so as to include same-sex marriages whilst at the same time recognising that 'no cleric of this Church shall be obliged to conduct any marriage against their conscience'.[1204] Conversely, at present, the law of the Church of Scotland only allows ministers and deacons to marry opposite-sex couples.[1205] In 2018, the General Assembly of the Church of Scotland voted to instruct the Legal Questions Committee of the Church to prepare legislation which, if accepted, would allow ministers and deacons to apply for a licence to conduct same-sex marriages if they wished to do so. The Committee was due to report to the 2020 General Assembly although was unable to do so owing to the cancellation of the latter because of the disruption caused by COVID-19. It is likely, therefore, that the matter will be addressed during2021. Thereafter, consideration will have to be given by the Church of Scotland as to whether, and if so to what extent, its law on marriage should be changed.

§3. Divorce Law

I. General Position

538. In English and Scots civil law, a marriage is terminated by death, dissolution or annulment. A marriage (otherwise valid) is dissolved by a decree absolute when it is established that there has been an irretrievable breakdown.[1206] A marriage is null (invalid) when a declaration of nullity has been made by a competent court in the United Kingdom. Generally, the law of the State does not recognise religious divorces.[1207] A divorce effected exclusively under religious law will have no direct civil effect. Under civil law, following either a civil annulment or a civil dissolution, parties are free to enter a second marriage. If parties obtain a religious divorce, they might regard themselves as free to contract a second marriage, but the State, in the absence of a civil divorce, will regard the parties as still legally married and a second marriage will be regarded as bigamous.

539. Divorce law, generally, came under public scrutiny as a result of the proceedings which led to the judgment of the Supreme Court in *Owens v. Owens*.[1208] Although divorce petitions are rarely defended, *Owens* was a case to the contrary. Whilst the trial judge found as facts that: (i) the marriage had broken down, (ii) Mrs.

1204. Scottish Episcopal Church Code of Canons 2019, Canon 31.

1205. Recognition of Marriage Services Act (Act I 1977).

1206. *See* Matrimonial Causes Act 1973, s. 1: this is evidenced by proof of: adultery; unreasonable behaviour; desertion; two years separation; or five years separation. Divorce in Scotland is regulated by the Divorce (Scotland) Act 1976; irretrievable breakdown is evidenced by the adultery of the defender, unreasonable behaviour, non-cohabitation for one year combined with the defender's consent to divorce and non-cohabitation for two years. It is also a ground for divorce (or dissolution of a civil partnership) that either party has been issued with an interim gender recognition certificate since the marriage or civil partnership registration.

1207. The approach to religious divorces effected abroad, however, seems to be more liberal: *Qureshi v. Qureshi* [1971] 1 All ER 325.

1208. [2018] UKSC 41.

Owens could not continue to live with Mr Owens, and (iii) insofar as Mr Owens believed otherwise, he was deluding himself, the judge nevertheless concluded that the statutory criteria for granting a divorce had not been made out and refused the petition. Appeals to both the Court of Appeal and the Supreme Court were unsuccessful. The latter, however, observed that Parliament may wish to consider changing the law so as to enable people in the position of Mrs. Owens to obtain a divorce (i.e., without having to satisfy the present statutory criteria).[1209]

540. Consequently, the Divorce, Dissolution and Separation Act 2020 came into force on 25 June 2020. The Act effectively introduces the concept of 'no fault divorce' whereby either or both parties to a marriage can simply state that the marriage has irretrievably broken down without having to attribute blame. Moreover, there will be no opportunity to defend the request for a 'divorce order' as a statement by the applicant(s) that the marriage has irretrievably broken down will be conclusive evidence as to that fact.[1210]

541. The stance of some religious organisations in the United Kingdom towards divorce and remarriage is complex. While civil divorce is a necessity under civil law to contract a second valid marriage, civil divorce is not recognised by some religions as sufficient to dissolve a religious marriage. Under religious law (particularly Jewish law), parties may be required to obtain a religious divorce before remarrying in a religious ceremony. What follows is a discussion of two particular points of interest.

II. Remarriage in Church

542. In neither the Church of England nor the Church in Wales is there a prohibition against a second ecclesiastical marriage following a civil annulment. Unlike many other Anglican churches neither has a system of nullity.

543. However, as discussed above, it is commonly understood that there is a legal right to be married in the parish church of both churches. Section 8(2) of the Matrimonial Causes Act 1965 provides that no member of the clergy is to be compelled to solemnise the marriage of any person whose former marriage has been dissolved and whose former spouse is still living or to permit the marriage of such a person to be solemnised in his or her church or chapel.[1211]

544. Church of Scotland ministers may lawfully solemnise the marriage of a divorced person whose former spouse is still alive; however, this is not a matter of routine. A marriage in such circumstances should only take place after the minister

1209. *Ibid.*, para. 45.

1210. Divorce, Dissolution and Separation Act 2020, s. 1.

1211. *See* M. Hill, *Ecclesiastical Law* 5.48 & 5.49 (4th ed., Oxford University Press 2018). Although many diocesan bishops offer written guidance on the matter, the conscience clause is a legal right vested in the individual cleric. For discussion of the Church in Wales, *see* N. Doe, *The Law of the Church in Wales* 266–269 (University of Wales Press 2002).

has taken 'all reasonable steps' to obtain adequate information about the life and character of the parties to be married, the grounds and circumstances of the divorce case, facts bearing upon the future well-being of any children concerned, whether any other minister of religion has declined to solemnise the proposed marriage and the denomination to which the parties belong. Special care shall be taken in cases where one or both parties belong to a denomination whose discipline may differ from that of the Church of Scotland. The minister should also guard against any danger of scandal arising from the solemnisation of a remarriage. In any event, no minister is required to solemnise a remarriage against his or her conscience.[1212]

III. Religious Divorces in Judaism and Islam

545. Under Jewish law only a husband can divorce his wife (by giving a *get*). The refusal to give a get notwithstanding the fact that the wife had obtained a divorce under English law means that the woman was still seen as married in the eyes of the Jewish faith and therefore unable to remarry under Jewish law. The husband could withhold a get to seek advantage as to the financial settlement in the divorce.[1213] The Divorce (Religious Marriages) Act 2002, by substituting a new section 10A into the Matrimonial Causes Act 1973, overcame this by providing that if a marriage was solemnised in accordance with the usages of the Jews (or any other prescribed religious usages),[1214] the court can refuse to issue a decree absolute until a get has been granted.[1215] Section 3A of the Divorce (Scotland) Act 1976[1216] makes similar provision in relation to Scotland. In a high-profile case in January 2020, a woman in London obtained a get from her husband after commencing a private prosecution against him for controlling or coercive behaviour contrary to section 76 of the Serious Crime Act 2015 (*see* Part VII). The husband was due to face a Crown Court trial, but the woman discontinued proceedings after the get was granted.

546. With regard to divorce under Islamic law, the husband must repudiate the wife by *talaq*. This may take a variety of forms, the major differences being the length of time before the *talaq* takes effect: sometimes immediately after its pronouncement, sometimes three-and-a-half months later. Muslim women may divorce their husbands, but in very limited circumstances: usually, when provision is made for this in the marriage contract. A wife may also obtain divorce through mutual agreement, but must normally pay a sum in return for the agreement of the husband

1212. Act XXVI of 1959 (Anent Re-marriage of Divorced Persons) (as amended).
1213. *See*, e.g., *Brett v. Brett* [1969] 1 All ER 1007.
1214. As yet no other religious usage has been prescribed.
1215. *See* M. Freeman, *Is the Jewish Get Any Business of the State?*, in *Law and Religion* 365 (R. O'Dair & A. Lewis eds, Oxford University Press 2001). A practical example of this provision being used as a successful 'bargaining chip' in ancillary relief proceedings may be found in the judgment of Baker J in *AI v. MT* [2013] EWHC 100 (Fam). The court's powers in relation to a get are not, however, confined to those set out in s. 10A of the Matrimonial Causes Act 1973. The court has, for example, the jurisdiction to order periodical payments to continue until the husband has taken the steps necessary to secure the grant of a get- *see Moher v. Moher* [2020] Fam 160.
1216. Inserted by s. 15 of the Family Law (Scotland) Act 2006.

to release her.[1217] Although it would be open to use the mechanism provided in the Divorce (Religious Marriages) Act 2002 in relation to securing a *talaq*, the Muslim community has not yet requested this of the Government.

§4. Civil Partnerships

I. Formation

547. Historically, under the Civil Partnership Act 2004, a civil partnership was 'a relationship between two people of the same sex' which is either formed 'when they register as civil partners of each other' or 'by virtue of having registered an overseas relationship'.[1218,1219] The restrictions on who could enter a civil partnership replicated those for marriage but for the requirement that the partners had to be of the same sex.[1220] Civil partners must be over 16 years old. Those under 18 years old need parental consent. They must not be married or in a subsisting civil partnership. They must not be within the prohibited degrees of relationship.

548. The formation of a civil partnership is analogous to the solemnisation of a civil marriage but while in a wedding ceremony it is the exchanging of vows that form the marriage,[1221] a civil partnership is formed once both partners have signed the civil partnership document before witnesses.[1222] Moreover, as with civil marriages, 'No religious service is to be used while the civil partnership registrar is officiating the signing of a civil partnership document'.[1223] It was originally the case that civil partnerships could not be registered at religious premises. However, section 202 of the Equality Act 2010 removed this requirement and permitted Regulations to be enacted.[1224] Section 3A of the Civil Partnership Act 2004 now states that 'for the avoidance of doubt, nothing in this Act places an obligation on religious organisations to host civil partnerships if they do not wish to do so'.

549. A Pastoral Statement issued by the House of Bishops of the Church of England on 25 July 2005 'affirms' that clergy of the Church of England should not provide services of blessing for those who have registered a civil partnership but 'where clergy are approached by people asking for prayer in relation to entering into a civil partnership they should respond pastorally and sensitively in the light of the

1217. *See* R. Arlow, *The Secular Approach to the Religious Dissolution of Marriage* (University of Wales, LLM Dissertation 2003).
1218. *See* J. Humphreys, *The Civil Partnership Act 2004, Same-Sex Marriage and the Church of England*, 8 Ecclesiastical Law Journal 289 (2006) and M. Hill, *Church, State and Civil Partners: Establishment and Social Mores in Tension*, in *Law and Religion: New Horizons* 57 (N. Doe & R. Sandberg eds, Peeters 2010).
1219. Civil Partnership Act 2004, s. 1(1).
1220. *See* Civil Partnership Act 2004, ss 3 and 4.
1221. Marriage Act 1949 s. 44(1), (3).
1222. Civil Partnership Act 2004, s. 2(1).
1223. *Ibid.*, s. 2(5).
1224. This power was exercised in the Marriages and Civil Partnerships (Approved Premises) (Amendment) Regulations 2011.

circumstances of each case'.[1225] This has been interpreted as meaning that clerics are 'canonically restrained from blessing a same-sex union'.[1226] On the basis that the services normally thought of as 'Blessings' are otherwise titled in the official language of the Church of England as 'Services of Prayer and Dedication after Civil Marriage', one commentator contends that the ban on a blessing does not prohibit a service of prayer, especially since Canon B5 grants clergy of the Church of England a wide-ranging discretion in the conduct of 'Public Prayer'.[1227]

550. Since December 2019, civil partnerships have no longer been restricted to those in a same-sex relationship. This change was brought about as a result of the judgment of the Supreme Court in *R (on the application of Steinfeld and Keidan) v. Secretary of State for International Development*[1228] where the Court concluded that to the extent that the 2004 Act precluded opposite-sex couples from entering into a civil partnership, it was incompatible with both Articles 8 and 14 of the ECHR. This led to the enactment of the Civil Partnerships, Marriages and Deaths (Registration etc.) Act 2019 which required the Secretary of State to pass regulations amending the 2004 Act to allow persons who are not of the same sex to form a civil partnership. Those regulations were passed, and the Civil Partnership Act 2004 has now been amended.[1229]

551. Section 9 of the Marriage (Same-Sex Couples) Act 2013 provides that civil partnerships can now be converted into marriages. The procedure is set out in The Marriage of Same Sex Couples (Conversion of Civil Partnership) Regulations 2014 and includes, among other things, a requirement that the parties sign, in the presence of the superintendent registrar, a 'conversion declaration'.[1230] The 'standard procedure' for conversion is set out in regulation 6 and includes a requirement that the parties attend before the superintendent registrar to provide certain evidence and, of course, pay the requisite fee.

1225. *Civil Partnerships: A Pastoral Statement from the House of Bishops of the Church of England*. July 2005.

1226. M. Hill, *Church, State and Civil Partners: Establishment and Social Mores in Tension*, in *Law and Religion: New Horizons* 57 (N. Doe & R. Sandberg eds, Peeters 2010). It is interesting to note that other provinces in the Anglican Communion have specific liturgies for the blessing of some same sex couples.

1227. B. Lewis, *What Services Are Clergy Permitted to Offer Couples in Same Sex Relationships in the Church of England?* http://thinkinganglicans.org.uk/uploads/brianlewis.html. Following Publication of the Pilling Report (GS 1929), the College of Bishops met in January 2014 and invited the two Archbishops to commission a small group to examine this and other issues on human sexuality.

1228. [2018] UKSC 32. For a discussion of the campaign for opposite-sex civil partnerships as well as consideration of how equal civil partnerships address the disadvantages faced by cohabitants, *see* A. Hayward, *The Steinfeld Effect: Equal Civil Partnerships and the Construction of the Cohabitant*, Child and Family Law Quarterly 283 (2019).

1229. By virtue of The Civil Partnership (Opposite-sex Couples) Regulations 2019 (S.I. 2019/1458) and, in Northern Ireland, The Marriage (Same-sex Couples) and Civil Partnership (Opposite-sex Couples) (Northern Ireland) Regulations 2019 (S.I. 2019/1514).

1230. Regulation 3(1)(a).

II. Termination

552. Although the provisions of the Civil Partnership Act 2004 as regards termination 'mirrors, to a large extent the provisions contained in the Matrimonial Causes Act 1973'[1231] with a civil partnership ending only by death, dissolution or annulment,[1232] there are two main differences. First, while adultery is a ground for a divorce,[1233] it is not a ground for the dissolution of a civil partnership.[1234] Second, in relation to annulment, while section 12 of the Matrimonial Causes Act 1973 provides that a marriage may be voidable if one party petitions that the marriage has not been consummated,[1235] there is no equivalent provision in the Civil Partnership Act 2004.[1236]

553. There are two possible interpretations for these omissions.[1237] The first is to see the references to adultery and consummation as being omitted since they are inherently heterosexual concepts.[1238] Since consummation for the purposes of section 12 of the Matrimonial Causes Act 1973 requires heterosexual intercourse,[1239] its omission is justified on the basis that heterosexual sexual activity is not an element of a civil partnership. This argument has, however, lost some of its force because, as discussed above, those in an opposite-sex relationship can now form a civil partnership. The second interpretation is that the omissions indicates that genital intimacy of any type is not an element of a civil partnership. The amended Act itself says nothing other than that there must be a 'relationship between two people'.[1240] This interpretation is supported by Baroness Scotland's explanation of the omission: 'There is no provision for consummation in the Civil Partnership Bill. We do not look at the nature of the sexual relationship, it is totally different in nature.'[1241] The Grand Chamber of the European Court of Human Rights has stated that: 'Rather than the length or the supportive nature of the relationship, what is determinative is the existence of a public undertaking, carrying with it a body of rights and obligations of a contractual nature.'[1242]

554. On this second interpretation, registering a civil partnership is not of itself contrary to Church of England teaching as found in the doctrinal Statement 'Issues

1231. N. Gray & D. Brazil, *Blackstone's Guide to the Civil Partnership Act 2004* 25 (Oxford University Press 2005).
1232. Civil Partnership Act 2004, s. 1(3). The order of dissolution being equivalent to a divorce.
1233. Matrimonial Causes Act 1973, s. 1(2)(a).
1234. Although a relationship with a third party may constitute the ground of 'behaviour' under s. 44(1) of the Civil Partnership Act 2004.
1235. Owing to the incapacity of either party to consummate or that it has not been consummated due to the respondent's wilful refusal to do so: Matrimonial Causes Act 1973, s. 12.
1236. *See* Civil Partnership Act 2004, s. 50.
1237. *See* M. Hill, *Church, State and Civil Partners: Establishment and Social Mores in Tension*, in *Law and Religion: New Horizons* 57 (N. Doe & R. Sandberg eds, Peeters 2010).
1238. N. Lowe & G. Douglas, *Bromley's Family Law* 74 (11th ed., Oxford University Press 2015).
1239. *D-E v. Attorney General* (1845) 1 Rob Eccl 279.
1240. Civil Partnership Act 2004, s. 1(1).
1241. Baroness Scotland, House of Lords Hansard 17 November 2004: column 1479.
1242. *Burden v. United Kingdom*, [2008] ECtHR [GC] 29 April 2008 (Application No. 13378/05) para. 65.

in Human Sexuality',[1243] which states that while homosexual orientation is acknowledged and accepted, the active practice of such orientation in a same-sex relationship incorporating physical intimacy is regarded as incompatible with the clerical state. The clergy of the Church of England are free to enter a civil partnership since the act of registration does not of itself constitute a declaration of homosexual practice.[1244] The Pastoral Statement issued by the House of Bishops of the Church of England stated that the Act left 'entirely open the nature of the commitment that members of a couple chose to make to each other when forming a civil partnership. In particular, it is not predicated on the intention to engage in a sexual relationship'.[1245]

555. Following the amendment of the Civil Partnership Act 2004, the Church of England, in January 2020, published an updated pastoral statement which concluded that the principles underlying its earlier pastoral statement also apply to those entering into an opposite-sex civil partnership, with the consequence that the Church should not provide services of blessing for those who seek them following the registration of a civil partnership.[1246] This led to a public backlash, resulting in a joint apology being issued by the Archbishops of Canterbury and York who acknowledged that the pastoral statement had 'jeopardised trust' and caused 'division and hurt'. As part of its Living in Love and Faith project, the Church of England has produced resources 'that will help the Church to learn how questions about human identity, relationships, marriage and sexuality fit within the bigger picture of what it means to embody a Christian vision of living holy lives in love and faith in our culture.'[1247] It is anticipated that this project will result in greater understanding, compassion and unity on these issues, but much remains to be seen. A 'Next Steps group' has been formed, led by the Bishop of London, which will, among other things, encourage participation in using these new resources as widely as possible with a view to further decision making in 2022.

556. Litigation in discrimination law has illustrated the problems the Civil Partnership Act 2004 has caused for some religious believers. In *Ladele v. London Borough of Islington*,[1248] concerning a registrar who was required to register civil partnership ceremonies despite her objection on grounds of religious belief, the Court of Appeal held that there was no harassment or discrimination. There was no direct discrimination because the Council's insistence was not motivated by the

1243. *'Issues in Human Sexuality': A Statement by the House of Bishops of the General Synod of the Church of England*, December 1991 (Church House Publishing 1991). The Court of Appeal considered the doctrinal status of *Issues in Human Sexuality*, in the context of a discrimination and harassment claim, in *Pemberton v. Inwood* [2018] EWCA Civ 564.

1244. M. Hill, *Church, State and Civil Partners: Establishment and Social Mores in Tension*, in *Law and Religion: New Horizons* 57 (N. Doe & R. Sandberg eds, Peeters 2010).

1245. *Civil Partnerships: A Pastoral Statement from the House of Bishops of the Church of England*, July 2005.

1246. *Civil Partnerships – for same sex and opposite sex couples. A pastoral statement from the House of Bishops of the Church of England*, December 2019.

1247. www.churchofengland.org/LLF, accessed 26 May 2020.

1248. [2009] EWCA (Civ) 1357.

claimant's religious beliefs. There was no indirect discrimination since any disadvantage was justified. In *McFarlane v. Relate Avon Ltd*[1249] it was similarly decided that a Christian counsellor dismissed for failing to give an unequivocal commitment to counsel same-sex couples was not discriminated against on grounds of religion or belief. These two decisions were held not to be in breach of Article 9 ECHR in *Eweida and Others v. United Kingdom.*[1250]

557. In *McClintock v. Department of Constitutional Affairs,*[1251] a Justice of the Peace who resigned (since he could not in conscience make an order placing children with same-sex couples as permitted by section 79 of the Civil Partnership Act 2004) was unsuccessful in his claim of religious discrimination because he had never made it plain that his objection was underscored by a conscientious or religious objection.

1249. [2009] UKEAT 0106_09_3011 (30 November 2009); [2010] EWCA (Civ) 880.
1250. (2013) 57 EHRR 8.
1251. [2007] UKEAT/0223/07/CEA.

Chapter 2. Religious Family Law

§1. Historical Background

558. Another area where religion and family law interact is in the upbringing of children.[1252] Historically, at common law[1253] the rule was that unless there were exceptional circumstances[1254] children had to be brought up in the religion of the father.[1255] This was abolished by section 1 of the Guardianship of Infants Act 1925, which stated that although courts 'should pay serious heed to the religious wishes of the parents', this should not occur to the extent of infringing the welfare of the child. While historically the right to determine the child's religion 'would have been regarded as perhaps the most important aspect of that child's upbringing',[1256] and would have led to much litigation, such issues rarely arise now in reported cases.[1257] The well-known case concerning the poet Shelley[1258] who was denied custody of his child on the basis that he was an atheist was emblematic[1259] of a judicial attitude in the nineteenth century in which 'a Christian upbringing was seen as a clear advantage whereas other types were regarded with suspicion'.[1260]

§2. Current Legal Position

559. English law now not only recognises the equality of parental responsibility,[1261] but also continues to recognise that it may have a religious dimension: 'A person with parental responsibility has the right to determine the child's religious education, though there is no duty to give the child a religious upbringing.'[1262] This

1252. *See* generally C. Hamilton, *Family, Law and Religion* Chs 5 & 6 (Sweet & Maxwell 1995); P.W. Edge, *Legal Responses to Religious Difference* Ch. 9 (Kluwer Law 2002) and A. Mumford, *The Judicial Resolution of Disputes Involving Children and Religion*, International and Comparative Law Quarterly 117 (1998).
1253. *See*, e.g., *Hawksworth v. Hawksworth* (1871) LR Ch. App 539.
1254. *Ward v. Laverty* [1925] AC 101 at 108.
1255. On which *see* J.A. Robilliard. *Religion and the Law* 183–185 (Manchester University Press 1984).
1256. G. Douglas, *An Introduction to Family Law* 89 (2d ed., Clarendon Press 2004).
1257. J. Herring, *Family Law* 486 (3d ed., Pearson 2007).
1258. *Shelley v. Westbrook* (1817) Jac 266.
1259. *See also*, e.g., *Re Besant* (1879) 11 Ch. D 508.
1260. J.A. Robilliard, *Religion and the Law* 185 (Manchester University Press 1984). For a modern view of the family courts' attitude towards religion *see* Sir James Munby, President of the Family Division of the High Court, writing extra-judicially in J. Munby, *Law, Morality and Religion in the Family Courts*, 16 Ecclesiastical Law Journal (2014).
1261. As confirmed now by Children Act 1989, s. 2(1).
1262. *Re J (Specific Issue Orders: Child's Religious Upbringing and Circumcision)* [1999] 2 FLR 678 at 685 (decision upheld by Court of Appeal: [2000] 1 FLR 571). *See* A. McFarlane, *'Am I Bothered?': The Relevance of Religious Courts to a Civil Judge*, 41 Family Law 946 (2011).

parental responsibility continues up until the child reaches a sufficient understanding to make his or her own decision[1263] and is also protected by numerous human rights safeguards.[1264]

560. Under the Children Act 1989 the welfare of the child is paramount.[1265] While section 1(3)(d) of the Act requires a court to have regard to the age, sex, background, and 'any characteristics of [the child's] which the court considers relevant', these are factors to be weighed in the balance and are not a paramount consideration. While it would be a breach of the ECHR[1266] for a court to deny a parent the care of a child simply because of that parent's religious beliefs,[1267] those religious beliefs need to be balanced against the welfare of the child and the rights of the other parent.[1268]

561. There have, in recent years, been a number of high-profile cases which highlight the tension between the welfare of the child and the wishes of the parents. An illustrative example is that of Charlie Gard where the parents lost a legal battle to take their son to the United States for trial therapy, the consequence being that it was lawful for the hospital to withdraw his life-support, allowing the child to die.[1269] Not even the intervention of the Pope could sway the outcome.[1270]

562. Adoption cases concerning religion show further evidence of this 'shift in attention from adults to children'.[1271] While previously consent to adoption could be conditional on the child being brought up in a particular religion, this was changed by the Adoption Act 1976. Section 7 required adoption agencies to have regard as far as practical to any wishes of the child's parent or guardian. The Adoption and Children Act 2002 has extended this: section 1(5) now states more generally that adoption agencies 'must give due consideration to the child's religious persuasion, racial origin and linguistic background'. The decision in *Re P (A Minor)*

1263. *Gillick v. West Norfolk and Wisbech Area Health Authority* [1986] AC 112. Indeed, in *AB v CD and Others* [2021] EWHC 741 (Fam), the High Court observed that parental responsibility continues, irrespective of whether a child is '*Gillick* competent', although parental rights cannot be used to trump a *Gillick* competent child's decision.
1264. *See* R. Ahdar & I. Leigh, *Religious Freedom in the Liberal State* 195 (Oxford University Press 2005).
1265. *See* E. Butler-Sloss & M. Hill, *Family Law: Current Conflicts and Their Resolution*, in *Islam and English Law* 108 (R. Griffith-Jones ed., Oxford University Press 2013).
1266. *Hoffman v. Austria* (1993) 17 EHRR 293; *Palau-Martinez v. France* (App No. 64927/01), judgment 16 December 2003.
1267. G. Douglas, *An Introduction to Family Law* 90 (2d ed., Clarendon Press 2004).
1268. *See Re J (Specific Issue Orders: Child's Religious Upbringing and Circumcision)* [2000] 1 FLR 571 at para. 12.
1269. For the judgment of the ECHR, *see Charles Gard and Others v. the United Kingdom*, Application No. 39793/17: European Court of Human Rights (First Section).
1270. https://www.theguardian.com/world/2017/jul/02/pope-shows-solidarity-with-charlie-gards-parents, accessed 20 June 2020.
1271. *See*, e.g., N. Lowe & G. Douglas, *Bromley's Family Law* 6 (11th ed., Oxford University Press 2015).

(Residence Order: Child's Welfare),[1272] resisting an application that a Downs Syndrome child born to Orthodox Jews and fostered by non-practising Roman Catholics should be returned to her natural parents, shows that where parents are unable to care for a child themselves they cannot insist on the child being adopted or being placed with carers who share the same religion.[1273]

563. The court will not automatically assume that a child acquires a parent's religion,[1274] unless the child is very young:[1275] courts are likely to enable children to continue their own religious practices.[1276] However, the child's welfare continues to be of paramount importance: it takes precedence over considerations concerning their own religion; as Balcombe LJ made clear in *Re S:*[1277] 'if the court were to be bound by [the child's] religious beliefs it would … amount to an abandonment of the duty imposed upon it by Parliament, to decide what [the child's] welfare, viewed objectively, requires.'[1278]

564. Moreover, the impact of the parent's religion upon the question of determining the child's religious heritage cannot be disregarded: 'local authorities must not change the child's religion'.[1279] Determining what the child's religion is requires reference to be made to the religion of the adult: a Local Authority cannot cause a child in their care 'to be brought up in any religious persuasion other than that in which he would have been brought up had the order not been made'.[1280]

565. There is much judicial rhetoric of neutrality, stating that 'the court is perfectly impartial in matters of religion'[1281] and that it is not for courts 'to pass any judgments on the beliefs' of parents,[1282] This has been reiterated by Munby LJ in *Re G*[1283] in which he held that

> Religion – whatever the particular believer's faith – is not the business of government or of the secular courts, though the courts will, of course, pay every respect to the individual's or family's religious principles. … The starting point of the common law is thus respect for an individual's religious principles, coupled with an essentially neutral view of religious beliefs and a benevolent tolerance of cultural and religious diversity.

1272. [1999] 2 FLR 573.
1273. G. Douglas, *An Introduction to Family Law* 89, 171 (2d ed., Clarendon Press 2004).
1274. *Re J (Specific Issue Orders: Child's Religious Upbringing and Circumcision)* [2000] 1 FLR 571.
1275. *Re P (Section 91(14) Guidelines Residence and Religious Heritage)* [1999] 2 FLR 273.
1276. *See Re R (A Minor) (Residence: Religion)* [1993] 2 FLR 163; *J v. C* [1969] 1 All ER 788: *Re S (Minors) (Access: Religious Upbringing)* [1992] 2 FLR 313 *Re T and M* [1995] FLR 1.
1277. [1992] 2 FLR 313.
1278. *See* the discussion by P.W. Edge, *Legal Responses to Religious Difference* 280–281 (Kluwer Law 2002).
1279. G. Douglas, *An Introduction to Family Law* 89 (2d ed., Clarendon Press 2004).
1280. Children Act 1989, s. 33(6)(a).
1281. *Re Carroll* [1931] 1 KB 317, 336.
1282. *Re T* [1981] 2 FLR 239, 249.
1283. [2012] EWCA Civ 1233.

> It is not for a judge to weigh one religion against another. The court recognises no religious distinctions and generally speaking passes no judgment on religious beliefs or on the tenets, doctrines or rules of any particular section of society.[1284]

However, as Munby LJ noted, there is an important qualification to this principle. His Lordship held that: 'All are entitled to equal respect, so long as they are "legally and socially acceptable"'[1285] and not 'immoral or socially obnoxious'[1286] or 'pernicious'.[1287] In determining whether a belief is 'socially acceptable' a value statement is required. For example,[1288] in *Re B and G (Minors) (Custody)*,[1289] the Court famously not only ruled against the parent who was an adherent of Scientology but in so doing commented that scientology was 'immoral and obnoxious' and 'corrupt, sinister and dangerous'.[1290]

566. Cases have seen judges proclaim that the religious beliefs of one party may cause indoctrination[1291] and social isolation.[1292] Some cases have led to courts making the decision to remove a child. However, it is more common for an order to be made requiring the parent to be 'moderate' members of the faith and not bring the child up in that faith.[1293] For example in *Re H*[1294] a Jehovah's Witness mother had to give an undertaking that the child be allowed to take part in school activities and celebrate Christmas and Easter, while in *Re T*[1295] a Jehovah's Witness mother was permitted to teach her faith to her children but the children were to go to their father for Christmas.

1284. Paragraphs 35–36.
1285. Purchas LJ in *Re R (A Minor) (Residence: Religion)* [1993] 2 FLR 163, 171.
1286. Scarman LJ in *Re T (Minors) (Custody: Religious Upbringing)* (1981) 2 FLR 239, 244.
1287. Latey J in *Re B and G (Minors) (Custody)* [1985] FLR 134, 157.
1288. Bradney gives the further example of the case of *Re ST (A Minor)* (1995) Unreported, *see* A. Bradney, *Faced by Faith*, in *Faith in Law* 96–98 (P. Oliver et al. eds, Hart 2000).
1289. [1985] FLR 134.
1290. At 159. For an unusual case involving religious indoctrination and capacity, *see Re EOA* [2021] EWCOP 20.
1291. *Wright v. Wright* [1980] 2 FLR 276.
1292. *Buckley v. Buckley* (1973) 3 Fam Law 106; *Hewison v. Hewison* [1977] Fam Law 207.
1293. *See* A. Bradney, *Religions, Rights and Laws* 46 (Leicester University Press 1993).
1294. [1981] 2 FLR 253.
1295. [1981] 2 FLR 239.

Part XI. Religion and Culture

567. This final part examines, from a legal perspective, the relationship between religion and culture in the United Kingdom. It begins by looking at the legal framework concerning religion, art and the media, which now includes a rapid growth in social media applications, most notably Twitter. It then explores how religion interacts with civil society, paying particular attention to the law relating to chaplaincy. It concludes by exploring the very public debate concerning freedom of expression and freedom of religion in the context of issues affecting transgender individuals. This part needs to be read in conjunction with Part V which explored the institutional ways in which religion and politics interact in the United Kingdom.

Chapter 1. Religion and Art

568. There is little regulation of the content of the arts in relation to religion.[1296] Provided that it is not in breach of the criminal law,[1297] regulation depends on the responses of customers, retailers, and distributors and private or public funders.

569. One exception is that the system of certification by the British Board of Film Classification (BBFC) applies to cinemas. Its guidelines state that the strength and impact of discrimination (including religious discrimination), as well as the use of discriminatory language, should be taken into account as part of the classification decision.

570. The film *Visions of Ecstasy* (the story of Teresa of Avila, a sixteenth century nun who experienced powerful ecstatic visions of Jesus) was refused a certificate for public showing by the BBFC because of its erotic content, on the grounds of possible blasphemous libel. After an appeal failed before the domestic courts, the distributor took the case to the European Court of Human Rights, which held that the BBFC's refusal to give a classification to the video of *Visions of Ecstasy* was neither contrary to Article 10 ECHR (freedom of expression) nor disproportionate.[1298] The offence of blasphemy in England and Wales has since been abolished by section 79 of the Criminal Justice and Immigration Act 2008.[1299]

1296. J. Young, *Regulation and Representation of Religion in the Media in the United Kingdom*, in *The Portrayal of Religion in Europe: The Media and the Arts* 265, 284 (N. Doe ed., Peeters 2004).
1297. The law on obscenity is covered by the Obscene Publications Act 1959. Section 1 provides the definition of obscenity: an article is obscene if it is 'such as to tend to deprave and corrupt persons who are likely, having regard to all relevant circumstances, to read, *see* or hear the matter contained or embodied in it'. *See also* Part VII, Ch. 8. For a recent example of a successful prosecution under the 1959 Act, *see* the sentencing remarks of Whipple J in *R v. N (Female Genital Mutilation)* 2019 WL 01116252 (Central Criminal Court). Whilst the most serious offence was for one of female genital mutilation, contrary to s. 1(1) of the Female Genital Mutilation Act 2003, the Defendant was also convicted of offences under s. 2(1) of the Obscene Publications Act 1959 as a result of having sent to others, by the medium of WhatsApp, videos of adults engaging in sexual activity with animals.
1298. *Wingrove v. United Kingdom* [1996] ECtHR 60 (No. 17419/90) (25 November 1996).
1299. For an extended account of the development of the blasphemy law and events leading to its abolition, *see* R. Sandberg & N. Doe, *The Strange Death of Blasphemy*, 6 Modern Law Review 71, 971 (2008) and M. Hill & R. Sandberg, *Blasphemy and Human Rights: An English Experience in a European Context*, Derecho y Religión 145 (2009).

Chapter 2. Religion and Media

571. A number of legal and extra-legal provisions regulate both the religious and non-religious press and broadcasting.[1300] The House of Lords has stressed the degree of deference which is to be given to domestic decision-makers exercising statutory functions.[1301]

572. Historically, the print media in the UK had not been subject to centralised approval or regulation. The newspaper industry was self-regulated by the Press Complaints Commission (PCC) which had a Code of Practice which provided that the press 'must avoid prejudicial or pejorative reference to a person's ... religion' and 'must avoid publishing details of a person's ... religion [unless it is] directly relevant to the story'.[1302] However, in anticipation of severe criticism by the Leveson Report, the PCC unanimously agreed in March 2012 to enter a transitional phase in preparation for its own abolition and replacement. A Royal Charter was agreed by the Privy Council in October 2013 in order to create a watchdog to oversee a new press regulator. The Independent Press Standards Organisation (IPSO) was established in 2014 following the abolishment of the PCC. IPSO is now the largest independent regulator of the newspaper and magazine industry in the UK. It aims to 'hold newspapers and magazines to account for their actions, protect individual rights, uphold high standards of journalism and help to maintain freedom of expression for the press'. IPSO's Editor's Code contains similar provisions in relation to discrimination as the PCC's Code of Practice. In other words, details of a person's race, colour, religion, gender identity, sexual orientation, physical or mental illness or disability must be avoided unless genuinely relevant to the story. Where such characteristics are referred to, the press must avoid referring to them in a prejudicial or pejorative way.

573. The Communications Act 2003 provides that broadcast media is regulated by the Office of Communications (OFCOM) which also has regulation over aspects of the internet (e.g., relating to copyright infringement: Digital Economy Act 2010). One of OFCOM's Standards Objectives is that 'the proper degree of responsibility is exercised with respect to the content of programmes which are religious programmes'.[1303] Religious programmes must not involve 'any improper exploitation of any susceptibilities of the audience for such a programme; or any abusive treatment of the religious views and beliefs of those belonging to a particular religion or religious denomination'.[1304]

1300. *See* J. Young, *Regulation and Representation of Religion in the Media in the United Kingdom*, in *The Portrayal of Religion in Europe: The Media and the Arts* 265 (N. Doe ed., Peeters 2004) and M. Hill, *Law, Religion and the Media: More Spinned Against than Spinning*, in *Religion and the News* 193 (J. Mitchell & O. Gower eds, Ashgate 2012).

1301. *R (on the application of ProLife Alliance) v. British Broadcasting Corporation* [2003] 2 All ER 977. *See* M. Hill, *Freedom of Expression: Defining the Limits for Broadcasters*, 7 Ecclesiastical Law Journal 466 (2004).

1302. Article 12.

1303. Communications Act 2003, s. 319(2)(e).

1304. *Ibid.*, s. 319(6); *see* s. 4 of the OFCOM Broadcasting Code 2019.

574. Religious bodies are disqualified from holding certain licences granted under the Broadcasting Acts 1990 and 1996. In the case of other licences, a religious body may apply for a licence and OFCOM may grant the licence if it considers it appropriate for that body to hold a licence of that description.[1305]

575. Advertising, including religious advertising, is regulated by the Advertising Standards Authority which has Codes for TV and Radio.[1306] The Authority is a non-statutory body set up by the advertising industry itself as a measure of self-regulation.

1305. *Ibid.*, s. 348; Sch. 14 para. 15.
1306. *See* Broadcast Code, ss 10 and 15.

Chapter 3. Religion and Civil Society

576. Religious groups and institutions continue to play a prominent role in public life. This is evident in relation to State events such as coronations, royal weddings and funerals, public prayers and services of national thanksgiving and remembrance. The many different ways in which religious groups interact with civil society have been explored elsewhere in the text, especially in Part V. This chapter will thus focus upon a significant way in which religious groups contribute to public life, the provision of chaplaincy.

577. Religious organisations maintain chaplaincies to prisons, hospitals and to the armed forces. Military and prison chaplains are paid for by government: full-time hospital chaplains are usually paid for by the National Health Service (NHS). The following outlines the legal framework concerning these chaplains.[1307]

§1. Prisons in England and Wales

578. Prisoners have a legal right to the services of a chaplain. In addition to general religion law, the subject is governed by the Prison Act 1952 and by secondary legislation, the Prison Rules 1999. Every prison must have a chaplain and, if large enough, may also have an assistant chaplain.[1308] Both must be clergy of the Church of England (or, for prisons in Wales, of the Church in Wales).[1309] Chaplains are appointed by the Secretary of State but may only officiate under a licence from the bishop.[1310]

579. The Secretary of State may also appoint a 'prison minister' of a denomination other than the Church of England if the number of prisoners in any prison who belong to that denomination requires such appointment. If no such appointment has been made the Secretary of State may allow a minister of a denomination other than the Church of England to visit prisoners of his denomination; but no prisoner may be visited against his will by such a minister.[1311] As a matter of practice, in addition to the chaplain, a Roman Catholic priest and a Methodist minister are

1307. *See* generally, M. Hill, *Chaplaincy Services in Public Institutions in England: History, Law and Practice*, in *Spiritual Care in Public Institutions in Europe* 21–38 (J. Tretera & Z. Horák eds, Wissenschafts-Verlag, 2019).

1308. Prison Act 1952, s. 7.

1309. *Ibid.*, s. 53.

1310. *Ibid.*, ss 7, 9.

1311. *Ibid.*, s. 10. For an unsuccessful attempt to challenge pay disparity between Church of England and other chaplains *see Naeem v. Secretary of State for Justice* [2015] EWCA Civ 1264 which was affirmed, albeit on different grounds, by the Supreme Court in *Essop and Others v. Home Office (UK Border Agency)* and *Naeem v. Secretary of State for Justice* [2017] UKSC 27.

appointed to every prison and other ministers are appointed or called in as necessary. The Prison Service Chaplaincy, based at Prison Service Headquarters, is the central organisation responsible for religious activity in Prison Service establishments.[1312]

580. When a prisoner is received into prison, the governor must record the religious denomination to which the prisoner declares himself to belong.[1313] This has been held not to be an interference with the prisoner's Article 9 rights.[1314] Any minister appointed to the prison, or permitted to visit prisoners in the prison, must be given by the governor a list of those prisoners declaring themselves to belong to his denomination. That minister may visit only those prisoners.[1315] However, prisoners not belonging to the Church of England must be allowed to attend chapel or to be visited by the Church of England chaplain. If the prisoner is willing, the chaplain must visit any prisoner not of the Church of England who is sick, under restraint or undergoing cellular confinement and is not regularly visited by a minister of his own denomination.[1316]

581. The chaplain must visit prisoners belonging to the Church of England and a prison minister must do so as regularly as he reasonably can for prisoners of his own denomination. Where a prisoner belongs to a denomination for which no prison minister has been appointed, the governor must do what he or she reasonably can, if requested by the prisoner, to arrange regular visits by a minister of that denomination.[1317]

582. The chaplain must visit daily all prisoners belonging to the Church of England who are sick, under restraint or undergoing cellular confinement. A prison minister must do likewise, as far as he reasonably can, for prisoners of his own denomination. Also, the chaplain or prison minister must interview every prisoner of his denomination individually soon after the prisoner's reception into that prison and shortly before his release.[1318]

583. A prison chaplain must conduct divine service for prisoners belonging to the Church of England at least once every Sunday, Christmas Day and Good Friday, and such celebrations of Holy Communion and weekday services as may be arranged. Prison ministers must conduct divine service for prisoners of their denominations at such times as may be arranged.[1319]

584. Arrangements must be made so as not to require prisoners of the Christian religion to do any unnecessary work on Sunday, Christmas Day or Good Friday, or

1312. Prison Service Standing Order 7A.
1313. Prison Act 1952, s. 10(5).
1314. *X v. United Kingdom* (1983) 5 EHRR 487.
1315. Prison Act 1952, s. 10(5).
1316. Prison Rules 1999, reg. 14.
1317. *Ibid.*, reg. 15.
1318. *Ibid.*, reg. 14.
1319. Prison Rules 1999, reg. 16.

prisoners of other religions to do any such work on their recognised days of religious observance.[1320] So far as is reasonably practical, there must be available for the personal use of every prisoner such religious books recognised by his denomination as are approved by the Secretary of State.[1321]

585. Prisoners are entitled to a diet that accords with the demands of their religion as agreed between the religious body and Prison Service Headquarters.[1322]

586. Prisoners are expected to wear clothing provided by the prison.[1323] However, they must be allowed to wear religious dress which accords with the requirements of their religion as agreed between the religious body and Prison Service Headquarters.[1324] Strasbourg jurisprudence has confirmed that Article 9 does not include a right for prisoners to wear their own clothes.[1325] In *R on the Application of Bashir v. The Independent Adjudicator and HMP Ryehull and the Secretary of State for Justice*[1326] the High Court held that charging a prisoner with failing to obey a lawful order contrary to Rule 51(22) of the Prison Rules 1999 when he failed to provide an adequate urine sample as a result of a voluntary religious fast breached his Article 9 rights.[1327] In the recent case of *Korostelev v. Russia*[1328] the applicant, who was serving a prison sentence, complained that his rights under Article 9 had been breached when he was reprimanded for praying during the prison's mandatory sleeping period (10pm-6am). Russia argued that, given the variety of religious beliefs among detainees, it would be highly impractical to draw up tailormade schedules for individuals or to make special exceptions to the general schedule for each group of believers. It also submitted that a decision not to institute proceedings against a prisoner for a breach of discipline could result in disobedience among prisoners and lead to an increase in risks to the personal safety of the prisoners and prison staff. The Court observed that whilst it 'recognises the importance of prison discipline, it cannot accept such a formalistic approach, which palpably disregarded the applicant's individual situation and did not take into account the requirement of striking a fair balance between the competing private and public interests'.[1329] It found there to be a breach of Article 9 and upheld the applicant's complaint. The Court took the opportunity to reiterate that 'during their imprisonment, prisoners continue to enjoy all fundamental rights and freedoms, save for the right to liberty … Accordingly, on imprisonment a person does not forfeit his or her Convention

1320. *Ibid.*, reg. 18.
1321. *Ibid.*, reg. 19.
1322. Prison Service Order 4550: Religion Manual.
1323. Prison Rules 1999, reg. 23.
1324. Prison Service Order 4550: Religion Manual.
1325. *McFeeley v. United Kingdom* (1980) 3 EHRR 161. *See also X v. United Kingdom* (1982) 28 DR 5.
1326. [2011] EWHC 1108 (Admin).
1327. *See* para. 76 above.
1328. [2020] ECHR 314.
1329. *Ibid.*, para. 59.

rights, including the right to freedom of religion, so that any restriction on that right must be justified in each individual case'.[1330]

§2. PRISONS IN SCOTLAND

587. The Scottish Prison Service appoints chaplains in cooperation with the faith communities in Scotland to provide pastoral care and to enable prisoners to practise their religion. Under the terms of the Prisons and Young Offenders' Institutions (Scotland) Rules 2011, prisoners are guaranteed the right to practise their religions so far as reasonably practicable.[1331] At the very least, each institution has the service of a Church of Scotland minister and of a Roman Catholic priest, though many chaplains are part-time and combine chaplaincy work with work in a nearby parish.[1332]

588. The religious denomination of a new prisoner must be recorded by the Governor of the prison as soon as reasonably practicable following reception[1333] and the Governor must inform every prisoner of the prison's facilities for religious practice. Chaplains must visit each prisoner of their denomination as soon as practicable after reception and, from then on, at such other times as the prisoner and the chaplain may agree. A chaplain must conduct religious services or meetings at such times as he or she, after consultation with the Governor, considers appropriate and, with the approval of the Governor, make any other arrangements considered necessary for the provision of religious ministration to prisoners of the denomination in question. Arrangements are also made for visiting ministers not on the prison chaplaincy team to minister to prisoners of their denominations.[1334]

589. Unless removed from association under Rule 95, all prisoners may attend services or meetings of their own religious groups as arranged by the relevant chaplain with the consent of the Governor; however, the Governor may prevent a prisoner from attending if, in exceptional circumstances, the Governor considers it is necessary to do so in the interests of good order.[1335] Pastoral visits to prisoners by chaplains are private, except where the chaplain requests otherwise or the Governor considers that privacy would be prejudicial to the interests of security or the personal safety of the chaplain.[1336]

1330. *Ibid.*, para. 57.
1331. Rule 44(1).
1332. For example, one of the elements in the decision as to whether or not Ms Helen Percy, the pursuer in *Percy (AP) v. Board of National Mission of the Church of Scotland* [2005] UKHL 73, was 'employed' by the defender was the fact that part of her duties as an associate parish minister was to act as part-time chaplain at HMP Noranside.
1333. Rule 13(1).
1334. Rule 44.
1335. Rule 44(3).
1336. Rule 44(4)(b).

590. Prisoners must be provided with such literature and other materials 'as the Governor considers appropriate' for their religious needs and must be allowed, so far as reasonably practicable, to possess 'religious books, items and materials appropriate to [their] religious denomination' for personal use.[1337]

§3. THE ARMED FORCES

591. There are chaplains to the Regular Army, the Territorial Army Volunteer Reserve, Royal Navy and the Royal Air Force. The term 'Army chaplain' is defined as meaning a commissioned chaplain in holy orders to Her Majesty's military forces.[1338]

592. Chaplains are appointed by the Secretary of State for Defence on the recommendation of the Chaplain General following nomination by an accredited representative of the religious organisation. In the case of the Church of England, the accredited representative is the bishop; in the Church of Scotland it is the Committee on Chaplaincy to HM Forces; in the Methodist Church it is the Royal Navy, Army and Royal Air Force Board; in the Catholic Church it is the sending bishop, through the Catholic bishop to the Forces.[1339]

593. Differences are to be found in the way that sending religious organisations keep in touch with their chaplains.[1340] While Church of England chaplains relinquish their diocesan ties and come under the Bishop to the Forces, Church of Scotland chaplains remain on the roll of a Presbytery.[1341] Chaplains continue to come under the discipline and teaching of their own particular church authorities.[1342]

594. The duties of chaplains and officiating clergymen in the Army are regulated by the Queen's Regulations for the Army 1961.[1343] All chaplains, with the exception of Catholic chaplains, come under the Chaplain General in all professional matters. In relation to Church of England chaplains, the Bishop to the Forces exercises pastoral supervision on behalf of the Archbishop of Canterbury. Catholic chaplains come under the direction of the Principal Roman Catholic Chaplain to the Army. It is through the instructions from the Chaplain General or the Principal Roman Catholic Chaplain that chaplains are posted to units or establishments.[1344]

1337. Rules 44(1)(b), (2)(b).
1338. Army Chaplains Act 1868, s. 2.
1339. D. Bailey, *Legal Regulation of the Appointment, Ministry and Episcopal Oversight of Amy Chaplains* 16 (University of Wales, LLM Dissertation 1999).
1340. *Ibid.*, 19.
1341. Act VII 1942 and Act VI 1947 of the General Assembly.
1342. *See*, e.g., Queen's Regulations for the Army 1961, para. JF.274.
1343. *See* paras J1432–J1442.
1344. Queen's Regulations for the Army 1961, para. JF.274.

595. The duties of chaplains in the Territorial Army Volunteer Reserve are regulated by the Territorial Army Volunteer Regulations 1967.[1345] The duties of chaplains in the Royal Air Force are laid down in Queen's Regulations for the Royal Air Force 1964.[1346] The duties of chaplains in the Royal Navy are stated in the Queen's Regulations for the Royal Navy 1967.[1347]

§4. Hospitals and Healthcare in England and Wales

596. There is no specific legal right under domestic law to the meeting of spiritual needs in hospitals. Rather, the provision of spiritual care for patients and staff in hospitals is governed by State quasi-legislation; the subject is regulated by health service guidelines.[1348] *Religion or Belief: A practical guide for the NHS* (2009) recognises that religion and belief are 'important considerations for all patients and staff'. The guide 'sets out how equality issues in religion or belief relate to the principles that underpin our health objectives'. The NHS Chaplaincy Guidelines 2015 covers a vast range of aspects of chaplaincy care, ranging from the provision of space for worship, to dealing with emergency incident planning and bereavement services.

597. The NHS guidelines recommend the NHS to make every effort to provide for the spiritual needs of patients and staff. Failure to meet these rights generally falls within the investigative powers of the health service ombudsman. Health authorities should regularly review their chaplaincy needs. There is also a Network for Pastoral, Spiritual, and Religious Care in Health support group,[1349] and the European Network of Health Care Chaplaincy which has issued *Standards for Health Care Chaplaincy in Europe* (2002).[1350]

§5. Hospitals and Healthcare in Scotland

598. The published policy of the Scottish Government Health Department states explicitly that spiritual care is integral to healthcare generally; and responsibility for the employment of whole-time hospital chaplains lies with the National Health Service in Scotland.[1351] Part-time chaplains are paid fees based on the number of sessions which they devote to hospital work. In addition to chaplains, however, the national policy makes it clear that all Health Service staff are spiritual care providers.[1352]

1345. *See* para. 119.
1346. *See* para. 100.
1347. *See* Ch. 44.
1348. *See* the Department of Health website: www.dh.gov.uk/.
1349. http://network-health.org.uk/.
1350. www.enhcc.eu.
1351. The current policy is summarised in A. Richardson, *Spiritual Care Matters: An Introductory Resource for all NHS Scotland Staff* (NHS Education for Scotland April 2009).
1352. Health Department Circulars NHS HDL (2002) 76 and CEL (2008) 49.

599. Each Health Board has been required to draw up a spiritual care policy for its own area aimed at providing service which is equitable and accessible for people of any faith or of no declared faith. The current guidance proceeds from the assumption that spiritual care is usually one-to-one, is completely person-centred and makes no assumptions about personal conviction or life orientation, while religious care is given in the context of shared religious beliefs, values, liturgies and lifestyle: 'Spiritual care is not necessarily religious. Religious care should always be spiritual'.[1353]

600. The latest guidance also recognises the need to educate NHS staff in order to understand and improve the quality of the spiritual care that they provide. To that end, in its 2007 Corporate Plan of NHS Education for Scotland (NES) expressed the intention of creating a competency framework for healthcare chaplains and healthcare staff; and NES supports a Postgraduate Certificate in Healthcare Chaplaincy delivered by the Division of Nursing and Health Care at the University of Glasgow.

1353. Spiritual Care CEL (2008) 49 para. 6.

Chapter 4. Religion and Public Debate

601. Law and religion continue to intersect in increasingly varied and complicated ways. The nature of public debate continues to evolve, and increasingly often difficult and sensitive issues are regularly the subject of debate and comment through the medium of social media platforms such as Twitter. One of the difficulties with this particular form of communication is that, owing to the limit on how many characters a person can post in a tweet, remarks are often branded as ill-informed and inflammatory, hindering public debate rather than advancing it.

602. In recent years, one very public debate has concerned the relationship between freedom of expression and freedom of religion in the context of transgender issues.[1354] The clash between the exercise of rights under Articles 9 and 10 of the ECHR is nothing new and the courts have become all too familiar with having to resolve such issues, bearing in mind the observations of Hoffman J in *R v. Central Independent Television*[1355] that:

> It cannot be too strongly emphasised that outside the established exceptions, or any new ones which Parliament may enact in accordance with its obligations under the Convention, there is no question of balancing freedom of speech against other interests. It is a trump card which always wins.[1356]

603. Legislation which has sought to advance and protect the rights of transgender individuals, such as the Gender Recognition Act 2004 and the Equality Act 2010, has resulted in a new type of clash which the courts are now required to resolve, with transgender rights on one side and freedom of expression and freedom of religion on the other. On the one hand, there are many who are actively campaigning for rights which they say are still lacking. On the other, there are those who say that the tide has turned too far in favour of affording rights to transgender individuals, such that other people in society are now materially disadvantaged. Self-identification is a particularly thorny issue. Cisgender individuals (the term currently used to describe a person whose gender identity matches the sex they were assigned at birth) can sometimes be quite vocal in arguing that a person who has transitioned from one gender to another (or who self-identifies with a gender different to that which matches the sex they were assigned at birth) should not be considered for some, if not all, purposes as having acquired the status of their new gender and the rights and responsibilities that flow from that. It is often the case (though certainly not exclusively so) that it is ciswomen who feel particularly disadvantaged as a result of the recognition of transgender rights. There are numerous examples advocated as to why this is said to be so which are being discussed in the media (and, with increasing frequency, the courts): (i) the use of gender-defined toilets and changing facilities, (ii) prisons, (iii) support groups for vulnerable people,

1354. *See* C. Grout, *Freedom of Expression and Freedom of Religion in the Context of the Transgender Debate,* (2020) 185 Law & Justice 121-139.
1355. [1994] Fam. 192.
1356. *Ibid.*, at 203.

and (iv) the ability to compete in certain sports and athletic events, are all examples where transgender rights, as well as the rights of others, are the subject of fierce debate.

604. These public debates have occasionally found their way to the courtroom with Employment Tribunals grappling with the question of whether beliefs about gender identities ought to be protected. *Forstater v. CDG Europe and Others,*[1357] a judgment of the Employment Tribunal, concerned the Claimant's belief that sex is biologically immutable. She believed that there exists only two sexes – male and female – and that it is impossible for a person to change their sex. She refused to accept that a transwoman is, in reality, a woman or that a transman is a man. The Claimant had been a Visiting Fellow of the Respondents and had entered into a consultancy agreement with them. That agreement came to an end because, in the Claimant's view, she had expressed 'gender critical' opinions in line with her beliefs. The Claimant's contention was that her opinions constituted a philosophical belief and she had been discriminated against because of them.

605. Having considered the criteria set out in *Grainger plc v. Nicholson,*[1358] the judge observed that:

> the Claimant's view, in its absolutist nature, is incompatible with human dignity and fundamental rights of others. She goes so far as to deny the right of a person with a Gender Recognition Certificate to be the sex to which they have transitioned … if a person has transitioned from male to female and has a Gender Recognition Certificate that person is legally a woman. That is not something that the Claimant is entitled to ignore.
> Many trans people are happy to discuss their trans status. Others are not and/or consider it of vital importance not to be misgendered … The Claimant's position is that even if a trans woman has a Gender Recognition Certificate, she cannot honestly describe herself as a woman. That belief is not worthy of respect in a democratic society. It is incompatible with the human rights of others that have been identified and defined by the ECHR and put into effect through the Gender Recognition Act.[1359]

606. Although the judge acknowledged the right to freedom of expression, he concluded that 'people cannot expect to be protected if their core belief involves violating others dignity and/or creating an intimidating, hostile, degrading, humiliating or offensive environment for them'.[1360]

607. A similar decision was reached by a differently constituted Employment Tribunal in *Mackereth v. Department for Work and Pensions and Another.*[1361] In that

1357. Case No. 2200909/2019.
1358. [2009] UKEAT 0219_09_0311. *See* paras 334 et seq. above.
1359. At paras 84–84.
1360. At para. 87.
1361. Case No. 1304602/2018.

case, a Christian Doctor, who undertook a role as a health and disabilities assessor on behalf of the Department for Work and Pensions, brought a claim for harassment and discrimination arising out of his refusal to refer to certain individuals he was required to assess by reference to their preferred pronouns, titles or styles of address. He would not, for example, refer to a transgender woman as 'Mrs'. To do otherwise, he asserted, would be contrary to his Christian beliefs, notably:

> His belief in the truth of the Bible, and in particular, the truth of Genesis 1:27: 'So God created man in His own image; in the image of God He created him; male and female He created them.' It follows that every person is created by God as either male or female. A person cannot change their sex/gender at will. Any attempt at, or pretence of, doing so, is pointless, self-destructive, and sinful. ('Belief in Genesis 1:27').[1362]

608. Similarly, Dr Mackereth held, what the Employment Tribunal classified as, a 'lack of belief in Transgenderism' as well as a 'conscientious objection to Transgenderism'.[1363]

609. Applying the *Grainger* criteria, the Employment Tribunal concluded that, whilst the other criteria had been met:

> belief in Genesis 1:27, lack of belief in transgenderism and conscientious objection to transgenderism in our judgment are incompatible with human dignity and conflict with the fundamental rights of others, specifically here, transgender individuals.[1364]

610. Thus, in both cases, whether argued from a freedom of expression angle or a freedom of religion one, the rights of transgender individuals not to be discriminated against prevailed.

611. A different approach was taken by the High Court in *Miller v. College of Policing and Another*[1365] which concerned the lawfulness of the First Defendant's operational guidance on 'non-criminal hate speech' and the way in which a local police force had dealt with a complaint by a member of the public about things the Claimant had posted on Twitter concerning transgender issues. Having posted a number of tweets some of which, the judge acknowledged, 'contained profanity and/or abuse', the Claimant was contacted by a police officer and warned that if his tweeting escalated it may turn into a criminal offence. Counsel for the Respondents submitted that there had been no interference at all with the Claimant's free expression rights or, if there had, it was at a trivial level. The judge rejected this:

1362. *Ibid.*, para. 6.
1363. *Ibid.*
1364. *Ibid.*, para. 197.
1365. [2020] EWHC 225 (Admin).

> In my judgment these submissions impermissibly minimise what occurred and do not properly reflect the value of free speech in a democracy. There was not a shred of evidence that the Claimant was at risk of committing a criminal offence. The effect of the police turning up at his place of work because of his political opinions must not be underestimated. To do so would be to undervalue a cardinal democratic freedom. In this country we have never had a Cheka, a Gestapo or a Stasi. We have never lived in an Orwellian society ...
> ... Warning the Claimant that in unspecified circumstances he might find himself being prosecuted for exercising his right to freedom of expression on Twitter had the capacity to impede and deter him from expressing himself on transgender issues. In other words, the police's actions, taken as a whole, had a chilling effect on his right to freedom of expression. That is an interference for the purposes of Article 10(1).[1366]

612. The judge concluded that the police's treatment of the Claimant disproportionately interfered with his right to freedom of expression, which the judge described as 'an essential component of democracy'. As to the transgender debate more generally, having earlier made clear that he was 'not concerned with the merits of the transgender debate', the judge observed that:

> there is a vigorous ongoing debate about trans rights. [The] evidence shows that some involved in the debate are readily willing to label those with different viewpoints as 'transphobic' or as displaying 'hatred' when they are not. It is clear that there are those on one side of the debate who simply will not tolerate different views, even when they are expressed by legitimate scholars whose views are not grounded in hatred, bigotry, prejudice or hostility, but are based on legitimately different value judgments, reasoning and analysis, and form part of mainstream academic research.[1367]

613. Whilst the decisions in *Forstater* and *Mackereth* may appear inconsistent with the judgment in *Miller*, it has been argued that, in respect of *Miller*, whilst the Claimant's right to speak on transgender issues was protected by Article 10, it does not follow that the same views would qualify as a philosophical belief under the Equality Act 2010.[1368] In other words, having freedom of expression is one thing, protecting actions that manifest the belief that underpins the expression is another.

1366. *Ibid.*, paras 259–261.
1367. At para. 20.
1368. *See* P. Johnson, *'Gender Critical' Beliefs and the European Convention on Human Rights*, 2 European Human Rights Law Review 116–121, at 120 (2020).

614. Other cases have concerned how a transgender parent should be recorded on a child's birth certificate[1369] and how the term 'mother' is to be defined as a matter of law.[1370] *JV v. AM*[1371] concerned private law proceedings between the mother and father of five children, the father having left the family home in order to live as a transgender woman. The family were Charedi Jews, which the judge described as 'ultra-Orthodox'. Accommodating transgender people within the community was said to be entirely inconsistent with Charedi beliefs, such that the strong views of the community were that the father should have no contact with the children. The judge observed that:

> Many would disagree with this approach. Indeed, it is offensive to those who believe in a tolerant, diverse, pluralistic society. In a mature society, however, accommodations have to be found, and this includes recognising and respecting religious and cultural beliefs that are outside what might loosely be called 'mainstream opinion'.[1372]

615. Ultimately, the father did not pursue her contact application and so the judge was not required to rule upon it. The case is, however, yet another example of the circumstances in which transgender rights can clash with the rights of others.

616. Transgender issues have arisen (and will doubtless continue to arise) in a variety of other legal contexts. This chapter has highlighted the clash between protecting transgender rights on the one hand and freedom of expression and freedom of religion on the other. The public debate concerning transgender issues will doubtless continue and it will ultimately be left to the courts to determine where the balance should be stuck in individual cases.

1369. *See R (JK) v. Registrar General for England and Wales and Others* [2015] EWHC 990 (Admin).
1370. *The Queen (on the application of Alfred McConnell, YY (by his litigation friend Claire Brooks)) v. The Registrar General for England and Wales v. Secretary of State for Health and Social Care, Minister for Women and Equalities, Secretary of State for the Home Department, the Aire Centre* [2020] EWCA Civ 559.
1371. [2020] EWFC 3.
1372. *Ibid.*, para. 3.

Selected Bibliography

Books

Adam, W. *Legal Flexibility and the Mission of the Church*. Aldershot: Ashgate, 2011.

Addison, N. *Religious Discrimination and Hatred Law*. London: Routledge, 2006.

Ahdar, R. & I. Leigh. *Religious Freedom in the Liberal State*. 2nd ed. Oxford: Oxford University Press, 2013.

Bradney, A. *Religions, Rights and Laws*. Leicester: Leicester University Press, 1993.

Bradney, A. *Law and Faith in a Sceptical Age*. Oxford: Routledge-Cavendish, 2009.

Briden, T. & B. Hanson. *Moore's Introduction to English Canon Law*. 3rd ed. London: Mowbray, 1992.

Cruickhank, M. *Church and State in English Education*. London: Macmillan, 1964.

Davie, G. *Europe the Exceptional Case*. London: Longman and Todd, 2002.

De Marco, N. *Blackstone's Guide to the Employment Equality Regulations 2003*. Oxford: Oxford University Press, 2004.

Doe, N. *The Legal Framework of the Church of England*. Oxford: Clarendon Press, 1996.

Doe, N. *Canon Law in the Anglican Communion: A Worldwide Perspective*. Oxford: Clarendon Press, 1998.

Doe, N. *The Law of the Church in Wales*. Cardiff: University of Wales Press, 2002.

Doe, N. *Law and Religion in Europe*. Oxford: Oxford University Press, 2011.

Doe, N. *Christian Law*. Cambridge: Cambridge University Press, 2013.

Doe, N. *Comparative Religious Law: Judaism, Christianity, Islam*. Cambridge: Cambridge University Press, 2018.

Dingermans, J. et al. *The Protection of Religious Rights: Law and Practice*. Oxford: Oxford University Press, 2013.

Edge, P.W. *Legal Responses to Religious Difference*. The Hague: Kluwer Law, 2002.

Edge, P.W. *Religion and Law: An Introduction*. Aldershot: Ashgate, 2006.

Evans, C. *Freedom of Religion and the European Convention on Human Rights*. Oxford: Oxford University Press, 2001.

Evans, M.D. *Religious Liberty and International Law in Europe*. Cambridge: Cambridge University Press, 1997.

Hamilton, C. *Family, Law and Religion*. London: Sweet and Maxwell, 1995.

Selected Bibliography

Helmholz, R.H. *The Oxford History of the Laws of England. Volume 1, The Canon Law and Ecclesiastical Jurisdiction from 597 to the 1640s*. Oxford: Oxford University Press, 2004.

Hill, M., Doe, N., Helmholz, R.H. & Witte Jr, J. *Christianity and Criminal Law*. London: Taylor & Francis Ltd, 2020.

Hill, M. *Ecclesiastical Law*. 4th ed. Oxford: Oxford University Press, 2018.

Jivraj, S. *The Religion of Law*. London: Palgrave Macmillan, 2013.

Knights, S. *Freedom of Religion, Minorities and the Law*. Oxford: Oxford University Press, 2007.

MacLean, M.A. *The Crown Rights of the Redeemer: The Spiritual Freedom of the Church of Scotland*. Edinburgh: St Andrews Press, 2009.

McCrea, R. *Religion and the Public Order of the European Union*. Oxford: Oxford University Press, 2010.

Morris, R.M. *Church and State in 21st Century Britain*. Hampshire: Palgrave Macmillan, 2009.

Poulter, S. *Asian Traditions and English Law*. Staffordshire: Trentham Books, 1990.

Poulter, S. *Ethnicity, Law and Human Rights: The English Experience*. Oxford: Clarendon Press, 1998.

Rodger, A. *The Courts, the Church and the Constitution, Aspects of the Disruption of 1843*. Edinburgh: Edinburgh University Press, 2008.

Rivers, J. *The Law of Organized Religions*. Oxford: Oxford University Press, 2010.

Sandberg, R. *Law and Religion*. Cambridge: Cambridge University Press, 2011.

Sandberg, R. *Religion, Law and Society*. Cambridge: Cambridge University Press, 2014.

Taylor, M. *Freedom of Religion: UN and European Human Rights Law and Practice*. Cambridge: Cambridge University Press, 2005.

Vickers, L. *Religious Freedom, Religious Discrimination and the Workplace*. Oxford: Hart, 2008.

Edited Volumes

Ahdar, R. (ed.) *Law and Religion*. Aldershot: Ashgate, 2000.

Bussey, B. (ed.) *The Status of Religion and the Public Benefit in Charity Law.* London: Anthem Press, 2020.

Doe, N., M. Hill & R. Ombres (eds) *English Canon Law*. Cardiff: University of Wales Press, 1998.

Doe, N. (ed.) *Marriage in Anglican and Roman Catholic Canon Law*. Cardiff: Centre for Law and Religion, 2009.

Doe, N. & R. Sandberg (ed.) *Law and Religion: New Horizons*. Leuven: Peeters, 2010.

Doe, N. (ed.) *A New History of the Church in Wales: Governance and Ministry, Theology and Society.* Cambridge: Cambridge University Press, 2020.

Durham, W. Cole, & D. Thayer, *Religion and Equality: Law in Conflict.* Routledge, 2016.

Edge, P.W. & G. Harvey (eds) *Law and Religion in Contemporary Society: Communities, Individualism and the State*. Aldershot: Ashgate, 2000.

Ferrari, S. & R. Cristofori (eds) *Law and Religion in the 21st Century*. Aldershot: Ashgate 2010.

Ferrari, S., M. Hill, A. Jamal & F. Bottoni (eds), *Routledge Handbook of Freedom of Religion or Belief.* London: Routledge, 2020.
Friedner, L. (ed.) *Churches and Other Religious Organisations as Legal Persons.* Leuven: Peeters, 2007.
Basdevant-Gaudemet, B. & S. Berling (eds) *The Financing of Religious Communities in the European Union.* Leuven: Peeters, 2009.
Grillo, R. et al. (eds) *Legal Practice and Cultural Diversity.* Aldershot: Ashgate, 2009.
Griffith Jones, R. (ed.) *Islam and English Law.* Cambridge: Cambridge University Press, 2013.
Griffith Jones, R, & M. Hill (eds) *Magna Carta, Religion and the Rule of Law*: Cambridge University Press, 2015.
Hill, M. (ed.) *Religious Liberty and Human Rights.* Cardiff: University of Wales Press, 2002.
Hill, M. (ed.) *Religion and Discrimination Law in the European Union.* Trier: Institute for European Constitutional Law, 2012.
Hill, M. & R. Helmholz (eds) *Great Christian Jurists in English History.* Cambridge: Cambridge University Press, 2017.
Hill, M. et al. (eds) *Christianity and Criminal Law.* Routledge, 2020.
MacLean, M.A. (ed.) *The Legal Systems of Scottish Churches.* Dundee: Dundee University Press, 2009.
O'Dair, R. & A. Lewis (ed.) *Law and Religion.* Oxford: Oxford University Press, 2001.
Puza, P. & N. Doe (ed.) *Religion and Law in Dialogue: Covenantal and Non-covenantal Cooperation Between State and Religion in Europe.* Leuven: Peeters, 2006.
Robbers, G. (ed.) *State and Church in the European Union.* 2nd ed. Baden-Baden: Nomos, 2005.
Spencer, N. (ed.) *Religion and Law.* London: Theos, 2012.
Temperman, J., TJ. Gunn & M. Evans (eds), *The European Court of Human Rights and the Freedom of Religion or Belief: The First 25 Years Since Kokkinakis.* Leiden: Brill Nijhoff, 2019.
Tretera, J. & Z. Horak, (eds) *Spiritual Care in Public Insituititions in Europe.* Berlin: Wissenschafts-Verlag, 2019.

Journal Articles

Bakalis, C & PW. Edge. 'Taking Due Account of Religion in Sentencing' *Legal Studies* 29 (2009): 421.
Barber, P. 'State Schools and Religious Authorities: Where to Draw the Line?' *Ecclesiastical Law Journal* 12 (2010): 224.
Cranmer, F. 'Christian Doctrine and Judicial Review: The Free Church Case Revisited' *Ecclesiastical Law Journal* 6 (2002): 318.
Cranmer, F. 'Who Is Jew? Faith Schools and the Race Relations Act 1976' *Law and Justice* 164 (2010): 75.
Cranmer, F. 'Methodist Ministers: Employees or Office Holders?' *Ecclesiastical Law Journal* 15 (2013): 316.

Selected Bibliography

Cranmer, F. & S. Peterson. 'Employment, Sex Discrimination and the Churches: The *Percy* Case' *Ecclesiastical Law Journal* 8 (2006): 392.

Cranmer, F. & R. Sandberg. 'A Critique of the Decision in Conisbee That Vegetarianism Is Not "a belief"' *Ecclesiastical Law Journal* 22(1) (2020):36.

Cumper, P. & P.W. Edge. 'First Amongst Equals: The English State and the Anglican Church in the 21st Century?' *University of Detroit Mercy Law Review* 83 (2006): 602.

Cumper, P. 'The Protection of Religious Rights under Section 13 of the Human Rights Act 1998' *Public Law* (2000): 254.

Cranmer, F. & J. Oliva. 'Church-State Relationships: An Overview' *Law and Justice* 162 (2009): 4.

Doe, N. 'Ministers of Religion and Employment Law in the United Kingdom: Recent Judicial Developments' *Anuario de Derecho Eclesiâstico del Estado* (1997): 349.

Doe, N. 'The Welsh Church Act 1914: A Century of Constitutional Freedom for the Church in Wales?' *Ecclesiastical Law Journal* 22 (2020): 2–14.

Duddington, J. 'God, Caesar and the Employment Rights of Ministers of Religion' *Law and Justice* 159 (2007): 129.

Edge, P.W. 'Current Problems in Article 9 of the European Convention on Human Rights'. *Juridical Review* (1996): 42.

Edge, P.W. 'Determining Religion in English Courts' *Oxford Journal of Law and Religion* 1(2) (2012): 402.

Goodall, K. 'Incitement to Religious Hatred: All Talk and No Substance' *Modern Law Review* 70(1) (2007): 89.

Griffith, P. 'Protecting the Absence of Religious Belief? The New Definition of Religion or Belief in Equality Legislation' *Religion & Human Rights* 2(3) (2007): 149.

Grout, C. 'Marriage, Polygamy and the Criminal Law of Conspiracy' *Ecclesiastical Law Journal* 20 (2018): 3–15.

Grout, C. 'The Seal of the Confessional and the Criminal Law of England and Wales' *Ecclesiastical Law Journal* 22 (2020): 138–155.

Grout, C. 'Freedom of Expression and Freedom of Religion in the Context of the Transgender Debate' *Law & Justice*: (2020) 121–139.

Harding, M. 'Trusts for Religious Purposes and the Question of Public Benefit' *Modern Law Review* 71(2) (2008): 159.

Hare, I. 'Crosses, Crescents and Sacred Cows: Criminalising Incitement to Religious Hatred' *Public Law* (2006): 521.

Harlow, A., F. Cranmer & N. Doe. 'Bishops in the House of Lords: A Critical Analysis' *Public Law* (2008): 490.

Hill, M. 'The Permissible Scope of Legal Limitations on the Freedom of Religion of Belief in the United Kingdom' *Emory International Law Review* 19(2) (2005): 1129.

Hill, M. 'Church-State Relations and Social Welfare in the United Kingdom' *Faith and International Affairs* 7(3) (2009): 27.

Hill, M. 'Faith Hope and Clarity: Interpreting the New Religion and Philosophical Belief Regulations' *New Law Journal* (15 January 2010).

Hill, M. 'Terms of Service' *New Law Journal* (7 June 2013).

Hill, M. 'Religious Symbolism and Conscientious Objection in the Workplace' *Ecclesiastical Law Journal* 15 (2013): 191.

Hill, M. 'The Faculty Jurisdiction Rules 2013: Simplier Process, Equal Protection' *Ecclesiastical Law Journal* 16 (2014): 47.

Hill, M. 'Historical Hinterlands for Religious Freedom in the United Kingdom' *Studies in Christian Ethics* 33(2) (2020): 147–155.

Hill, M. & R. Sandberg. 'Muslim Dress in English Law: Lifting the Veil on Human Rights' *Derecho y Religión* 1 (2006): 302.

Hill, M. & R. Sandberg. 'Is Nothing Sacred? Clashing Symbols in a Secular World' *Public Law* (2007): 488.

Hill, M. & R. Sandberg. 'Blasphemy and Human Rights: An English Experience in a European Context' *Derecho y Religión* (2009): 145.

Humphreys, J. 'The Civil Partnership Act 2004, Same-Sex Marriage and the Church of England' *Ecclesiastical Law Journal* 8 (2006): 289.

Iwobi, A. 'Out with the Old, In with the New: Religion, Charitable Status and the Charities Act 2006' *Legal Studies* 29 (2009): 619.

Leigh, I. 'Hatred, Sexual Orientation, Free Speech and Religious Liberty' *Ecclesiastical Law Journal* 10 (2008): 337.

Leigh, I. 'Recent Developments in Religious Liberty'. *Ecclesiastical Law Journal* 11 (2009): 65.

Luxton, P & N. Evans. 'Cogent and Cohesive? Two Recent Charity Commission Decisions on the Advancement of Religion' *Conveyancer and Property Lawyer* (2011): 144.

Mumford, A. 'The Judicial Resolution of Disputes Involving Children and Religion'. *International and Comparative Law Quarterly* (1998): 117.

Munro, C.R. 'Does Scotland Have an Established Church?' *Ecclesiastical Law Journal* 4 (1997): 639.

Newark, F.H. 'Public Benefit and Religious Trusts' *Law Quarterly Review* 62 (1942): 234.

Petchey, P. 'Legal Issues for Faith Schools in England and Wales' *Ecclesiastical Law Journal* 10 (2008): 174.

Quint, F. & P. Hodkin. 'The Development of Tolerance and Diversity in the Treatment of Religion in Charity Law' *Charity Law and Practice Review* 10 (2007): 1, 2.

Rivers, J. 'In Pursuit of Pluralism: The Ecclesiastical Policy of the European Union' *Ecclesiastical Law Journal* 7 (2004): 267.

Rivers, J. 'The Secularisation of the British Constitution' *Ecclesiastical Law Journal* 14 (2012): 371.

Sandberg, R. 'Church-State Relations in Europe: From Legal Models to an Interdisciplinary Approach'. *Journal of Religion in Europe* 1 (2008): 329.

Sandberg, R. 'Laws and Religion: Unravelling *McFarlane v Relate Avon Ltd*' *Ecclesiastical Law Journal* 12 (2010): 361.

Sandberg, R. 'Clarifying the Definition of Religion in under English Law: The Need for a Universal Definition', *Ecclesiastical Law Journal* 20(2) (2018): 132–157.

Sandberg, R. & N. Doe. 'Religious Exemptions in Discrimination Law' *Cambridge Law Journal* 66(2) (2007): 302.

Selected Bibliography

Sandberg, R. & N. Doe. 'Church-State Relations in Europe' *Religion Compass* 1 (2007): 561.

Vickers, L. 'Religious Discrimination in the Workplace: An Emerging Hierarchy' *Ecclesiastical Law Journal* 12 (2010): 280.

Warburton, J. 'Charities and Public Benefit: From Confusion to Light?' *Charity Law and Practice Review* 10 (2008): 1.

Watkin, T.G. 'The Vestiges of Establishment: The Ecclesiastical and Canon Law of the Church in Wales' *Ecclesiastical Law Journal* 2 (1990): 110.

Index

The numbers here refer to paragraph numbers.

Index

Index

Index

www.ingramcontent.com/pod-product-compliance
Lightning Source LLC
LaVergne TN
LVHW011123300926
849160LV00008B/490
* 9 7 8 9 4 0 3 5 3 4 9 5 4 *